Praise for *Br*

"This is Erin Lowry's best
about money by providing a
life examples for practicall
After reading *Broke Millennial Talks Money*, you'll no longer shy away
from money discussions with your coworkers, friends, family members,
or romantic partners. You'll be ready to talk!"

—Cameron Huddleston, author of *Mom and Dad, We Need to Talk: How
to Have Essential Conversations with Your Parents About Their Finances*

"Learning how to talk about money is the first step in making more of it.
While the focus may be on money, this book is really about the relationships we have with one another and what we value in our lives. It is
straightforward, engaging, and relatable. I highly recommend it for
everyone—not just millennials!"

—Claire Wasserman, founder and author of *Ladies Get Paid*

"Money conversations aren't the sexiest tactic in personal finance, but
they're fundamental to reaching your financial goals. If you've been stall-
ing, this book takes 'I don't know where to start' off the table. . . . The
scripts aren't abstract or colorless—they're the kind of insights that can
only come from thousands of thoughtful interactions over time. I walked
away from this book feeling seen. I was able to recognize my own conver-
sational shortcomings and gain a greater appreciation for the struggles
that everyone faces. There's no shortage of tips and tricks to get unstuck
regarding financial goals, but a productive conversation remains un-
matched. I'll be referencing this book every time I need to get out of my
own head and just talk!"

—Kiersten Saunders, cofounder of *Rich & Regular*

"In *Broke Millennial Talks Money*, Erin makes messy and awkward money conversations easy and straightforward. No matter if it's talking money with our boss, friend, or parents, she gives us scripts we can use as a guide, shares important context about why talking about money is difficult to begin with, and cheers us on to have these important conversations (see ya, pay gaps!). We all need to read this book!"

—Ashley Feinstein Gerstley, founder of *The Fiscal Femme* and author of *The 30-Day Money Cleanse*

BROKE MILLENNIAL
Talks Money

BROKE MILLENNIAL
Talks Money

Scripts, Stories, and Advice to Navigate Awkward Financial Conversations

Erin Lowry

A TarcherPerigee Book

tarcherperigee

An imprint of Penguin Random House LLC
penguinrandomhouse.com

Most TarcherPerigee books are available at special quantity discounts for bulk purchase for
sales promotions, premiums, fund-raising, and educational needs. Special books or book
excerpts also can be created to fit specific needs. For details, write: SpecialMarkets@
penguinrandomhouse.com.

Library of Congress Cataloging-in-Publication Data

Names: Lowry, Erin, author.
Title: Broke millennial talks money: scripts, stories, and advice to navigate awkward
    financial conversations / Erin Lowry.
Description: New York: TarcherPerigee, Penguin Random House, 2020.
Identifiers: LCCN 2020021204 (print) | LCCN 2020021205 (ebook) |
    ISBN 9780143133650 (trade paperback) | ISBN 9780525505440 (ebook)
Subjects: LCSH: Finance, Personal. | Self-confidence.
Classification: LCC HG179.L697 2020 (print) | LCC HG179 (ebook) | DDC 332.024—dc23
LC record available at https://lccn.loc.gov/2020021204
LC ebook record available at https://lccn.loc.gov/2020021205

Printed in the United States of America
10 9 8 7 6 5 4 3 2 1

To every person who engaged in an intense money discussion with me. I appreciate you.

Contents

Introduction

ON A SURPRISINGLY warm New York City winter night in 2020, Peach and I were exiting a recording studio when he said, "I think it's important to make sure people know we don't always reach a clean, easy solution to our money disagreements."

The two of us had just completed a rare media interview together. Over the course of my then-seven years being "Broke Millennial," Peach—my pseudonym for my husband—had been a character in my work. He had the authority to decide if and how he wanted his image and information shared, but he usually wasn't the one being interviewed.

We'd been asked to do an interview for a podcast about the experience of getting a prenuptial agreement—a highly taboo subject that almost always elicits an immediate reaction from people. (You probably just had one yourself.)

Before the interview, we'd had several conversations about our own boundaries and what we were and weren't comfortable letting the world know. I share a lot with you in my books and on social media, but, perhaps surprisingly, there are morsels I keep for myself.

Because we'd gone into the interview knowing where we drew the line—and we were more than a year removed from our prenup process—it had started to come off like we'd just flawlessly navigated the experience with nary a speed bump. That was, of course, not the case.

We had disagreements that sometimes escalated to fights with hurt feelings. We learned things about each other and our relationships to money, possessions, and perceived ownership and entitlement. We still have one reoccurring debate that has yet to be settled. (Don't worry, we're going to talk a lot more about prenups in part 4!)

Even though Peach and I don't always see eye to eye on finances, we do one thing a lot: talk.

Talking about money is critical.

WHY I WANTED TO WRITE *THIS* BOOK

A few years ago, I noticed a trend in what people were asking me to speak about at events and in the media. They really wanted to learn how to talk about money. Okay, no one phrased it that way. They'd ask specific questions about awkward interactions that were seemingly only made uncomfortable because of money. For example, getting a Venmo request from a friend asking you to split the cost of the wine she purchased for the movie night she invited you to. Or how to travel with friends when everyone is on a different budget. Or whether you should help pay off your boyfriend's student loans. Or whether you really need to [*you can fill in the blank with anything about wedding season here*].

This got me thinking about the fact that there really wasn't a definitive guide out there on how to navigate these conversations. There was a smattering of information here and there in other books, but none of them offered scripts and stories and advice on how to actually talk about money.

It took a long time to figure out how to explain this book to people (honestly, I'm still trying to be more succinct). When you say, "It's a book about relationships and money," people immediately translate that to romantic relationships.

So I pivoted to saying, "It's a book about how to talk about money with all the important people in your life." The response? Blank stares.

Then I tried: "It's a book that helps you talk about money at work, with family, with friends, and with your romantic partner."

"Oh, I need that book!" was the general response.

HOW IT'S STRUCTURED

This book is split up into four sections:

Part 1: Talking About Money at Work
Part 2: Talking About Money with Friends
Part 3: Talking About Money with Family
Part 4: Talking About Money with Your Romantic Partner

Each section is split up into chapters.

You don't need to read this book in a linear fashion. Feel free to flip around and read the sections that apply to you right now. One thing I would encourage is that you don't skip reading the other side, especially in part 2, "Talking About Money with Friends." For example, in chapter 4, "What Happens When You're in Significantly Different Financial Situations?," if you are the friend who earns more, then you still need to read about what to do when you earn less.

There will also be specific suggestions on language to use to initiate conversations, which will be noted with the 💬 symbol.

Truthfully, though, no matter what the section, there's one universal truth: it all comes down to boundaries and communication.

That doesn't simplify navigating these discussions, but keep those themes in mind as you journey along.

Before we leap into how to talk about money with other people, let's quickly address one key concept . . .

HOW DO YOU TALK ABOUT MONEY WITH YOURSELF?

"Ninety percent of the things we need to navigate in our financial lives are not terribly complicated," says Amanda Clayman, a financial therapist. "The complicated pieces are in the emotional and behavioral element of it. What we find is that our parents didn't teach us how to pay attention to money without getting really anxious about it. Or they imposed a limiting belief structure, specifically around scarcity—about there never being enough money. When they apply that belief system to their own lives, people see that they're not getting good results."

Money Scripts

We all have an emotional relationship with money and hold beliefs about it that are rooted in our upbringing. For those who read *Broke Millennial*, you may remember my Krispy Kreme donut story where I sold donuts at a yard sale, and my dad came and took back the amount he'd spent to buy the donuts (and made me pay my little sister) to teach me a lesson about net profit. It's a money memory that's seared into my brain, and it's one of many. But even if you don't have this sort of cut-and-dried memory about your parents and money, chances are that you picked up on signals.

"When someone says, 'Why didn't they teach me about money?' what they're really saying is 'Why didn't they teach me something different about money?'" says Clayman.

Dr. Brad Klontz, professor of financial psychology at Creighton University, has studied money scripts, the unconscious beliefs we hold about money that, like Clayman mentioned, are rooted in childhood.

In simple terms, these beliefs are:

- Money avoidance: a tendency to believe money is bad and the wealthy are greedy and corrupt.
- Money worship: a tendency to believe money is the key to happiness and the solution to your problems.

- Money status: a tendency to link your self-worth to your net worth.
- Money vigilance: a tendency to be alert and watchful over your financial health and not believe in being given financial handouts.

You likely exhibit tendencies of more than one money script. It's probably not surprising that I, someone whose career is rooted in understanding money, tend to fall into the money status and money vigilance camps over avoidance and worship. You'll learn more about money scripts in chapter 12, "Fighting Fair About Money."

"For most of us, our money scripts are unconscious, but they drive all of our financial behaviors," says Klontz. "Awareness isn't everything, but it's an important component because it helps reduce shame."

Our money scripts can tie into something more serious: a money disorder.

Money Disorders
"Money disorders are chronic patterns of self-destructive financial behavior," says Klontz. "We know better, but we just can't seem to stop ourselves."

Money disorders include:

- Financial dependence
- Financial enabling
- Financial denial
- Financial enmeshment (blurring of boundaries between adults and minors)
- Financial infidelity
- Excessive risk aversion (being so afraid of loss that you sabotage your chances to earn money before you really start)
- Overspending
- Underspending
- Gambling disorder
- Hoarding disorder

- Compulsive buying disorder
- Workaholism (Klontz admits to struggling with this, and when I did the Klontz Money Behavior Inventory, so did I—which surprises no one in my life.)

Klontz cites overspending as the most common money disorder for Americans, especially when you consider how low savings rates are in the United States.

Extreme frugality (underspending) is another example of a money disorder, where people are so anxious about money they don't even want to spend on something they need, even if they can afford it.

You can give yourself a money disorder assessment by going to www .yourmentalwealth.com/assessment.

A small way to get a handle on emotional spending is to never fully trust your instincts, says Klontz. You should second-guess yourself before making a financial decision or a purchase. But that doesn't need to be as stressful as it may sound. Doing something simple like waiting a full twenty-four hours before making a purchase gives your brain time to really process the choice.

Another important practice is to set aside time once a month or once a week to look at where your money went. "A lot of times people are really shocked in the beginning there, because their spending isn't aligned with their perceived values and goals," says Klontz.

SET YOUR GOALS

You probably picked up this book because there are people in your life you want to communicate with better when it comes to finances. It could be telling your friends that you can't keep spending like they do because you're prioritizing student loan payments. It might be asking your parents if they have enough money set aside to actually retire. Or maybe you want to finally set some actionable financial goals with your partner, like saving up to move to a new city or taking a dream vacation together.

Whatever your reason, I'd like you to fill in the following blanks (or grab a pen and paper if this is a library book).

I want to talk to _____ about

_____ by _____.

I want to ask _____ about

_____ by _____.

I want to tell _____ about

_____ by _____.

Come back to these as you navigate this book and learn the techniques to have these conversations, and hold yourself accountable to those deadlines.

Now, let's get to talking about money!

Part 1

Talking About Money at Work

WHEN I FIRST pitched the idea of this "relationships and money" book, a lot of my friends were surprised that I wanted to include a section about work. Romantic partners, family, friends—all that made sense to people as important relationships in which we needed to discuss money. But work? Who wants to talk to their coworkers and bosses about money, outside of maybe asking for a raise? It's so awkward! And that awkwardness is exactly the reason it's critical that a book dedicated to the idea of how to talk about money tackle workplace relationships.

The social dynamics of a workplace are filled with tense money conversations—everything from asking a coworker how much they earn to negotiating with your boss for a raise to being honest that you can't afford to go out to lunch at that bougie new spot near the office.

In this chapter, you're going to find actual scripts for:

- How to ask your coworkers how much they make
- How to (politely) confront a manager about a pay gap
- The best ways to successfully negotiate
- Ways to handle imposter syndrome (which does include talking to yourself . . .)

FREELANCERS/CONTRACTORS/SELF-EMPLOYED PEOPLE— DON'T JUST SKIM THIS SECTION!

To all my fellow 1099ers, you may have a knee-jerk reaction to just skim over this section because it seems as if it's being written only for the traditionally employed. It's not. In fact, it's just as critical, if not more critical, for those of us who operate outside the traditional employment bubble to have these salary conversations.

While I was writing this book, Jackie Lam, a fellow freelancer in the personal finance realm who runs the site Hey Freelancer, sent me an email with the subject line "Question about writing rates."

I clicked to find a perfectly crafted script asking me how much I earned working for a particular client. Jackie gave me permission to reprint the email here for you.

Hi Erin—

Hope all is well with you! I have been a regular contributor to the Brooklyn* blog for about a year and a half now. I noticed you've done some writing for the Queens blog.

I just renegotiated rates with my contact there, and wasn't sure if

---

*Names of the actual clients have been changed to New York City boroughs.

I charged enough. At the risk of coming off blunt, might I ask what rate you charged? If you don't feel comfortable giving a specific number, was it under or over $600 for about 1,000 words?

Did you include sharing out to your social media platforms in the rate?

Best,
Jackie

Jackie set up everything perfectly. First, she identified that I'd be a good person to ask because I wrote for a similar company's blog on a similar topic (and these companies were owned by the same parent company). Second, as an icebreaker, she acknowledged it was a potentially awkward question to ask. Third, she offered me the option of just giving a ballpark on my rate instead of specifics. Her particular style is actually a strategy known as the over/under method, which we'll discuss in more depth later in this chapter. Finally, Jackie further clarified what else could've been included in the rate to increase the value and cost.

Within the hour, I responded to Jackie and shared that not only had I made more than twice what she'd charged for the same work, I knew someone with the same credentials as myself who'd made nearly twice what I had. I'd come to learn about the other writer's rate from doing exactly what Jackie had done with me: asking the awkward question to the fellow freelance friend. After finding out my friend made almost twice what I did, I asked for a sizeable increase when I renegotiated my own contract.

In addition to sharing specifics about the contract for which Jackie had inquired, I also gave Jackie some specifics about general rates I charge on other work, for good measure. In my opinion, it doesn't hurt me when I share information like this. Instead, it ultimately helps. If other high-caliber writers are undervaluing their work, then it's harder for me to get paid what should be market rate because clients can get away with paying less. To use a cliché, "a rising tide lifts all ships," and sharing rate information is one way we can raise that tide.

Granted, Jackie and I both write about money professionally—so talking about rates may be a tad less awkward for us than for most. But don't worry; no matter your work situation, we're going to figure out the best way you can ask the "how much do you make" question!

Chapter 1

"How Much Do You Make?"

THE CASE FOR ASKING ABOUT SALARIES

"HOW MUCH ARE you willing to pay to avoid an awkward conversation?"

Alexandra Dickinson, a negotiation expert, posed this question, and my expression might as well have been that mind-blown emoji.

It's such a simple question, and it's truly at the heart of this entire chapter.

"If it's a five percent raise, are you willing to pay that much to avoid the ten seconds of awkwardness it would take to ask about it?" continued Dickinson. "And also, the worst they can say is no."

As if this simple question weren't enough to reframe anyone's thinking when it comes to discussing salaries with coworkers, Dickinson went on to share a story about a client of hers, a story so nearly unbelievable that it has the potential to morph into an urban legend. I can already hear it being cited at happy hours a decade from now with the starting line "Well, my best friend's cousin's coworker . . ."

A client of mine, who worked at a global company where there were many, many people in her role across the organization, spoke to her colleagues who'd been hired around the same time and had similar education credentials. My client found out that she was making $10,000 less, and she went into her boss's office and said, "I happen to know some folks around here are making a lot more than me and I'm curious about that." Her boss responded that he was surprised to hear that because there is a pay grade in place and salaries shouldn't be that far off from each other. The boss double-checked the salary and it turned out there had been a typo when she was hired. Someone simply typed in the wrong number in the payroll system and that was it. She got back pay, she got a raise, she got everything.

What I love about that is that she was respectful and evidence based. She didn't go in guns blazing and she didn't jump to conclusions. She went in with information and questions and an open mind and had a conversation that led to a result that she should've had to begin with—plus it strengthened the relationship.

—Alexandra Dickinson

Obviously, not every salary disparity will be quite so straightforward. But what I do love is that Dickinson's client could've gone on for years, perhaps her whole career, earning significantly less than her coworkers and much less than she deserved if she hadn't just faced the potential awkwardness of directly asking, "How much do you make?"

In my own life, asking fellow self-employed friends how much they've made, are making, or would charge for certain work has brought me tens of thousands of dollars more than I would've otherwise negotiated. Literally.

The first time I had a revelation about how much I was lowballing myself came about a year after I started speaking at events and conferences.

At the time, I was working a full-time job and just getting a feel for how to value my work as Broke Millennial in my spare time. This included speaking engagements, brand partnerships, and writing articles. Working full-time also gave me far less urgency when it came to pricing my services because it wasn't my primary means of income. Every bit of additional income that came my way through Broke Millennial just felt exciting. Basically, I wasn't treating it like a business. I give you all this background so you can understand my mindset at that point in my career.

The woman in charge of hiring me for a panel discussion had pitched the idea to me on the phone and then directly asked how much I would charge to fly across the country and speak. My answer: "Um, $3,000 plus travel expenses?" I even phrased my response as a question. "Oh yeah, that works great for us," she said.

A friend of mine was hired to speak on the same panel. We had similar experience levels. We were both traveling from the same city to this speaking engagement. We were both women and nearly the same age. It was as if all the possible factors for why we might get paid different amounts had been deliberately controlled for in this particular case just to teach me a lesson.

Over dinner, and after a little liquid courage, I directly asked my friend how much she was getting paid for speaking on the panel. "Ten thousand dollars," she told me.

My jaw dropped. She was making $7,000 more than I was for the same work! While a little bit of envy crept into my brain, I was mostly so appreciative that she'd shared that information because it showed me what was possible.

But finding out you're making $10,000 less than a coworker or negotiated for $7,000 less than a friend isn't the worst that could happen, because a fear of discussing salary isn't always as black-and-white as the worry that you'll be rejected or judged by your coworker. The real concern could be potential backlash directly from your employer. Before we discuss how to even ask your coworkers how much they make, let's first address the perceived (and sometimes real) risk of talking salaries.

Can You Get Fired for Asking Someone About Their Salary?

In short, no. Well, probably not. In the United States, it is illegal under the National Labor Relations Act for most employers to bar their employees from discussing salaries, and it's illegal to fire them for doing so.[1]

There are, of course, exceptions to that rule. According to the National Labor Relations Board website, "the NLRA does *not* apply to federal, state, or local governments; employers who employ only agricultural workers; and employers subject to the Railway Labor Act (interstate railroads and airlines)."[2] In addition, those in the role of supervisor or independent contractor are also not covered.

If your job doesn't fall into any of those categories, you still need to proceed with caution before gabbing about salaries. You really need to know your office climate and whether your employer tries (possibly illegally) to prevent these conversations from happening. It may be illegal to fire you for striking up conversations about salaries, but that doesn't mean it's illegal to find another cause to justify giving you the axe. Plus, your employer may be willing to take the gamble that you aren't going to hire lawyers to fight them over your dismissal.

Even if your company culture is one that makes the idea of discussing salary as enticing as living without Internet for a month, there are still plenty of ways you can ask other people about their salaries.

Who to Actually Ask "Hey, How Much Do You Make?"

Before we dig into the how, we need to first address the who. You can't just go around your office indiscriminately asking people what they make. You should really consider who *you specifically* should ask. While you might want to know what the vice president makes, it probably doesn't benefit you directly unless that's the next level up for you.

Who You Should Ask

Dickinson recommends asking three types of people:

1. Someone who does your role at your company or at a similar company
2. Someone who has been promoted out of your role recently
3. Somebody who hires for your role

It's also important you ask both men and women. She advises asking three men and three women as a stronger sample size and to try to control for any sort of gender wage gap. If you are Black, indigenous, or a person of color, then you should also be sure to ask BIPOC men and women as well as white men and women to attempt to control for the racial wage gap.

Alison Green, founder of the website Ask a Manager and author of a book of the same name, advises you to consider someone who not only is in a similar role but has also been at the company for a similar amount of time. Length of time at a company is often a legitimate reason for a pay disparity between two people doing the same job.

You also have to be honest with yourself about the quality of your work, which isn't always easy. Green points out that if someone who is otherwise the same as you in terms of title and years in a role is an absolute rock star at their job and you've been struggling a bit, then it's probably not the right comparison to make.

How to Actually Ask "How Much Do You Make?"

Dickinson has a three-sentence script to get through the potential awkwardness of bluntly asking someone how much they make.

> Sentence 1: *"I'm doing research because . . .* [insert your reason]." For example, the reason could be that you're about to ask for a raise, trying to determine if your salary is within the standard range, or interviewing for a new position.
>
> Sentence 2: *"And I think you have some information that could help me."*
>
> Sentence 3: *"Would you be willing to share your ballpark salary with me?"*

Alternatively, if you're asking someone who hires for your role, is a mentor or a former boss, or is just generally in a higher position in the company, then Dickinson recommends amending the line to *"I'm thinking of asking for X. Does that sound reasonable to you?"* After all, asking a person who drastically outranks you what they make doesn't exactly help you and may not be an appropriate question.

"Each of those things are really specific," explains Dickinson. You're doing research and not just being nosy. You're asking this person because it directly correlates to your job, either because they do or did your job or because they hire for your job. And asking for a ballpark gives them an out.

There is also an optional fourth sentence Dickinson likes to add: *"I'd be happy to follow up with you and let you know how it turns out."* It's designed to play on our natural curiosity and get the person to discuss salary with you because they're then interested in the outcome.

Green recommends saying:

> *"I am getting ready to ask for a raise. I want to make sure that my expectations aren't too high or too low. I was hoping you could help me calibrate what to expect at our company."*

"If you're driven by concern that you might be underpaid compared to men in your office or white people in your office, you can be pretty direct about that if you want to," says Green.

> *"I am getting the sense that I'm significantly underpaid compared to the men on our team and I'm hoping you can help me test that assumption."*

If the person you're asking immediately seems to balk at the question, then you can proactively promise confidentiality by saying, *"I'm really just looking for data and background here. I won't use your name."* On one hand, that could make it more likely that you can get pretty precise numbers given to you. But Green is wary of starting the conversation with the confidentiality promise because then you're boxed into that promise and it may be helpful in the future to be able to speak in specifics (a point we'll discuss in a bit when we talk about unearthing pay disparity).

The Power of the Cold Pitch

While you can turn to websites such as Glassdoor, Salary.com, the Muse, and Career Contessa for details about salary information, Green isn't a fan of trying to digitally crowdsource salary information as a primary source of data. She points out that the ranges on these sites are too broad because job titles can vary drastically by company.

You also don't have to keep your insights strictly within the walls of your office. In fact, it could be really helpful to ask people outside of your company how much they make, especially if you don't feel it's a shrewd move to ask a colleague. The cold pitch is also helpful if you're interested in transitioning into a new field or moving to another city.

Now, obviously this is only helpful information in your quest if the person you're asking holds roughly the same position at a similar-size company in the same place you live (or want to move to). Consider this: if you're working a job in Boise, Idaho, and cold-pitch someone doing the same job in San Francisco, those aren't comparable situations based on cost of living.

Before you panic about where to find these people to cold-pitch, don't worry. Social media totally has you covered.

Dickinson recommends cold-pitching on LinkedIn or reaching out to your school's alumni network.

Caitlin Boston, a UX designer, used the LinkedIn cold-pitch strategy when collecting data for her own salary negotiation.

Of course I was initially uncomfortable with the idea of just emailing flat-out total strangers, "What are you making?" or "What do you think I should be making?" or "What's the salary range that's appropriate for my job background?" But I also realized that out of the dozens and dozens of people I reached out to, there's probably not going to be many people who even read this message. So this is just a numbers game.

I really just distilled it down to thinking, "This is what the platform is built for, and I'm uncomfortable, but it's okay to be uncomfortable." I do that a lot when I'm about to have a hard work conversation. I tell myself, "It's okay to be uncomfortable. This is why you're uncomfortable, and it's because you need to get to XYZ place. You're not there yet. And you have to have this conversation to get to this place and it's all part of a process."

Then I just did it because I knew if I didn't I'd be putting myself at a disadvantage for my next series of negotiations that I was about to go into. I didn't want to do that again. I wanted to be operating from a place of strength.

Also, I thought to myself, "Do I want to be uncomfortable now with anonymous people on the other side of the screen who will never meet me, or do I want to be uncomfortable in a negotiation with someone who will dictate the next five years of my salary trajectory?"

Boston wrote a succinct email laying out the situation with various levels of detail, depending on the recipient:

Hey—I'm a UX researcher and I just found out I'm really grossly underpaid compared to some of my coworkers. As I go into the next round of job interviews, it would be helpful if you could share what you think I should be making or what salary you think I should ask for.

If her recipient was a woman, Boston would mention that she was underpaid compared to a male coworker, and if the recipient was a woman of color, she'd mention it was a white, male coworker. She wanted to provide context that would be meaningful for people.

Boston pitched dozens of people on LinkedIn who worked in her industry and were based in either New York, the Bay Area, or Los Angeles. She ended up hearing back from three people: one man and two women (one woman also being a woman of color like Boston).

All the responses were really short and basically said, "This is the salary you should be making, this is the salary you should ask for, and this is what someone with your background should expect to make. Good luck."

THE GENDER AND RACIAL WAGE GAPS

For much of my early working life, I lived in a blissful bubble where the gender pay gap didn't penetrate my reality. My stint in public relations was at an office dominated by women all the way up the ranks to CEO, and then when I worked for a start-up, I was the only employee in the office for a long time and the next employee brought in was also a woman. It really wasn't until I was self-employed that I first witnessed a blatant example of gender bias in the workplace.

A woman at a financial services company was interested in bringing me in to speak at an event, but I kept getting passed up the internal hierarchy for approval. Finally, I had a phone call with a decision maker and she asked me about my credentials. I told her about my book (at the time, *Broke Millennial* was about to be published), where I'd done speaking engagements previously (which includes Fortune 500 companies, major festivals, and Ivy League universities), and my media experience.

Then she asked about my finance credentials. I was honest that I wasn't a certified financial planner, and while I'd worked for a start-up in the financial services space, I didn't have years of experience working within a financial institution. Instead, I did a lot of research and positioned myself as more of a "translator," distilling the confusing jargon of the financial world into something relatable and digestible.

Then she said, "Oh, well, that won't work for us. We can only work with people who have more credentials."

My inner monologue started ranting immediately because I knew they'd hired a man for a talk who had the exact same credentials I did: he had no direct experience in the financial world and a degree that wasn't in finance, but he had written a book about money. I had to wonder, what was the difference aside from our gender?

My actual response was along the lines of: "Okay, well, I'm sorry to hear that. Please stay in touch if you ever are looking to expand your pool of speakers."

Thankfully, I kept that internal rant in my brain during our call. Keeping it professional meant I didn't risk the relationship with my original point of contact and instead kept in touch with her. This was a move that served me well, because I ended up working with that company multiple times in the future, after that particular decision maker had left. Making a flippant retort about the perceived injustice I felt at the time could've cost me literally tens of thousands of dollars.

Sex-based wage discrimination is illegal in the United States under the Equal Pay Act. Specifically, the EPA "prohibits sex-based wage discrimination between men and women in the same establishment who perform jobs that require substantially equal skill, effort and responsibility under similar working conditions."[3] Title VII of the Civil Rights Act of 1964 prohibits wage discrimination based on race, color, religion, and national origin.

Even after it was deemed illegal, the legacy of gender- and race-based pay disparity didn't magically go away.

There are numerous studies and surveys attempting to both prove and disprove gender and racial wage gaps. For example, in 2018 the Pew Research Center found that women earned 85 percent of what men earned, and it would take thirty-nine extra workdays for women's salaries to catch up with men's.[4] Both men and women can experience a racial wage gap, with Black and Latina women seeing the most drastic disparities.[5] A 2018 research paper written by Valentin Bolotnyy and Natalia Emanuel, both in the Department of Economics at Harvard, controlled for many of the traditional reasons for workplace discrimination by examining why female workers were earning 89 cents for each male-worker dollar, and later 94 cents, at a unionized workplace (bus and train operators for the Massachusetts Bay Transportation Authority) where tasks, wages, and promotions were identical for both genders.[6] The findings suggested that "women's choices" were part of the reasoning, with women preferring time and flexibility over their male coworkers' willingness to work split shifts or pick up overtime. Oftentimes this wasn't so much tied to "women's choices" as it was to the necessity for women with dependents, especially single mothers, to have regular work hours. Women with dependents were less likely than men to accept an overtime opportunity, particularly on weekends and after regular work hours, due to the limitation of childcare options.

While Bolotnyy and Emanuel's research wasn't specifically trying to disprove the existence of a wage gap, certain nonbelievers have clung to "women's choices" as a rallying cry for why women do run up against a wage gap. But this book isn't focused on how and why both genders should partake in the rearing of children and how historically female-dominated fields are often underpaid, with men dominating the top positions even though they're the minority in the field (e.g., teaching).

Let's redirect to what to do about bringing up a wage gap.

What becomes incredibly awkward is unearthing how a pay gap is impacting you directly and then discussing it with your manager. It's such a potentially awkward situation that you may just avoid it entirely and try to negotiate your way to closing the gap all on your own.

"If you've uncovered a significant gender pay gap of twenty percent or more, it's possible you could take care of it just by asking for a raise and without getting into the fact that your male coworkers earn more," says Green. "But twenty percent is a really big raise, and most people don't get raises that are that large. So you could get into a position where they give you a raise, but the gender gap is still there and you have to go back and have a second conversation, and that'll seem weird because your employer might wonder why you didn't just say what you were asking about to begin with."

As a general guideline, Green recommends that if you're addressing something specific like a gender pay gap or other payment inequality, you do it head-on.

Wage Gaps Outside of Gender and Race

On the flip side, if you find out that a coworker of the same gender or race is drastically outearning you, then Green suggests using that as background data about what it is possible to earn in your company for that type of work as opposed to bringing it up in your negotiation.

"Managers still really bristle at people comparing their salaries to others'," says Green. "And they shouldn't, because it's a perfectly reasonable thing to do. Now, if there's a legal issue involved, like a gender or race disparity, they can't bristle at it because legally they're required to address it. But if you take that stuff out, it's just a coworker earning more than someone else."

In the next chapter, we'll talk about how exactly to initiate a negotiation conversation.

Reporting an Issue

It's always best to try to deal with a wage-gap issue in-house first by speaking directly with your manager and/or human resources contact. However, if you've tried to rectify the situation and nothing has changed, then you could consider escalating by filing a lawsuit and/or filing a claim with the Equal Employment Opportunity Commission.[7] Just keep in mind that a lawsuit can take years and may be costly. That doesn't mean it's the wrong decision. You should just calculate the financial ramifications.

Chapter 2

Asking for More Money
(a.k.a. Time to Negotiate)

JUST A FEW DAYS before I received the email from Jackie using the "over/under" strategy, a BuzzFeed article featuring a woman dancing in a purple latex one-piece and declaring herself debt-free went viral.

I watched the entire video, enthralled at the challenges this woman had overcome and how she'd managed to pay off over $200,000 in student loan debt without any assistance from her parents or a partner. Then the real kicker came: she'd increased her salary by 41 percent. Her simple tip: ask your coworkers how much they make using the "over/under" method.

The woman in the video was Caitlin Boston, the same woman who used the cold-pitching strategy on LinkedIn. Boston is a UX researcher based in New York City who paid off $222,817.26 in student loans, including interest, thanks in part to her shrewd negotiating skills.

Here is her story.

While living with my parents between grad school and getting a paid internship, I realized I should probably figure out my student loans. My mom came out of her room with papers and folders over half a foot tall and handed it to me, saying, "These are your student loans." The stack was all the paperwork my parents had accrued over the past five or six years for both undergrad and grad school. They cosigned all the loans for me and had taken out the loans in my name. I had no idea what the initial number was going to be.

Boston went through all the paperwork and figured out she had about $147,000 in student loans spread across at least nine different loans, half of which were private, with high interest rates between 9 and 12 percent. Her monthly minimum payment was just under a whopping $1,400. Boston freaked out because she'd planned to do a paid internship followed by working for Teach for America. But her teaching placement was in Tennessee with a salary of $20,000—which wasn't tenable with her staggeringly high monthly student loan payments. She ended up having to drop out of Teach for America and cobble together different part-time jobs on top of her paid internship for a while to make her payments. Eventually, Boston ended up starting her career in the nonprofit world.

I was working in nonprofits and really enjoying the work because it was fulfilling in a base emotional way, but I had such significant debt. I think a lot of the people that go into those fields and stay long term either have a lot of economic privilege and come out of school with no debt, or they're in a financially comfortable situation where they don't have to manage a precarious financial situation.

I had to make a hard choice, because I realized I'd never pay off these loans or be financially stable if I stayed doing something I really enjoyed. That's when I realized I needed to pivot. I had to figure out what skills I had that I could transfer.

Boston sat down and made a list of the characteristics and qualities she wanted in her next job and future career. One was to be in a field where she'd have recruiters trying to find her and not the other way around.

It was all very clearly designed. None of it was by accident. I took distinct and deliberate steps over the past five years to get to where I am now. People always think it happens overnight, and it doesn't. It's chess, not checkers.

After switching out of the nonprofit world and starting at a design agency, Boston continued to play chess. One key way she did this was to arm herself with data, especially after she made the startling discovery that she and a few of her female coworkers, who had a lot of experience, made the same salary as a significantly junior white woman.

Most of these women were women of color, and I knew I needed to find out what a white, male coworker of mine was making so I could accurately tell if everyone was being screwed equally or if it was the women and, more specifically, the women of color. So, I went to go talk to my white, male coworker who is also a friend of mine—not just some random person in my department—that I could confide in.

I asked if I could chat with him about salary around the time of performance reviews, so it wasn't a strange question to ask. When I started asking flat out, "What are you making? I found out that X, Y, [and] Z and I are all making the same and I'm trying to find out how disparate the range is here." He got really uncomfortable, as you would expect when getting asked what you're making flat out. I recognized in that moment that if I didn't want to lose him, I needed to soften my approach in a way that's going to get me the information I need, but is going to be more strategic. So, then I said, "If I just ask you if you're making over or under a certain number, could you just tell me yes or no?"

The answer made it clear Boston and her coworkers were being underpaid.

After talking to her manager and other people in her company about
the raises and promotions they'd received, Boston realized if she wanted
to make a big jump it would be necessary for her to switch to an entirely
new company.

> The company I was interviewing for gave me a range and I picked
> a number that was $10,000 above the high end, and that's how I
> got up to the 41 percent [increase in pay]. I really held the line at "I
> want X for my salary. I'm not going anywhere beneath X." Statisti-
> cally it's also proven that you're going to get a higher raise by leav-
> ing your company than staying.

Boston had the advantage of doing telephone-based negotiations, so
she was able to have sheets in front of her that enumerated all her stats at
her current job. She was also working with recruiters, and one had even
turned her down due to her salary demands, but it didn't deter her.

Boston would say, "Based on [*insert stats about performance*], I'm at
the upper end of the range here, and also X is my salary expectation. And
compared to what I'm making now, I'm not prepared to move for less
than X."

She also didn't share what she was currently making, and it's illegal in
New York State to ask.

In addition, she also tried to get the recruiter to say a number first.
When asked about the salary range she wanted, Boston would counter
with "Why don't you tell me what you think I'm worth."

Now, before you mentally dismiss the relevance of Boston's achieve-
ments to your own life, I did ask her for a rebuttal for all the internal
scripts of "Well, I don't work in tech, so this doesn't apply to me." Because, to be honest, I totally have felt that way while reading stories like
this one. As has Boston!

I was that person for nine of ten years of my debt repayment journey. I had a Google search tag that would send me articles about debt payoff stories just so I could take them apart.

I never thought this would be my path. I literally started off as a woman of color in a nonprofit in a major urban city with parents who would die in debt. I am definitely not coming from good financial literacy.

Anyone could do what I did, which is leveraging their existing skill set to figure out the industry that's most likely to pay you the most. Then leverage the position you get in that one place to the next job. People think about this like A to B and it's not. It's an A-to-Z-level journey, and you're just constantly trying to level up to your next step and trying to keep evolving based on what you've currently got.

Then you have to be relentless and ask people for help along the way to find out how you can get to where you want to be.

WHAT TO DO IF YOU FIND OUT THAT YOU'RE UNDEREARNING

When you go through an experience like Boston's and find out that you're being paid unfairly compared to another coworker, it can be tempting to name-drop to a manager as part of your negotiation technique. Depending on the situation, that could actually be the right move.

A decade ago, Alison Green, founder of the website Ask a Manager and author of a book of the same name, would've advised you to avoid bringing up a coworker's salary in your own negotiations because people could be outearning you based on negotiating better or bringing in a qualification you don't hold. But the increased awareness around the gender pay gap in recent years made her pivot her line of thinking.

"There are times when women in particular have to be able to cite what men in their company are making if there is a disparity," explains Green. "I think if it is a case like that, when you're thinking there is a disparity by gender or by race, it's okay to say it."

Green recommends using this script:

> *"I wanted to talk to you about my salary. I'm being paid X and I've learned that John, who does the same work that I do and manages a group of the same size* [or insert your comparison here], *is being paid twenty percent more than that. I'm trying to understand the reason for the difference."*

This language avoids your accusing your manager or company of deliberately violating the Equal Pay Act. Green does point out that there could be a perfectly legitimate reason for the pay disparity, like John's dealing with especially difficult clients or more complex projects, or seniority in the company that gets rewarded on a merit-based system, so it's best not to escalate to being adversarial at the start of the conversation.

Don't Wait Until Your Employer Offers You a Raise

It's easy to just wait until review time to go in and make your case for why you should get a raise or why you deserve more than the company's standard 2 or 3 percent, but if you wait until then it could be too late if you work for a company that offers raises on a specific schedule.

"Often by the time they're offering you a raise, your department budget has already been set and there isn't much wiggle room for them to go back and get you more," says Green.

If you work for a company with a set schedule of when raises and promotions are offered, then you shouldn't wait until the topic of a raise gets raised by your boss (oh yeah, wordplay!). Green recommends you get proactive. Start by figuring out the timeline on which your company operates. Do performance reviews and raises get discussed every March, or is your company more of an end-of-year-wrap-up organization?

Whatever the timeline, you need to advocate for yourself before the budgets for the next year are set if you're looking for more than a standard raise.

Confused about figuring out when those budgets get set? Green advises you to ask directly. You can bring it up with a manager or someone else in your department who has been around for a while. And since a majority of companies will tie raises into performance review discussions, you usually know when a performance review is on the horizon and you can backwards-plan your ask for a raise from there.

Curious about how to time your big ask? Green recommends asking three or four months ahead of when raises are typically offered. Meaning, if reviews and raises get discussed in December, then you should be asking for a raise in September or October. And don't get discouraged by a no, because at least your request is on your manager's radar.

Proving That You Earned That Raise

"I think a lot of people worry that they have to go in with a really formal case to justify their raise," says Green. "But in a majority of cases, you don't need to do that."

Odds are strong that if it's annual performance review time, then your manager probably knows that you're hoping for, if not expecting, a raise. Green points out that it's completely natural to start the conversation with:

> "I'm hoping we can revisit my salary; it's been [insert time here] since it was last set and I'm hoping we might be able to increase it."

However, it never hurts to be overprepared, and no one wants to see a dead-fish-eyes blank stare from their boss after asking for a raise, so you might as well have some data to back up your big ask.

Green recommends reflecting ahead of time on how your contributions have increased since the last time your salary was set. But let's be honest: our memories are incredibly fallible, which is why it's important to collect data along the way instead of trying to have perfect recall months or even more than a year later.

Success Folder

I personally like to utilize a system called "the success folder." Not a particularly clever or unique name, but it works. This is a folder I keep on my computer and use to track triumphs as they unfold so I'm not scouring my inbox or trying to recall victories months (or even a year-plus) later.

Examples of what to put in your own success folder include:

- Metrics proving you performed better on a project than anticipated
- Proof of personal growth in your position over the year
- Picking up new responsibilities
- Doing tasks that are above your designated title to prove you're ready for a promotion
- Praise from clients, managers, or coworkers

Even as a self-employed person, this can be an incredibly useful technique to use when you're telling clients about new rates. You should certainly just be able to raise rates, but it never hurts to remind them of your growth and how you've brought value to their lives/businesses/bottom lines.

The Bullet-Point List

Now that you've gathered the data on your success and growth over the year, Green advises that you write out a bulleted list with the highlights to take into the meeting with your manager. She doesn't necessarily recommend you hand this list over to your boss, but it's more of a cheat sheet to help you structure your own thinking.

Asking for Constructive Criticism

One of the simplest ways to prove that you've earned a raise is to ask for direct feedback and then prove you've exceeded expectations. Obviously, this particular tactic has to be deployed months before you're gearing up to ask for more.

"I'd like to discuss what I can do to move up to [insert position here]. *Any constructive criticism or recommendations on skills to build or improve would be really appreciated."*

Asking for a road map from your boss makes it much easier for you to track progress toward the next promotion and/or raise.

Have a Sponsor (Which Is Different from a Mentor)

Sitting in the audience at a conference, I heard a panelist mention the difference between a mentor and a sponsor. She defined a sponsor as the person at work who could help you navigate the internal company structure and help you reach the next rung on the metaphorical ladder in your career. This sponsor may not look like you and may not relate or even empathize with the set of challenges you face, but they will advocate for you.

A mentor, as she defined it, is the person in front of whom you can cry and be your most vulnerable self. Your mentor may look like you and understand your lived experience. Your mentor, in this case, doesn't work in your office.

When it comes to negotiating, the sponsor is the person you want.

"Typically, a sponsor is [someone] much higher up in the company who has power and prestige and will say good things about you to other people who matter within the organization," says Veronica Dagher, host and cocreator of the *Wall Street Journal's Secrets of Wealthy Women* podcast. "For example, a sponsor may use their political capital within the organization to recommend you for a raise or promotion. Sponsors are especially crucial for women, who typically face a pay gap and have a more difficult time landing raises and promotions when they ask for them for themselves."

There's no one-size-fits-all way to find this person, but asking thoughtful questions of higher-ups and seeing who is more engaged in answering and helping you is one way to start vetting.

These people, especially a sponsor within your company, may also be helpful in vouching for you when the higher-ups are determining raises. Again, this comes back to understanding how your company decides on and manages raises.

Handling Your Self-Doubt

One of the trickiest factors going into a negotiation is to feel in your bones that you deserve what you're asking for. Problem is, a lot of us battle a mean little inner critic that's hell-bent on convincing us we're not worthy. Imposter syndrome will be discussed in more detail later on in this chapter, but for the sake of negotiating, it's important you know how to get a handle on it before you're at the metaphorical negotiating table.

"The best antidote to anxiety is preparation," says Melody Wilding, licensed social worker and executive coach for sensitive high achievers, who also gave a TEDx talk about how to stop fighting your inner critic for good. "One of the most helpful ways to do this is to remind yourself of past wins," advises Wilding. "Remind yourself of when you've been in similar situations in which you've had to stand up for yourself or rally your strength to advocate for something that mattered to you."

Wilding says to reflect on how you prepared for a situation in which you ultimately came out feeling really good about the outcome. It's not just to give yourself all the positive feels but also to provide information and insight about how you can go into this new situation with strength and confidence.

"Use the doubt to motivate you," she says. "Doubt functions because there's a perceived gap between our capability and the demands of the challenge in front of us."

This gap can be used to help you focus on where you need to go digging for more information, like finding out your coworkers' salaries or about the negotiating style of the person with whom you'll be meeting.

Why Are You Freaking Out?

Preparing to ask for a raise, especially a big one, can be a really stressful and emotional experience—if we allow it to build up in our brains. But one of Boston's friends and coworkers made an excellent point as she prepared for her own big negotiation that put things into perspective.

"Why are you freaking out? This is just business. Get it together," said Boston's friend. "You know what you're worth. You're really good at your job. So tell them why you should be making X and then go ask for it. You're acting really emotional about something that's not emotional. This is just how work works."

Mental Reframing

All too often, negotiating gets positioned as you versus them, and someone is going home a loser. Claire Wasserman, founder of Ladies Get Paid and author of a book of the same name, has a different thought process: negotiating is about "finding a creative solution that satisfies everyone."

"You're not asking for money so much as you're asking for an investment," says Wasserman. "They're investing in you, and you're bringing returns to the company. They're not going to employ you if you're not somehow making them money."

This reframing can be particularly powerful for women because, as Wasserman points out, we're often socialized to be accommodating or people pleasers who value relationships. Negotiating can feel like a risk with the potential to disrupt the relationship, unless you think of it as an investment in you as opposed to a fight with winners and losers.

This mindset can also be supported by the use of a certain type of language in your negotiation.

Common Negotiating Tactics
Language You Can Use

Wasserman advises that you can negate that back-and-forth, winner-and-loser fight from the start by using "we" language:

 "How can we figure out a solution that works for everybody?" or *"No doubt we can come to a compromise that everyone is happy with."*

And compromise is key for all parties to reach a happy end point. Another approach is to start by being direct.

"One of my all-time favorite lines is 'I would like,'" says negotiation expert Alexandra Dickinson. "It's not 'I want,' 'I need,' 'I deserve,' and it's not 'I was wondering . . .' It's not demanding or wishy-washy, it's right down the middle."

 "I would like . . ."

Dickinson recommends using it frequently in life, joking that she says, "I would like you to take out the trash" to her husband—who is totally wise to the ploy. Using it in day-to-day life can also help it feel like the frankness and directness is less awkward.

Should You Talk First?

Honestly, I think I might've heard the whole "Don't be the one to speak first in a negotiation" idea from Jack Donaghy on *30 Rock*, but it is common negotiating advice. One of the first times I went in for a big negotiation (and by "big," I mean I was asking for a $20,000 raise), I remember feeling really stressed that I wasn't supposed to talk first—but also I'd been the one to initiate the meeting, so that seemed like an incredibly unrealistic expectation and tactic.

When I asked Green her thoughts on the "Don't be the one to speak first in a negotiation" technique, she chuckled and said, "I think if you're asking for a raise, you have to be the one to speak up first."

But talking first and overtalking are two very, very different things.

Silence Is Powerful

"Speech is silver. Silence is golden," says Dickinson. "People hate silence. We call it awkward. We try to fill it. There is hardly a moment of your day without sound." This simple truth can be a powerful ally for you in a negotiation.

"I've done my research, and according to what I've found, the market rate for this kind of role is X, and for all the reasons that we've discussed about my performance and contributions, I'd like a raise of X percent."

And then just shut up!

"I'm not saying it's going to work one hundred percent of the time," says Dickinson. "But people really dislike silence, and you might get responses like 'Okay, let me look into that and get back to you,' or 'Oh, sure, I think we can do that.' Because if you can just hang a little longer—like five seconds in silence—you may be able to get a better result."

Wasserman also sees talking too much as a common negotiating mistake.

When I asked her about mistakes she'd made in negotiating for herself, Wasserman admitted she'd spoken so much that she'd talked herself down with language like "This is my number but I'm extremely negotiable."

Wasserman cites a difference between undercutting yourself by talking too much and quoting a number to let a potential client or employer know your value and then adding a clarification like "But depending on your budget, I can work with you." The latter can be a useful tactic for self-employed people or small-business owners.

But don't twist the "leaning into silence" strategy into a belief that you should never make the initial offer in a negotiation.

Is It Okay to Make the First Offer?

"Don't make the first offer" is a classic piece of negotiating advice that Dickinson herself was taught. This is rooted in the concept that if you make the first offer and ask for exactly what they were going to pay you (or less), then you have left money on the table.

However, Dickinson strongly disagrees.

"The only time that you would not make the first offer is when you have absolutely no idea what the number should be and you don't have time to find out how much something like this would pay," says Dickinson. "An example might be a brand-new role in a brand-new start-up that is doing something no other company has done before."

She recommends starting on the high side, within reason and based on research, and letting your potential or current employer counter and talk you down.

"If you've done your research and are asking for something relative to the income range in the industry and your location, then you have the benefit of anchoring them to a higher number and letting them know where you are," says Dickinson.

Wasserman also agrees that it's not always best to allow the employer to offer the first number, especially since you may already feel uncomfortable and awkward about having to be negotiating in the first place. Best just to make it as painless as possible for yourself. She recommends you start by stating the salary (or raise) that you want.

"It's not a random number," says Wasserman. "You have research to back it up. You have a case of why you're a top performer and should get the top dollar."

> *"In my market research I found that the top performers in this field make X amount.* [Insert context about what makes you a top performer.] *I'm looking for X amount or as close as possible to it. Is that something that's doable on your end?"*

Wasserman points out that with this strategy you're showing your value and anchoring to a high number, which enables the conversation to start and center there as opposed to having to potentially negotiate them back up to what you wanted in the first place. You've also provided context to justify your ask.

Unfortunately, these well-deployed strategies won't always result in the raise you want, which is when it's time to consider asking for something outside of extra dollars in your paychecks.

What You Can Negotiate for Other Than Salary

"If you ask for a raise and you don't get it, the subtext is always that maybe you're dissatisfied and will start looking somewhere else," says Green. "So if you can explicitly say, 'Here's this other thing that would make me happy,' often that's good incentive for them to give it to you."

> *"It's really important to me to raise my salary. I think something like X dollars would be more in line with the market, but if you can't do that, it would be a great benefit to me to be able to to [insert request here, e.g., have flex time or professional development funds]."*

Here are common things for which you can negotiate outside of salary:

- Vacation time
- Working remotely
- Flex time, especially if you need to come in later or leave earlier one day a week to pick up or drop off a child
- More funds for professional development or education
- An intern
- Increased parental leave
- Leadership opportunities

You can also consider asking about perks such as pre-tax transit cards or reimbursement of your cell phone bill, especially if you use your personal phone for company work (and let's be honest, most of us are checking our email on our phones after work hours).

Dickinson recommends considering places where you may be saving your company money and how you'd like that benefit potentially applied elsewhere. For example, if you're covered by your spouse's healthcare and therefore your company isn't paying a premium for your healthcare costs, you could ask for that to be applied as a bonus or put toward other perks. There's no guarantee, but it could be worth an ask.

"I'm covered under my spouse's healthcare plan, so I don't need healthcare coverage here. Could you increase my salary or give me a one-time bonus?"

Practice, Practice, Practice

If you're traditionally employed, then you probably aren't going to have the chance to practice negotiating your salary consistently. And not everyone's job involves negotiating (looking at you, lawyers), so it's a skill that may feel difficult to improve.

Luckily, our lives are full of opportunities to practice the skill of negotiating, and as Dickinson says, "practice makes permanent."

If you're buying something at a store, you could say, *"Hey, I really love this dress, but it's pretty expensive. I was wondering if you could give me a discount on it."* Then let the silence hang.

This strategy of simply asking for a discount worked for Dickinson while she was shopping at Barneys. The sales clerk ended up giving her 10 percent off!

Dickinson also suggests practicing the silence strategy in your day-to-day life—for example, with roommates. If someone eats your food, you can say, "Hey, I put chocolate cake in the fridge and I noticed it's gone." And then just be quiet! Somebody is going to pipe up. Allowing yourself to feel these potentially uncomfortable moments periodically before going into a negotiation really lays the groundwork for when you are asking for more money.

"Just getting comfortable asking for things with no expectation of getting them can be really illuminating, because you get over the feeling of 'What's going to happen?!'" says Dickinson.

Plus, it primes you for the possibility of rejection.

What If You're Turned Down?!

"If you ask for a raise at your current job and you're turned down, you don't just want to slink away with your head down," says Green.

"Can you give me a sense of what it would take for me to earn that raise?"

Green points out that if your manager is struggling to answer that simple question, that lack of an answer is really important information to you. You want your manager to at least be able to come up with something, because it indicates that if you can't have the raise conversation now, it's a possibility in the future.

"If she's so vague that, reading between the lines, it seems like she's saying that would never happen, that's really important for you to know," says Green.

But the ideal scenario out of asking that question is that your manager ultimately provides you with a blueprint of how to improve your skills or take on new responsibilities to prove yourself.

Battling Imposter Syndrome

During the book tour for my second book, a woman in San Francisco approached me and made some polite small talk before she finally asked, "Did you have imposter syndrome at all when you wrote your first book? And if you did, how did you get over it?"

My honest reaction was to laugh. She looked startled, so I quickly explained that not only did I have it writing the first book, but I had a nasty case while writing the second book too. "Imposter syndrome hasn't gone away for me, it's just evolved. I worry about new things each time," I told her.

That's the thing about imposter syndrome. It's insidious, and even with mounting evidence that you're capable, qualified, credentialed, and deserving, your brain still spins a narrative that you aren't worthy. It's an ailment that can hinder negotiating, interviewing for a new job, or generally progressing in your career (and life). And while this book focuses on how we communicate with other people about money, it's also important to focus on how we talk to ourselves. Imposter syndrome can be one of the cruelest internal monologues, preventing you from taking a risk, asking for more money, sharing your salary information, or being vulnerable with your loved ones.

"I would define imposter syndrome as the feeling that you're a fake or a fraud," says Melody Wilding. "And it really comes down to an inability to internalize your accomplishments. It's living in fear of failure and inadequacy."

But if you've experienced imposter syndrome, you're not alone. In fact, it'd be strange if you haven't. Wilding points to recent research that shows that at least 70 percent of people experience it at some point in their career.[1]

"The reason imposter syndrome is called a phenomenon and not a diagnosis is because self-doubt, to some degree, is normal and healthy," explains Wilding. People will often come to her and describe starting a new job and feeling like a fake who has no clue what they're doing. She points out that of course they don't know what they're doing. They're starting a new job they've never done before, and that's perfectly normal; they're exactly where they're supposed to be.

"It's important not to internalize that information as a sign that you are broken or weak," says Wilding. "It's a normal response to the situation."

The way I dealt with imposter syndrome was fairly unhealthy, because I put a lot of value on other people's opinions and feedback about my work. That external validation is what helped me feel worthy. It's not the mentally or emotionally healthy way to battle your inner critic. Instead, try these strategies that Wilding recommends:

Change Your Thinking

Wilding describes this as the most long-lasting solution to imposter syndrome, but it's much, much easier said than done. She recommends that you focus on gaining more self-awareness around your thoughts and the inner monologue you have with yourself, and question the accuracy of those thoughts and how much they're helping you reach your goals.

In my example of experiencing imposter syndrome while writing and publishing a book, the inner monologue became something like "What gives you the right to write about this subject when you never studied this in school or professionally worked in this field?" First, it's easy to deduce that this is rooted in an insecurity about the level of education I have (bachelor's degree) and the fact that I didn't go to a prestigious university. Second, when I allow myself to step back from that criticism and evaluate it, I remind myself that I'm functioning in a reporter capacity— and I am trained to be a journalist. Then I point out that the foundation of my work as Broke Millennial is to figure out how to "translate" jargon and make a complicated subject more relatable, actionable, and palatable for people. Finally, it's important for me to remember I've done this twice before, and both books did well and helped a lot of people. That line of thinking proved illogical then, so what would make it logical now?

See? Much easier said than done.

Separate Feelings from Facts

"Just because you feel stupid doesn't mean you are stupid," says Wilding. The fancy psychology term for this kind of irrational thought is cognitive distortion, also known as an unhelpful thought. She cites as an example all-or-nothing thinking, like the idea that you need to be perfect or you're a failure. (I can't help but think of Ricky Bobby's dad saying, "If you ain't first, you're last," in *Talladega Nights*.) Other examples would be overgeneralization, such as "I got rejected for a raise once, so I'll never get another raise again," or catastrophizing: "If I mess up at my job, I'll get fired and then end up broke and on the street."

Use the Rule of Five

In moments of battling with your internal critic, Wilding advises you to look at your hand and force yourself to generate and count off five other ways to view the situation.

For example:

1. "What would a friend say in this situation?"
2. "If I knew all the answers, what would I do?"
3. "What can I learn from this?"
4. "What if everything *does* work out?"
5. "How realistic is this thought on a scale of one to ten?"

"The goal is to learn how to question your thinking and create alternative, healthier ways to view the situation," says Wilding.

Build Habits to Recognize Your Accomplishments

Akin to the aforementioned success folder, Wilding has her clients create what she calls a "brag file." You can add in your own daily successes as well as praise from coworkers, clients, or a boss. The strategy is to take in and celebrate your accomplishments instead of minimizing them or pushing them away. Which also leads to . . .

ACCEPT PRAISE

Just take the compliment! It's so common to deflect or minimize praise with lines like "It was good luck" or "It was a team effort." Wilding says you need to just say thank you or "Thank you for recognizing that" as opposed to pushing it away.

INTENTIONALLY TAKE ON RISKS

"The only way you get more confident is to put yourself in situations where you feel uncomfortable and expose yourself to that type of situation and learning so you can get through it and survive it and grow from it, and next time it won't feel as scary," says Wilding.

NAME IT AND REFRAME IT

Similar to how personal finance experts will advise you to track your spending by writing it down and how fitness professionals will tell you to track everything you eat, Wilding suggests you actually track your inner critic.

"Write it down," she says. "I will have clients track the thoughts they're having and what they're saying to themselves, then weigh the evidence for and against it. Negative thoughts stick around because there is often some kernel of truth to them, but there's also a lot of evidence against that thought. The only way to change your thinking is to specifically identify what you're telling yourself that's not serving you and actively start to rewrite that dialogue and practice telling yourself different stories."

An example Wilding gives is to flag when you use extreme words like "always" or "never." For example, "this always happens" or "nothing ever works out for me."

This Isn't "Fake It Till You Make It"

Trust me, I've employed this mentality plenty over my career, but Wilding personally isn't a fan of the "fake it till you make it" mantra.

"It's very invalidating," explains Wilding. "Because the suggestion to me is that I'm not good enough as I am and I need to act like or behave like someone else. And I found in my case that faking it is really stressful and draining, especially to someone who is more sensitive."

She also dislikes how the expression implies that there's some sort of end point where you'll unlock total freedom from self-doubt. In her professional experience, that's not how it works.

"New level, new devil," jokes Wilding. "If you're someone who's continuing to challenge and grow yourself, you're going to continue to have doubt, but you can have a healthier relationship and response to it."

Using Your Inner Critic for Good

"Your inner critic is really there to protect you," explains Wilding. "Evolutionarily speaking, our brains try to keep us safe and out of danger. The inner critic is a mechanism for doing that." She recommends that instead of trying to fix it or make it go away, we should listen to our inner critic and use it to identify our own limiting thoughts. That's not to say we take our inner critic's advice and avoid taking risks. Rather, we should listen to it to find out why we're scared and look closer at the beliefs and thoughts that aren't serving us anymore.

WHEN YOU'RE INTERVIEWING FOR A NEW JOB

At the start of my professional life, there was no grand vision or actionable plan in place to build a career. To be honest, I just followed the money. And meager money at that. I had the scarcity mindset of just wanting to have a steady paycheck with benefits and didn't really analyze how to take steps to get where I wanted to go. I didn't reflect much at all on my eventual end point—only on the fact that I wanted to be financially sound.

Then came an opportunity to build a job from scratch with a start-up company. The work opportunity excited me, and my potential employers were totally fine with my continuing to work on Broke Millennial as a side hustle. Plus, the job was in the financial technology services realm, so I'd actually have a lot of learning opportunities.

At the time, I was earning $37,500 at my job, and I had brought home $23,000 working multiple jobs the year before that. All this while living in New York City. So, I decided to go big on this salary negotiation and asked for $50,000. It sounded like such a big number compared to my current anchor points, but not so big a number that I'd price myself out of the job.

I didn't even get a counteroffer. The bosses said okay on the spot. It was one of my first experiences negotiating and I felt elated, but then I realized the fact that they hadn't countered meant I'd likely sold myself short. My previous low salaries had skewed my perception of what I deserved.

It can be tough to figure out how to come up with your ask in a negotiation, which is why it's so critical to speak to people in order to collect information about salaries. It also helps you avoid falling into a common negotiation trap when interviewing for a job: giving the person in charge of hiring an anchor point based on your current salary.

Should You Provide a Salary Range?

"I do think you need to be prepared to talk about how much you're look-ing to earn at this new job," says Green. "I don't think you should talk about salary history, and I don't think that's anyone's business other than your own. There's lots of data that shows discussing salary history has historically suppressed wages of women and people of color. They start out being paid less, and then their salaries at new jobs are based on their past salaries, and it pulls their wages down."

It's important to know your rights. In fact, some states have passed laws making it illegal for employers to ask about salary history. At the time of this writing, the following states have a statewide ban prohibiting employers from requesting salary history from job applicants: Alabama, California, Colorado, Connecticut, Delaware, Hawaii, Illinois, Maine, Massachusetts, New Jersey, New York, North Carolina, Oregon, Pennsyl-vania, Vermont, and Washington. In addition, Puerto Rico also has a commonwealth-wide ban.

Depending on where you live and the job for which you're applying, there could be a local city ban on requesting salary history information, generally if you're applying for a local government job.

So, if you don't live in one of those areas (or if someone breaks the ban), you may be wondering, "How do I avoid the question?" It's one thing to know you shouldn't give salary history, but it's another to actu-ally dodge the question entirely.

Green recommends you employ the old politician pivot. Don't answer the question you were asked, answer the question you wanted to be asked! In this case, you'd answer with how much you're looking to make in this new job as opposed to how much you have been making.

"Based on market rates and my skill set, my desired salary for this position is $80,000."

"The employer is asking a BS question, frankly," says Green. "They already have a salary range they're willing to pay and they're not going to change it dramatically in an upward direction just because you ask for more. It's a coy little game employers play, and they should be up front about what the salary range is."

Self-Employed Life—When You're Constantly Interviewing for New Jobs

Freelance and contractor work is essentially just one job interview after another. Sometimes you're interviewing and negotiating for jobs multiple times a month! But a lot of the same factors hold true in self-employed work as they do for the traditionally employed. In fact, I'd argue it's even more important for us all to talk to each other about money because there aren't as many options to visit websites with aggregated information.

But we also have the advantage of getting *a lot* of experience with negotiating, which can help improve this skill set quickly.

One of my favorite pieces of advice about negotiating as a freelancer comes from my friend and fellow author Kristin Wong of *Get Money*, who says to always tack on 15 percent to whatever number you come up with. We have a tendency to undervalue ourselves, and this is a quick, measurable way to combat that inclination. Plus, it's great to gut-check with fellow freelance friends on what they'd charge for a project.

What If You Get Turned Down?

It's quite possible your negotiation for more money in a job interview process will end with a hard no. Green recommends you decide ahead of time whether or not you're still willing to take the job so you're not fumbling for a way to respond. If you do want to accept, here's an option:

"You know, I really appreciate your considering it, but I'm excited about the job and I'd love to accept regardless."

Hold Up, Can I Negotiate for My First Job Ever?

Why yes, yes you can. In fact, you probably should. I remember when I graduated college in 2011 it was just a couple years after the Great Recession, and people were panicked about getting any sort of job. It became the softly spoken advice to just accept what you were offered and don't dare counter. So, I didn't. In fact, it was many years before I negotiated for the first time. This failure to ask for more can cost people tens to hundreds of thousands of dollars over the course of their careers when you factor in the power of compound interest over decades.

When I asked Dickinson if people should negotiate when offered their first job ever, she emphatically said, "Oh my God, yes! People should negotiate for every job they have from day one forever."

And this isn't a woman who is just giving this advice in retrospect, looking back at failures. She actually negotiated her first job ever, a high school job she got at fourteen working at McDonald's! Her gumption paid off, and she ended up getting an extra ten cents an hour *and* opened up her first Roth IRA. Absolute baller status.

Naturally, the critic inside all of us would say something along the lines of "I have no leverage and no experience. Why would this employer ever agree to pay me more than what's been offered?"

Dickinson offers a simple way to reframe that nasty inner-critic narrative, especially to those entering the workforce right out of college or a vocational program.

"You're showing your employer that [negotiating] is a skill that you have and that you value your own training and expertise," says Dickinson. "You may not have full-time job experience for your first job other than maybe an internship, but you are bringing the latest and greatest in education. You're the most newly educated and your training is the freshest."

Ultimately, negotiating helps prove your confidence, and it shows potential employers that it's yet another skill you have in your arsenal.

Do You Tell Your Boss About Your Side Hustle?

In February 2014, I was working in public relations earning $37,500 a year at my day job and starting to bring in side-hustle money from free-lance writing. I was eager to move up to a better salary, but there didn't seem to be much room for growth at my current agency. So, I started sending out feelers and secured an interview with a top public relations firm in New York City—a firm that wanted me on a team working for a big bank. It paired perfectly with the personal finance writing I'd already started to do on the side, which they knew about. It was part of the reason they'd brought me in for the interview.

First came the phone interview, in which I was asked about my salary expectations, and then the in-person interview, and finally the phone call to offer me the job.

"The position would be account executive," the hiring manager told me. "And we'd be able to offer you $45,000."

I mentally high-fived myself and then heard her say, "But there's a problem with you continuing to run your blog."

"Okay, does that mean you'd need me to stop writing there entirely?" I asked.

"Yes," she said.

"And what about freelance writing?" I asked.

"No," she said. "I'm sorry to say our client isn't comfortable with you doing any work at all in the finance industry outside of your day job."

"Would you be able to provide a higher compensation package then?" I countered. "Freelance writing does bring in a fair amount of additional income."

"Unfortunately not, $45,000 is our final offer," she said.

"Okay, I understand. I'm going to have to pass, then," I responded without taking a moment to really consider all the options.

"Wait, are you sure?" said the hiring manager. She seemed startled that I'd responded so quickly and rejected the offer.

"Yes, I'm sure."

At the time, I really wasn't sure. But I wasn't terribly excited about the prospective new job, and I felt confident I could pick up an extra $7,500 in freelance writing that year—bringing my total pay to $45,000—and that giving up my side hustle would actually cost me a lot more in the long run. (I was right.)

"Some companies will require that you run any side job past them to make sure there's no conflict of interest," says Green, who advises you check your employee handbook to see if such a rule exists. While it might sound like an overreach on the part of your company to ask you to run a side job by them, there really could be a conflict-of-interest issue, depending on your job and/or what your company does.

However, if there's absolutely no rule written down or even an unspoken rule in the office, Green suggests you go the classic "Ask for forgiveness, not permission" route when it comes to having a side hustle while gainfully employed. But use your brain! If your side-hustle job has zero overlap with your day job, great! But if you're using skills from your day job to moonlight on the side and then a potential client approaches you who also works with your employer, well . . .

You probably don't want to be putting your day job in jeopardy unless your side hustle is now earning enough to replace that income plus benefits.

WHEN YOU SHOULDN'T BE ASKING FOR MORE

Okay, I've spent pages going on and on about how to advocate for yourself and ask for that raise! And that is all critical information to have and an important step to take. But it's also important to know that there are moments when it's not appropriate to sit down with your manager and make your case for a salary increase. Those moments are few, but it's still wise to know them.

"When you just started," says Green, acknowledging that if you're only a few months into a job, it is not the right time to renegotiate.

She also points out that if you've been getting a lot of critical feedback and really struggling with performance issues at your job (or at least your manager is interpreting that you are), it's likely not an opportune time to negotiate.

"Sometimes I get asked if it's okay to ask for a raise when a company is going through a difficult financial time, like just having layoffs," says Green. "And that's tricky because you don't want to seem thoughtless, like you haven't noticed what's going on around you. At the same time, if you haven't had a raise in a couple years and your contributions have increased, it's unreasonable to continue being compensated inappropriately for the work that you're doing." Green says there is no definitive answer, and you truly do have to read each situation and evaluate it on a case-by-case basis.

CHALLENGE

It's really easy to read a book like this and just never take action. So, I've created simple (not easy, but simple) challenges for you at the end of each part with the hope that you'll actually start to implement some of what you've learned.

Challenge 1: Send out six cold emails via LinkedIn (or a similar tool) to ask people about their salaries. Even if you're not gearing up for a negotiation, it's good to start collecting info, and it's easier than asking a coworker.

Challenge 2: Practice two negotiating strategies in your daily life within the next week.

Suggestions:

→ Ask for a deal at a store. Here's a really simple strategy. Go to a café near closing time and ask if you can get a pastry for free with your drink. After all, they'll probably throw out whatever's left anyway.

→ Let silence hang. Whether it's with roommates or coworkers or the person with whom you try to negotiate at the store, you need to make your ask and then let it hang for at least five seconds without following up.

Bonus challenge: Directly ask a coworker how much they earn using the "over/under" strategy.

Next up, we discuss how to get really honest with your friends about money.

Part 2

Talking About Money with Friends

"SHOULD I MAX out my HSA?" Maggie texted me.

"Probably, but it's hard for me to figure it out without knowing the full picture," I typed back. "What's your income for this year? And remind me how much you're paying in student loans?"

"Honestly, I don't really feel comfortable sharing that information anymore because it's not just me," she responded.

Maggie had recently gotten married and, rightfully, felt as if she should have her husband's consent to share their financial details. When it was just her information, then it was her decision about what she would and wouldn't share. But if her husband felt uncomfortable with friends' knowing their combined income or net worth or debt numbers—well, he had both a right to feel that way and a right to privacy.

Instead of being more open and honest with friends as we age, the reverse is far more common. You might've once felt comfortable sharing specific numbers or at least generalizations about salary, spending habits, or debt with a friend, but over time, something shifted. You could be clamming up because you merged your financial life with someone else's, like Maggie. Or maybe it's because you and a buddy used to earn the same modest paycheck, but now you're balling and rarely stress about money, and that's just a jerk thing to admit. Other times it's because you feel left behind. Your job doesn't pay what your friends' jobs do—or you needed more education to progress in your career and that student loan debt is gobbling up the cash you'd otherwise put toward all the adulting your friends seem to be managing.

Whatever the reason, deciding when and how to talk money with friends and stand up to friends about your money (hello, birthday dinners . . .) is intimidating. There's no secret language to strip away the discomfort.

In this section, we're going to discuss how to push through the awkwardness, pain, resentment, judgment, and fear to learn how to have an open, honest talk with our friends about money. We're going to evaluate if and when you should share your numbers. We're going to tackle the big question, which is one I've been asked time and time again: how do you handle it when you and your friend(s) make significantly different amounts of money?

An important consideration before you continue: still read the sections of the chapters that you feel don't apply to you. For example, if you're the one who earns less in a friend group, well, you may be inclined to skip the section about when you earn more. Don't. Read it, because it can help provide insight into your friends' side of the social dynamic. You don't have to agree, but it's always good to understand.

Chapter 3

Should You Share Your Numbers with Friends?

BEFORE WE CONTINUE, let me just clarify something. *PARTS OF THIS CHAPTER WILL PISS YOU OFF!*

Or, to use a trendy term: trigger warning. This is my third book about money, and I've never once thrown the words "trigger warning" at the top of a chapter. Honestly, I write and talk about money for a living. Quite literally, every day I'm in some sort of personal finance discussion. Despite my comfort with the topic, I found it hard to avoid getting defensive while conducting some of the interviews for this chapter, and my hackles were still raised when listening to them later. There are going to be some extreme truth bombs dropped here, and you're going to think, "No way. I'm not like that. My friends aren't like that. This would never be a problem for us."

The harsh reality is, you're probably wrong.

What I ask of you is that you read this chapter, even if it really pisses you off, and let it sit with you. The statements that are made in these pages aren't a judgment of you, nor are they prophetic. Instead, your mere awareness of what usually happens when financial power dynamics shift in friendships may be exactly what helps you become a better communicator about money with your friends. Because open, honest communication is the real antidote to many of our relationship and money woes.

"At this point, it's tired to say people don't like to talk about money," says Lindsey Stanberry, author of Refinery29's *Money Diaries* and deputy managing editor of CNBC's Make It, who has read and edited hundreds of people's stories about how they spend their money in a week. "People are really eager to talk about money, especially when they can talk about it with a stranger."

From the tens of thousands of hours I've logged on planes, trains, and automobiles, I can attest that this is true.

Sitting on a Greyhound bus, I once had a seatmate tell me he'd just been released from prison. He talked openly about his fears of reentry into society. It ranks as one of the most intense conversations I've ever experienced, and I couldn't even tell you this man's name. Years later, I probably couldn't pick him out of a crowd. His face has been distorted to more of a fuzzy outline by both time and a malleable memory. Clearly, he needed to talk to someone about his feelings, and I, a complete stranger he'd never see again, provided a safe space in which to share those feelings.

It's logical that you'd be more likely to share an intimate secret with a seat buddy on an airplane or bus than your best friend. You'll probably never see the stranger again. The risk of judgment won't rock the foundation of your relationship because you don't really have a relationship. However, a stranger can't provide the type of long-lasting support you might need for your confession. Your friends can.

THE UNPLEASANT TRUTH OF REACHING ADULTHOOD

"I had no idea that people had different money situations, which is so weird," admits Gaby Dunn, author of *Bad with Money* and host of the *Bad with Money* podcast. "I thought that I just wasn't working hard enough, which is so toxic. I came out to LA and I thought, 'Oh wow, all these people can afford to make these short films and afford to not have a day job and just write all day and they're going to be more successful than me.' And I really thought it was because I didn't work hard enough. Then at twenty-five or twenty-six, one of my friends said something about her parents' owning the condo where she lives, and I said, 'You don't pay rent?!' and she said, 'No.' And I know it sounds crazy, but it had never occurred to me that people's parents give them money. I had never, ever thought about it. All of a sudden I realized that all my friends and I had different amounts of money in the bank."

One of the most uncomfortable truths in adulthood is the reality that you and your friends are not in the same place financially. It can leave a particularly nasty taste in your mouth if you once shared a common financial script. The change happens for a myriad of reasons. Sometimes it's that you didn't know your friend came from money. It could be that you suddenly started earning a lot and your friends are in less lucrative jobs. Or maybe some friends chose to make life-altering decisions earlier, like marriage or having children or moving to an expensive city.

Arriving at this realization, whether it's in a dramatic fashion like Dunn or just a natural progression, does beg the question: should you be speaking in specifics when it comes to your money?

SHOULD YOU SHARE YOUR SALARY WITH YOUR FRIENDS?

"What, that's awesome! How much would you be making?!" I asked my friend Charlotte when she told me about her new job offer.

She paused for a moment. It was brief, but there was a distinct pause before she shared her new salary. It was a big number. The kind of number that could certainly make people feel a range of emotions from envious to uncomfortable.

Charlotte and I had gone to college together, majored in journalism together, and then both moved to New York City. We'd started out as scrappy twenty-two-year-olds not earning enough from our primary jobs and having to work side hustles to make ends meet. We lived in the same outer-borough neighborhood that had started out really affordable and suddenly gotten trendy in recent years. We'd always been comfortable talking to each other about money. Probably because we'd met at a time when we went from debating the world's issues in the dining hall to leaning on each other in the "real world." Even before I started Broke Millennial, Charlotte was the kind of friend I'd talk to about numbers. And as our careers diverged in our mid-twenties, she transitioned into the tech world, and I took a leap into self-employment. There could've easily been a natural tension over the "how much do you make" question.

But I think because our careers went in such different directions, it remained easier for us to communicate about money. We're not in comparable fields. So, if Charlotte gets a promotion, a raise, or a new job, it's not a frustration for me. Now, when other self-employed friends of mine score a big contract or negotiate a much better deal on the same gig, you betcha I get a little green with envy. Which really begs the question, *should* you ask your friends how much they make?

Dr. Brad Klontz, a financial psychologist and professor at Creighton University, says sharing your salary with friends is generally an enormous risk.

"The risk is that they are going to look at you differently now," says Klontz. "Typically, in a negative way. I think it's fairly universal for people to have some negative feelings or automatic thoughts about those who have more than them."

In order to determine if there's more to gain than lose by sharing salary numbers with a friend, Klontz recommends you think through a few questions first:

- Are you an open book on everything with your friend, and that's something you're used to?
- Were they friends with you before you found success?
- How are they going to take it?
- Will it be perceived as bragging?

"In personal finance there is a push to be transparent and share all the details about what you're making, but sometimes I think it's not productive and just voyeuristic in some cases," says Kristin Wong, author of *Get Money*. "It's not bad if you don't want to share every number. If it can be productive and help your friends, then it makes sense."

Wong herself is very transparent with those in her life when it comes to sharing numbers, but it could be a by-product of writing about money for a living. She doesn't expect others to reciprocate or be as open.

How to Determine Whether Sharing Your Income Is Helpful

Determining whether or not sharing your income (or net worth) with a friend is helpful all comes down to context, context, context. Reflect on why you are sharing this information. Are you providing insight that will help your friend feel motivated to pay off debt, negotiate for a higher salary, pick up a side hustle, or start saving more? Or should you be honest with yourself and recognize that you might be flexing a bit and offering up a not-so-humble brag?

With that in mind, when you're the one asking for a friend's salary information, you should open the conversation with context. Why exactly are you asking a friend how much they earn? And be honest with yourself: Do you really need to know how much a friend makes as insight for your own career or financial goals? Or are you curious about whether your friend is actually affording their lifestyle or just financing it on credit? The former can be helpful; the latter is none of your business unless they bring an issue directly to you. If you are in the "Seriously, that info would be helpful to me" camp, then here are some ways you can initiate the conversation:

 "I'm planning to ask for a raise soon and wondered if you've had any success negotiating your salary."

If your friend works in the same industry and knowing a ballpark (or specifics) about their salary would actually be helpful, then you can use the over/under strategy from the work section.

"I'm starting to get the sense I might be underpaid in our field. This might be an awkward question, but how much do you make?"

Then, if your friend is acting awkward or uncomfortable, you pivot to the over/under strategy . . .

"It's okay if you don't want to give an exact number, but is it over or under [insert number here]?"

Another option is to ask upon hearing about a promotion or raise.

"That's so awesome you got the job offer! Are you getting a good pay bump?"

A good way to lay a foundation for this conversation is to consider speaking more broadly, with percentages instead of actual numbers—for example, sharing your savings rate or the percentage of your income you put toward retirement or other investing goals. You should proceed with as much caution about sharing your total net worth as you would about sharing your salary.

"There's a lot of emotion tied to money, so you don't want to feel like you're bragging or making your friends feel bad if you have more saved for retirement than they do," says Wong.

None of this is to say you shouldn't share. Sharing can be powerful, just like asking coworkers about their salaries. However, once shared, that information can't be unlearned. It's really obnoxious when a friend gets a sense of your salary and then feels entitled to make judgments about what you can and can't afford, or how you should or shouldn't be spending your money. You need to really evaluate if and how it could impact your relationship before sharing. Should you decide that being open about your salary and/or net worth isn't a good idea, then just be straightforward. You could even make a counteroffer to soften the blow:

"To be honest, I'm not really comfortable sharing my exact numbers, but I'm happy to share the percentage of my salary I save and invest each month if you think that would be helpful."

What About Your Debt Number?

After pages of saying, "Eh, be careful about sharing your salary," I'm going to make a bold claim. You should seriously consider sharing your debt number, or at least the existence of debt, with your friends. "Uhhh, why?!" I can hear some of you screaming at me. Well, because it gets a lot easier to do something like this:

"By the second or third year I was dealing with loans, and people were picking up in their careers, I had to just be really honest that I didn't have the money to spend on dinners out or other recreational expenses," says Caitlin Boston, a UX researcher who paid off six-figure student loan debt. "Or say, 'Hey, if we're going to do this, then this is what I can spend, and I don't know if it's realistic for me to come.'"

I know, I know—sharing your debt number is an incredibly scary proposition. There is so much shame and emotion tied up in debt, and it can make you feel truly vulnerable to say to a friend, "Listen, I've got $35,000 in student loans and $5,000 in credit card debt." You risk being judged, especially when it comes to consumer debt (a.k.a. credit card debt and personal loans).

There is often a belief that student loans or a mortgage is "good debt" while consumer debt is "bad debt." Frankly, I could write an entire book about the issues we've created in America by intertwining morality and debt. But this isn't that book! Instead, I challenge you to forgive your past self for any debt-generating decisions that were made. It's done. Today you can focus on making a plan for how to handle the debt—and if you're struggling to do that, I recommend the first book in this series: *Broke Millennial: Stop Scraping By and Get Your Financial Life Together.* (Why yes, that is a rather self-promotional plug.)

Being vulnerable and open with your friends about your debt can help deepen the bonds and intimacy of your friendship. It can provide helpful context to them about why you may react in a certain way to a financial situation, decline invitations, or even experience levels of general anxiety. Another reason I advocate sharing your debt journey is simple: built-in accountability.

Be Accountability Buddies

Personal trainers and gym classes are popular in part because they provide a layer of accountability. You've already paid for a session and someone is expecting you to show up. Sharing your debt payoff plan (or general financial goals) with a friend can have the same effect, especially if they are also trying to pay off debt. Having someone else who's aware of your goals and asking about your progress can keep you on the straight and narrow. Now, I'm not saying it'll keep you from slipping up here and there, but it certainly helps motivate you to cross the finish line.

If your brain is screaming, "Oh, hell no!" or maybe you even muttered that out loud reading this section, you could still find anonymous accountability on the Internet. There are hundreds (probably thousands) of blogs and Instagram accounts dedicated to people anonymously sharing their financial mistakes, milestones, and debt payoff journeys. Search hashtags like #debtfreecommunity, #debtfreejourney, #studentloans, #debtpayoff, and #debtfreedom to find them.

People Might Not Share Outright, but I Bet They're Providing Context Clues

"There are so many ways we talk about money without actually talking about money," says Lindsey Stanberry. "I was at a dinner recently and all the conversation was about money. Someone was talking about moving to New Jersey and struggling to find a house they could afford, and another woman was talking about having a second kid and timing it so her other child was in school and she'd only be paying for one child's care cost. While none of those were explicitly about money, they were all about money."

Don't be discouraged if you would like to engage in a money talk with a friend and you initially get shot down. It could be simply planting a seed for a conversation your friend might bring up in the future. Or you can just be on the lookout for other ways in which your friends discuss money without actually discussing money. Those context clues can also provide insight for how to navigate the almighty "What happens when my friend and I earn very different salaries?" conversation.

Chapter 4

What Happens When You're in Significantly Different Financial Situations?

"Let's do a steak house," one of my friends suggested while our group debated activities for our three-day trip to San Antonio.

It was Texas, after all, and a steak house felt like a must-do. Problem was, not everyone in the group saw value in the fairly hefty price tag that would accompany a visit to a steak house. So, my friend immediately solved the problem by offering to heavily subsidize the meal. That way he'd get what he wanted and those who didn't see the value wouldn't feel cranky that someone else was deciding how to spend their money.

This is just one scenario that becomes more common as you get older. As you age, three significant things begin to happen with friends.

First, people's value sets begin to change. You might've all been fine with drinking boxed wine and cheap beer in college, but now some of your friends fancy themselves self-taught sommeliers and others only drink local craft brews. And that's fine. You're allowed to start wanting nicer things—but just because you're okay dropping $40 on a bottle of wine without a second thought, it doesn't mean your friend, who hasn't yet developed a palate for a full-bodied red, is wrong for drinking an $8 bottle of Moscato.

Second, life events occur on differing timelines. Your friends will get married and therefore merge their financial lives with other people's—people who also have a say in how money is saved, invested, and spent. They may start having babies or need to support family members, and could have less discretionary income to spend on going out or taking trips than those who don't have these same obligations.

Third, people in your inner circle of friends may begin to earn significantly different amounts of money. Or, if you're all earning about the same, people's financial goals will vary, which means spending patterns will no longer align.

For the friend who earns more, it can feel really frustrating that you're being anchored to the person who earns the least amount of money, has the highest debt situation, or just doesn't want to spend money. For the friend who isn't as flush with cash, it can be embarrassing or can even result in credit card debt in an effort to keep up.

All these factors can combine to slowly breed annoyance or even resentment with each other if you don't address the situation.

This is a tough pill to swallow, but as you mature and enter different life situations, you tend to go through a self-selecting process in which you begin to narrow your friendship circles to those who, in many ways, reflect your own experiences and views.

"As you get older, you want to be friends with people who are similar to you and date people who are similar to you," says Gaby Dunn, author and host of the *Bad with Money* podcast. "As I've gotten older, my group has become queer people and people with similar backgrounds."

Married people will look around one night at a gathering and realize most of their friends are also married or in long-term, committed relationships. Parents often prioritize fellow parents as friends over those who are child-free because there's an instant understanding there. Heck, I'm friends with more dog people than cat people! (I jest. Sort of.)

But it isn't just about life situations and experiences. Surprise, surprise—it all ties back to money.

This self-selecting process often extends to socializing with those in a similar socioeconomic class. This isn't to say you cut out old friends, but you may naturally start to see less of each other and go from bosom buddies to the occasional catch-up session. I'm not saying it's the right thing to do, but it's a common occurrence, especially if you aren't willing to be honest with your friends. It can be really, really awkward to have these money talks, so you may find yourself subconsciously phasing someone out in lieu of having that tough talk (or find that a friend is doing it to you).

WE ALL HAVE A FINANCIAL COMFORT ZONE

Dr. Brad Klontz, a financial psychologist and a professor at Creighton University, developed the idea of the "financial comfort zone" (FCZ) to better explain this natural drive we have to seek out what we already know. Klontz likens your financial comfort zone to culture in that there are certain rules and ways things are done that mirror circumstances from your upbringing and are comfortable to you.

To use my upbringing as an example of how our FCZ often plays out in our adult lives: I grew up in an environment in which there wasn't a lot of money stress, largely as a by-product of my parents' being on the same financial page. They weren't big spenders. Frugality and saving were modeled and encouraged, except when it came to travel. Both of my parents valued travel and would spend more lavishly there than in any other area. To this day, I'm frugal in many areas of my life, but not so much when traveling. Arguably, I'm frugal so I can travel.

"Now, the further you get out of that zone, the more psychological pressure there is to get you right back to that zone," says Klontz. "It totally explains why people win the lottery or get a big bonus and then totally blow all the money."

When Klontz works with a client who recently came into a large sum of money, he'll somewhat facetiously say, "You have two choices right now. Number one, get rid of all your money. Or number two, get rid of all your friends. Because the middle ground is going to take a tremendous amount of work, and you can do it, but people have a tendency to do one of the other two things."

For most people, coming into a large sum of money is a gradual experience that happens as a two-pronged attack of living well below your means and moving up in your career. But whether it's at twenty-five or thirty-five or forty-five or fifty-five, you may reach a point in your life when you and your friends have significantly different financial situations.

So, let's talk about this shift and how to do the "tremendous amount of work."

WHEN YOU EARN LESS (OR YOU'RE IN A LOT OF DEBT)

"We're hardwired to dislike people who have more than we do," says Klontz. "The likelihood of you experiencing envy toward your friend [who earns more] is really high, and that envy can destroy your relationship if you're not careful."

The Psychology of Envy, a.k.a. You'll Want to Get Judgmental
"Are you okay with your friend talking to you about their financial stress?" asks Klontz.

Just because your friend earns more than you do doesn't mean they are without financial stress. But it could be difficult for you to listen to your friend go on and on about a money woe when you earn less or are struggling with more debt. "You'll start to nitpick at your friend and judge how they're spending money and possibly feel like they're somehow undeserving," says Klontz.

Don't Let Your Friend Keep Picking Up the Tab
It's likely that your friend could start to feel self-conscious about how much they have, which can lead to your friend's offering to pay. At first,

you might take them up on the offer—after all, they're making so much and can totally afford this. And they wouldn't offer if they didn't want to pay, right? But Klontz advises that you also reciprocate by offering to pay the next time. He warns that constantly accepting your friend's generosity can lead to your friend's feeling awkward about it, regardless of what they're telling you.

You also don't have to reciprocate on the same financial level; it's often about the gesture, Klontz points out. You do need to be honest in order to make the relationship work.

> *"I want to pay next time, but I can't afford this restaurant. Are you okay with our eating at a cheaper place?"*

Your friend also might keep offering to pay because it's their love language, and even if it's coming from a purely altruistic place with zero strings attached, it might not make you feel warm and fuzzy inside. Paco de Leon, founder of The Hell Yeah Group, a financial firm focused on creatives, recommends you be honest about how it makes you feel, but start off with a positive.

> *"I appreciate the kind gesture, but it doesn't feel good for me."*

It's Okay to Spend Money, Even When You Have Debt

You do not—I repeat, you do not—have to sacrifice absolutely everything in your life in the pursuit of paying off debt. In fact, it's probably going to do a number on your mental health if you eschew all earthly pleasures for years in the dogged pursuit of complete debt freedom (or a big financial goal).

"I was never that person who was going to eat potatoes and rice and live a monastic existence and not go out ever," says Caitlin Boston, who paid off $222,817.26 in student loans. "One thing that really helped me is that I gave myself one vacation a year."

Boston didn't spend lavishly on vacations either. She picked countries that were more affordable than many European destinations, or even domestic trips, and then would earmark part of her monthly budget as savings for the trip.

"I needed a release valve," explains Boston. "You can't have that amount of pressure on you all the time and not feel like you have a way to excise it. That's a way I felt really healthy in managing my debt. It also made me realize I can spend money and it's not going to completely derail me financially."

In addition to travel, Boston would give herself permission to save up for purchasing new clothing. Usually about twice a year she'd buy herself a nice pair of pants or a sweater or jacket.

"It's okay if I have small luxuries now and then, just not all the time," she says.

It's natural to feel judgmental or even resentful at times, but good, close friends in healthy relationships discuss their feelings and express their needs. It's not dissimilar to a romantic relationship in this way. You can still go out and have a good time with your high-earner friends. You can maintain just as close of a connection if you utilize these techniques to prevent negative feelings from driving a wedge.

When You Make More

"I try to be cognizant of the income disparity and not be a dick about it," jokes de Leon. "If I know my friends are struggling and cobbling together their existence, I'm not going to invite them to the new sushi restaurant that's going to cost $150. I'm going to save that for my bougie friends. And you should have a nice spectrum of people you're friends with—because it makes you a better person."

While de Leon's "Don't be a dick" mantra when it comes to friends and finances is both giggle inducing and practical, a cognitive dissonance can also occur for people who either always had or came into wealth.

"As you have more money than other people, you're automatically distanced emotionally from their experience," says Klontz. "It's easy to say, 'Rich people don't care about people who have less than them.' Well, how much time do you spend worrying about people who have less than you in another country?" asks Klontz.

He cites this as a normal thing that happens because it's easier to see what's happening above us, but it's harder to understand an experience someone is having that's lower on the socioeconomic scale.

Understand the Flip Side of the Psychology of Envy

Envy is usually the by-product of someone's having more than you do (or something that you covet). If you aren't envious of your friends' financial situations, it could be that you're all in similar income brackets, or that you appear to all be in the same situation because someone is leveraging debt unbeknownst to you.

"It's really common for people to judge you or have a negative opinion of you," says Klontz. "So be conscious of what your friend can afford, because you could be in the position to create stress or minimize it. If you're at a really different income level, be conscious and aware of the fact that your friend may not be able to afford going to certain places or doing certain things."

So, what does that look like in action? Here are a few ways you can avoid crushing your friend's budget and help reduce the psychology of envy.

Offer to Pay (Sometimes)

Similar to my friend and the steak house, Gaby Dunn will offer to cover her friend's meal if she wants to go to a particular restaurant.

"I got some good professional news, and I said to my friend, 'I want to celebrate and I want to go to this restaurant, so I will pay for you.' And she said, 'Oh no, you don't have to. It's fine, I can cover it.' But I told her, 'I want to celebrate here and I want you to come and I'm not going to make that your problem.'"

That idea of not making it your friend's problem is a really key point.

One of the growing pains in earning more than your friends is accidentally establishing the expectation that you'll always pick up the tab. Especially if your friends are well aware that you are in a more stable financial position. There's a delicate balance between being generous when your decisions financially impact your friends (e.g., you want to spend time with them and eat at a fancy restaurant) and always paying just because you feel awkward about earning more.

Give your friend a reason for why you want to engage in a certain activity, then offer to pay. If/when your friend resists the idea of your paying, you can further explain that you're picking up the tab because you want to do the activity that you want to do instead of compromising, so you're not going to also expect your friend to pay. Here's an example:

> *"I just saw that the Backstreet Boys are doing a surprise reunion tour concert this weekend. I really want you to come with me, so I'll buy the tickets."* [Friend resists.] *"I hear you, but I know you were more of an NSYNC fan, so I'll get these tickets because I really want you to experience the Backstreet Boys!"*

But You Don't Always Have to Pay . . .

Just because you earn more doesn't mean you have to bankroll your group of friends. In fact, you shouldn't. Such behavior can ultimately breed resentment and distrust. You're probably going to start questioning your friends' motives for being around you and get cranky that you're always picking up the tab. And your friends might feel disrespected that you always insist on getting the bill. You think it's generous, but to them it could read as your believing they can't handle their finances or pay for a meal.

"I do like to be generous when I can, but also I know my friends don't expect that," says Melanie Lockert, author of *Dear Debt* and cofounder of the Lola Retreat. Lockert has experienced both sides of this equation, as she transitioned from being one of the lower earners in her group of friends to a higher earner.

She advises that you determine for yourself the level of generosity with which you're comfortable.

"By 'comfortable,' I mean a level of comfort where you can let this go and you're never going to think, 'Oh wow, remember this one time when I covered that?'" says Lockert. "You're not keeping tabs. Keeping tabs will kill you and ruin your friendships."

Still Invite Your Friends

It can become tempting to just avoid inviting certain friends to events if you're worried they can't afford the price tag. But it's not your job to make the decision for your friend.

"You have to extend the invitation," says Klontz. "They're going to see it on Instagram anyway, and you have to at least have the conversation about it because it's going to get back to them and they're going to feel pretty hurt. Twenty years ago it might not have gotten back to them, but now it will."

The only way to avoid phasing a friend out, especially if it's just over some awkwardness, is to be open and honest with each other.

Have the Explicit Conversation

To harken back to a point Klontz made earlier in this section, the awkwardness, tension, and ultimately distancing happens when you want to scale up your lifestyle and your friend can't afford to (or doesn't want to).

Klontz uses the example of going on a group vacation with friends. What happens if you want to fly first-class and they can only afford economy? Are you going to stay in a budget hotel because that's all your friend can afford?

"If you do that, are you going to want to go on vacation with them next time?" asks Klontz. "Did you sacrifice so much that you're uncomfortable on the trip and wishing you hadn't gone?"

It's critical to find your happy medium with each other, but Klontz advises that can only happen when you have an explicit conversation and commitment to each other that you won't let money mess up the friendship.

> *"I care about time with you and I want to ensure we don't lose our friendship with each other."*

From this opening line, you can work together to brainstorm creative ways to spend time together that are enjoyable for both of you but don't hurt either person's bank account. It can even become a fun challenge between you two, like finding free events in your city or town, or who can come up with the best "friend date" itinerary within a certain budget.

In 2019, I did a no-spend challenge in the month of February, but I also didn't want it to keep me from socializing. In order to mix it up and not just say, "Want to come over and I'll make dinner?" each time my friends hung out, I started to scour event listings for free museum hours and other free activities. It became fun for my friends, with some of them joining in the search. The New York Public Library's free one-hour tour of the Schwarzman Building (the iconic library with the two lions out front) is one of my favorites in the city.

When Your Value Sets Just Don't Align

Tension over money in a friendship isn't always about disparate incomes. It really could be about different value sets. In the aforementioned example of flying first-class and flying coach, both friends may be able to afford to fly first-class, but both may not see the value equally. Friend A may want the seat that reclines fully into a bed and the proper silverware and semi-decent food, while Friend B would rather save the money, pack a yummy snack, and then take a ZzzQuil to sleep through the flight. Neither friend is right or wrong. They just have different value sets.

The issue comes to a head when you have to say to your friend that you don't want to spend money on a particular item, activity, or accommodation—especially when they know you can afford it. It's awkward because the underlying implication (whether you mean it this way or not) is that you are judging what your friend values.

Instead of talking about values, Klontz suggests you eliminate that language from the conversation, because it comes off judgy, and instead refocus to bring up your goals as your reason for making a certain decision. Talk in terms of your goals instead of values.

> *"Oh, we'd love to go on vacation with you, but we're trying to save up for* [insert thing here]."

It also never hurts to provide a counteroffer. Maybe you can't afford the full-blown vacation, but what about a weekend getaway nearby?

Before you get too alarmed, none of this information is meant to deter you from staying friends with people you grew up with or your best pals from college. Rather, it's good to be aware early on so you can start to address the situation before any resentment, frustration, or animosity begins to simmer below the surface of your seemingly amicable relationship.

Creating a Plan to Work Through All This and Stay Friends

It will be remarkable if you make it through life without having money cause some level of tension with a friend—even if it's as simple as deciding how to split a dinner bill! Whether you've had a few minor annoyances start to accumulate or you're feeling left out because your friend isn't inviting you to the posh events she attends, you have to open up.

Learn How to Talk It Out—Even When It's Awkward

"Identify the distress and communicate," says Amanda Clayman, a financial therapist. "What is your worry about how money is going to impact this relationship? Start to communicate that worry to the other person."

Clayman advises that you first reflect on your worry (identify the distress). Then you have to communicate that worry to your friend in a kind and loving way. Clayman recommends you always start off the conversation with something positive.

"I love you and I want to spend time with you, and your friendship means a lot.

"I worry that as we move into this next phase of our lives when I'm a teacher and you're a banker, we are going to have different lifestyles, and it will get harder for us to just naturally hang out like we used to.

"I don't want that to be a factor in whether we stay friends."

"And then figure out if your friend shares this concern, which it's very likely that they do and they just don't know how to bring it up," says Clayman. "Next, start to talk about your thoughts and feelings. We're not rushing to a solution. We are using this as an opportunity to codevelop and cocreate what makes both people feel respected, seen, and validated."

However, it is important to consider that even after introspection and some solid talks, you and your friend's relationship might eventually fizzle out and become the "occasional coffee date" kind of friendship.

"Not every friend you make is going to be a friend for life, and sometimes we need to let that go," says Clayman. But she advises that you don't just let a friendship phase out because you don't know how to have a conversation about this new, uncomfortable dynamic.

Chapter 5

Setting Boundaries

OKAY, WE'VE TALKED about when and how to share numbers with friends and what to do when you're in different financial situations. Now it's time to talk about boundaries and learning how to say no.

But before we get to the actual strategies, let's acknowledge one thing: This can be awkward. Really, really awkward. Having to straight-up tell someone your budget limitations is fundamentally uncomfortable. However, *Dear Debt* author Melanie Lockert reframes this situation perfectly: "You have to weigh which will win out: the embarrassment or the resentment. Is it going to be more embarrassing to own up to your financial situation or will you be resentful for three days because you said yes when you really can't afford it?"

In a classic how-to-split-the-dinner-bill-at-a-birthday-party situation, Lockert did this analysis in her head and realized she wouldn't see most of the people at the dinner again, her friends there would still love and care for her, and the resentment would certainly outweigh the embarrassment of advocating for herself in the moment.

STRATEGIES TO SET FINANCIAL BOUNDARIES WITH FRIENDS

The previous two chapters have focused largely on the hypothetical and psychological elements of friendship dynamics. Now let's talk about practical strategies (and actual language to use) when you need to gently, but firmly, set boundaries with your besties.

Counteroffer

When your friend asks you to come to happy hour, take a trip, get dinner, be in a wedding, or have a spa day and you want, or need, to say no, there's a special technique to make the entire exchange palatable for both parties.

"You have to have the courage to have a counteroffer," says Dr. Brad Klontz, a professor of financial psychology at Creighton University. "Especially if your friend has more money than you. There's nothing worse than 'Hey, do you want to do this?' 'No.' Because then I'm left to make up some sort of reason about why you said no."

Personally, I go for the counteroffer with the compliment sandwich, because you sandwich the bad news in between a compliment or a thanks and a compliment plus a counteroffer.

"I really appreciate the invitation . . .

"But I'm focused on paying off my student loans by the end of this year," or *"It's a little out of my budget.*

"I definitely do want to spend time with you though. Would you want to come over for game night instead?"

If your friend is inviting you to something that's already set—like a concert—then you can pick a specific night to add to your counteroffer.

"Would you want to come over next Wednesday for cocktails and game night?"

UX designer Caitlin Boston also deployed the counteroffer technique a lot, especially in the first eight years of her debt repayment journey. Oftentimes she wouldn't ask for a change of plans but rather offer another solution. For example, if her friends were going out for dinner, then Boston would say the following:

"I'm busy, but I can come meet you for a drink afterward."

Share Your Reason

"I had a friend who started just saying to people, 'I'm saving money right now. I can't go to the restaurant. Can we eat at your house?'" says Gaby Dunn, host of the *Bad with Money* podcast. Her friend's openness empowered Dunn to do the same. "She is a very confident person who just has that straight-shooter way of talking, and I thought, 'Wow, she's a genius.' But really she's just being honest with people."

Before you go freaking out that you couldn't be that direct with your friends, Dunn points out that she has never been upset with a friend for advocating for herself.

"You can ask, 'Can we change the plan?' and nobody is ever going to be mad," says Dunn. "If anything, I started coming to her with ideas, like, 'Hey, do you want to go on a hike?' I started pitching her free activities."

Now, while I'd love to say that your friends will always be that accommodating, I'll be honest that routinely asking to change plans can tick people off, especially if you don't give them notice and you request a change of plans at the eleventh hour. It's important to advocate for yourself, but you also have to be okay with your friends' deciding to do the originally planned activity. Just because you elect to opt out doesn't mean they have to too.

Perhaps you currently don't have the confidence of Dunn's friend to be up front that you're saving for a big goal or trying to pay down debt, but it really can help to open up and share your "why." It provides context for your friends, which helps them better understand you and your decisions.

"I think people should talk about those things," says Lindsey Stanberry, author of Refinery 29's *Money Diaries* and deputy managing editor of CNBC's Make It. When she was in her twenties, Stanberry and her husband set an aggressive savings goal of $100,000 to buy an apartment in New York City. The two would constantly turn down invitations from friends in their pursuit to save.

"We didn't really talk about it back then. We just looked cheap," says Stanberry.

Another common reason to avoid extra expenses: babies.

"Having a kid is definitely an excuse," says Stanberry, pointing out that the cost of a babysitter in addition to the activity really adds up. Plus, it's about not just money but spending time with your child, especially if you both work.

Of course, I'm not advocating that you have a child just for the excuse of declining social invitations—but it is helpful to contextualize for your friends that going out isn't as simple as it used to be. People only know their lived experiences, and while, sure, they get that you'd need to hire a babysitter, they might not recognize that you and your partner's coming to a birthday dinner for four hours would cost the price of dinner plus the $80+ for the babysitter (depending on rates of babysitters in your area).

Take Control in Order to Manage Expectations

Being the self-appointed party planning committee helps, and making the social decisions in your friend group enables you to stay within your budget. But that sounds like a friend dictatorship, and that isn't conducive to a good friendship. Instead, you can directly set expectations.

"Could we pick a dinner spot that's no more than $20 each? I actually have a few ideas."

Tying back to the counteroffer concept, it's always a stronger case if you can provide options when you're trying to manage expectations. Do your research ahead of time and go in ready with a pitch.

Lockert advises that you set expectations on the amount of time you're willing to be there or the amount of money you can spend before the event happens.

> *"I'd like to come out tonight, but I'm probably only going to have one drink because I'm on a budget."*

Plus, if you've also shared your goals (like debt payoff or saving up for a house) or you've been honest about your budget restrictions, it does help make a stronger, more empathetic case.

"My best friend is quite a bit more affluent than I am, and we had really honest conversations in which I would tell her the maximum amount I could spend," says Boston.

In her experience, Boston found her friends always had an empathic response rather than a negative one when she needed to manage expectations. Either they adjusted their plans to accommodate her or they agreed she'd just join next time when it fit into her budget.

I've said it before, but it bears repeating: your friends don't have to change their plans to accommodate you, but that doesn't mean they're having a negative reaction to you either. They just want to do whatever fun event they planned, and that's okay.

Bring a Snack (or Otherwise Reduce the Cost)

Having to constantly play defense can get really tiring. I get it. Sometimes you want to just be the go-with-the-flow person who eagerly accepts your friends' invitations. You can, but it might take a little extra work to reduce the potential damage to your bank account.

"I'd always bring snacks with me because I wouldn't have eaten yet, or people would be eating and I didn't want to be tempted to spend money," says Boston. "If it was going to be a longer night, I'd bring an actual sandwich and say, 'Oh, I'm really hot, so I'm going to go outside for a minute,' and then go eat the sandwich outside."

The answer isn't always to bring a snack, but consider the ways you can lower the overall cost for yourself. For example, skip the drinks at the bar ahead of the concert and make a deal with yourself that you can only buy one drink there and no merch. I always bring sealed bottled water with me to sports events (after checking ahead of time to see if the arena allows them to be brought in) because I don't want to spend $7 for a water and a lot of arenas won't allow you to bring in reusable water bottles.

Unfortunately, group dinners are the enemy of these hidden tactics.

Can't Afford to Split the Bill

Group dinners were invented to test your ability to set boundaries. Splitting the bill evenly is the smoothest way to handle a group dinner, but it's not the most fair and equitable.

Barring the ability to intercept people's minds and make everyone volunteer to simply cover their portion of the bill, there's no easy way to navigate this situation. You're going to have to advocate for yourself and have the potentially awkward conversation. But I'm willing to bet at least one other person at that table will be relieved and leap at the chance to just pay for what they ordered.

(Counteroffer strategy) + (managing expectations) + (sharing your excuse) = the ideal way to navigate the splitting-the-dinner-bill conversation.

Reduce the day-of tension by setting those expectations early. Let's use the common birthday dinner situation. Tell your friend ahead of time (we're talking as much time as possible) that you'd like to come, but you really need to only pay for your portion of the bill.

It's even better if you can give your friend a ballpark of how much you're able to spend so they can keep it in mind when picking a restaurant. Don't be shy about providing your reasons—"I'm saving up to buy a house," "I'm really working on paying off half my student loan debt by the end of the year," or "It's been a slow year financially and I'm really on a strict budget."

"I'm excited to celebrate your birthday with you, but I'm really aiming to make a $500 payment toward my student loans this month, so I have to be mindful of my budget. Would it be possible for me to cover just what I order and chip in a little for your meal?"

Granted, it's not entirely fair to ask your friend to restrict options to what's in your budget, or she may already have made her selection. In either case, you can come in with a counteroffer.

"The restaurant you picked is delicious but a little out of my budget. I really do still want to celebrate with you, so I'll just come for dessert or an after-dinner drink if that's okay."

You can also volunteer to be the person at the end of the dinner who steps up and figures out how to split up the bill evenly.

Paco de Leon, founder of The Hell Yeah Group, recommends looking for fast-casual–style restaurants where you order and pay, then go sit down, especially if splitting the bill is known to be a pain point.

Don't Accumulate Credit Card Debt for Other People's Special Moments

One of the toughest parts about setting boundaries with your friends is that you're going to have to opt out sometimes, especially if participating would get financed on credit cards.

"You might be upset for a little bit, but you should consider that you don't want to be hundreds of dollars in debt for something you can't afford," says Boston, who set a big goal to avoid credit card debt while she was paying off her six-figure student loans.

It's one thing if a medical emergency arises or you need to fly home to be with a loved one in a time of crisis. But do not let other people's special moments (weddings, birthdays, graduations) drive you into consumer debt.

There can be a compromise. For example, you don't have to opt out of the wedding entirely—because I understand wanting to be there to celebrate this moment with your friend. But maybe you have to forgo the bridal shower and bachelorette party in order to be at the wedding. (Don't worry, we have an entire chapter dedicated to weddings on deck!)

Be Vulnerable with Your Friends

"Honesty is the best policy," says Dunn. "And maybe you'll lose friends or you'll find out that your friends were faking it too."

> A friend I lived with in grad school got married right after graduation, and I had less than zero dollars at that point. Her family was from Austria, so they were getting married in Austria. At the time I wasn't as vocal about my financial situation, so I told her, "I'm prepping for this big thing and I can't get out of work," and I never told her I couldn't afford to go to her wedding. I felt really bad about that too, because I've never lived it down when I see her [her friend always teases her a bit about not attending her wedding]. Now that everything has come out that I had these massive student loans, it's become more clear that I wasn't being inconsiderate, I just had no money.
>
> —Caitlin Boston

Being vulnerable with a friend takes a lot of trust and love, but sharing your truth also prevents your friend from thinking the worst. If one of your closest friends told you she couldn't come to your wedding because of work, that would be hurtful. But if she said, "I have six-figure student loan debt and just can't afford an international plane ticket," that would be completely understandable. You might still be sad, but at least you would understand the why.

Sharing your financial vulnerabilities may also illuminate which friendships are meant to be lifelong bonds and which ones will undergo the natural phase-out. If a friend is throwing a hissy fit that you can't afford an international plane ticket, well, maybe she's not such a solid pal.

Boston found that being honest with her friends about her debt led to her having a support system, because she could finally talk about managing her debt and how it was affecting her, and provide context for why she couldn't do certain activities. And they never gave her a hard time about it.

"I'm now in a position where I'm doing the same thing with some of my friends," says Boston. "They'd say, 'Can we eat dinner in the house or can we cook together?' and I think it creates a really healthy openness that leads to better intimacy."

Get off Social Media—or at Least Set Some Restrictions

This one is about setting a boundary for yourself and your own mental health. And I'm fully aware that no one reading this is going to go delete all social media (myself included). But it is important to try to at least limit your exposure to social media if it's causing harm either mentally, to your budget, or to your relationships. It is painful to see a group of friends out together that didn't invite you. It will make you jealous when your bestie posts jaw-dropping landscape photos from her latest travel adventure.

Our parents' generation may have used McMansions and over-the-top purchases to "flex for the 'gram" before the advent of social media, but chronicling your every experience is also a way to showboat.

"It's a piece of technology that's being leveraged for capitalism, and it's exploiting our normal dopamine response system," says de Leon about social media.

Like I said, I'm not expecting anyone to actually completely opt out of social media based on a couple of paragraphs, but consider setting boundaries. That could mean taking one full day a week in which you don't log on. Or maybe it's muting people on your feeds (or unfollowing them entirely if it won't damage a relationship). Keep reminding yourself that social media is a carefully curated version of another person's life and doesn't represent reality.

You should also stop obsessively checking the fun your friends are having if you chose not to attend a trip or event due to budget restrictions. Put your phone away and engage in a budget-friendly activity instead.

How to Decline an Invitation

Saying no to a friend's invitation is *hard*, especially for life events like birthdays and weddings. Sure, you can probably say no to brunch or happy hour with ease, but giving a hard pass on being a bridesmaid or groomsman? Well, good luck.

> I never wanted to be a bridesmaid. I was one in my early twenties and after that I managed to avoid it. I never had been on a bachelorette trip until this year, and I always thought that when it came up I'd say no because it's not how I want to spend my money. And then when it happened to me, I just said yes and grumbled about it a lot behind the scenes. It was unfair because I had the money to be able to afford to do those things now [compared to my early twenties], but it's just not how I wanted to spend my money at all. At all, at all. But I did it and really felt like a hypocrite for not being able to protect myself.
>
> —Lindsey Stanberry

Next up is a chapter dedicated to handling the finances of being in weddings, because let me tell you what, being asked to be in a wedding can quickly become one of the biggest sources of tension in a friendship!

Whether you're trying to say no to a college-friends reunion or to attending a baby shower, one of the key moves is to decline sooner rather than later. Don't be the person who backs out at the last minute, especially if other people are depending on you to financially contribute.

As for the how, it's similar to the compliment sandwich. You want to offer a consolation prize.

"It's important to acknowledge how much you care about them so it doesn't seem like you're just dismissing their friendship," says Kristin Wong, author of *Get Money*. "Then try to find some other way of celebrating with them."

 "Sorry I can't come on the reunion trip, but I'd love to join digitally for a group happy hour one of the nights you're all there."

Or:

 "I'd love to take you out to dinner to celebrate your new adventure."

"Whatever you offer, make sure that it's not going to be stressful for them and that it helps make them feel like you want to be a part of their celebration," says Wong.

You can also send a small gift as a token to offset any sting from your declining, especially if it's a close friend. For example, one of my go-to baby shower moves is to send my favorite book to read as a kid (with a note explaining that) and a small gift for mom, like nice bath salts or lotion.

While it's perfectly understandable to bow out of the financial obligations attached to certain functions, you do always want to be careful to strike a balance so that you're also investing in your relationships.

Invest in Friendships Too

"Want to go to Adam's parents' house this weekend out on Long Island? We thought it'd be a fun getaway and cool to see where he grew up," my friend Emily texted me.

"Okay, well, I'm still waiting to hear back about a babysitting gig—so I'll let you know if I can come by Thursday," I responded.

This was a fairly standard response to social invitations for me in my early twenties. I was living my dream of moving to New York City and making it on my own. So many people around me were being financially supported by their parents, and I took great pride in achieving the first rung of financial independence: getting off parental welfare. (Also, it's not like my parents were offering any, either!) Plus, I was in a long-distance relationship and needed to save up every extra penny to be able to go visit Peach, my then-boyfriend, now husband.

But this constant prioritization of earning money over building relationships started to take a toll. I became an unreliable friend who frequently turned down social invitations if the opportunity to pick up an extra shift at the coffeehouse or secure a babysitting gig came my way.

In retrospect, this is now something I regret, because I failed to invest in friendships, and it came with serious repercussions. I had to rebuild my social circle in my mid to late twenties. I have only a couple friends today who are people I knew in my early twenties. Certainly some of this is a natural by-product of living in a city where people often move away— but it's also because I didn't invest in friendships.

By the way, that trip to Adam's parents' house turned into a weekend those friends constantly referenced as "epic."

When You Say No Too Often, People Stop Inviting You

Conversations about rejection are usually linked to romantic relationships—the fear of asking someone out or the awkwardness of turning down someone's advances. But really, no one likes to get rejected in any scenario. Platonic, romantic, work . . . it always sucks when someone tells us no.

When [my husband] Ken and I were saving up our money to buy an apartment in our twenties, we probably lost friends because we never, ever went to brunch. We just didn't spend the money. We'd have people over for dinner, but we wouldn't go to restaurants. I think people thought that was weird, but we'd made that decision. And people stopped inviting us to things. Ken's best friend got engaged and he and his fiancée really loved to go out to eat. They had this huge engagement dinner and they just didn't invite us. They invited us to the drinks afterward. By then we even owned our apartment. We'd reached our goal—we just had a reputation at that point.

—Lindsey Stanberry

Fortunately, there's a simple solution.

Have a Friend Fund

Set aside money each month to put into a "friend fund" and give yourself permission, especially if you're in aggressive debt payoff or savings mode, to invest in time with your friends. Go to happy hour, go to the movies, get a coffee, grab dinner, or just have some extra money to host friends for dinner at your place.

This is also a useful fund for those moments when your spending values aren't necessarily in alignment with a friend's. Sometimes you need to compromise and engage in what your friend wants to do, especially if it's important to them or a way to show support. This makes me flash back to all those nights of attending bad improv and sketch comedy shows! But I know that not all my friends want to come to personal finance events—and yet they will to support me.

While I do advocate investing in your friendships, let's be clear that it's not the same as loaning your friends money.

Should You Lend Money to Friends?

Do you want to stay friends?

I say that somewhat facetiously, but to be honest, it's simply the truth. Loaning money to friends can be a quick way to lose them.

"I was in a situation in which I loaned money to a friend and didn't set any terms other than 'Pay it back when you can,' because we didn't think we'd be those friends who would have a falling-out over this," says Wong. "But we did. It was because he was making purchases that I was silently judging. In my head I was still accounting for the money I had loaned him. In his head he was just living his life, and we weren't communicating what those terms were. We had very different expectations. I think if we'd just laid those expectations out from the start, everything would've been fine."

Unless you're truly able to loan money without the expectation of getting paid back and without the natural inclination to judge your friend's spending habits, it's best to not offer it up in the first place.

It's also okay to be honest about your own financial restrictions.

"If you can't afford to do it, it's okay to say, 'I can't afford to do this,'" says Stanberry.

In part 3, I'll further elaborate on how to go about giving a loved one a loan. But when it comes to your friends, my advice is simple: don't, unless you can truly reframe it as a gift in your mind.

Chapter 6

Let's Talk About Weddings

"You don't know who your friend really is until she starts planning a wedding." This thought is shared by every veteran bridesmaid. (It happens to the men too! Groomzillas are very real.)

In my mid-twenties, I was unceremoniously ushered into a phase of life in which everyone around me decided now was the time to legally bind themselves to another person. Weddings dominated both social conversation and my bank account.

After a year with five wedding invitations and no end in sight, I decided it was time to stop trying to "make it work" within my regular budget and instead made "Other People's Weddings" its own savings account. Seriously, I opened up a savings account and nicknamed it "Other People's Weddings." It wasn't meant to be snarky or a dig at Peach—I wasn't ready to get married. It truly was a way to play defense against the onslaught of invitations to weddings, most of which I wanted to attend. It simply made sense to proactively save up for other people's weddings.

Previously, the money I was funneling into my "Other People's Weddings" fund would have gone into my travel savings account, but considering most of my vacation time had been co-opted by attending ceremonial commemorations of true love, it was logical to just transition the money to that purpose too.

I set a goal to have between $2,000 and $4,000 in the "Other People's Weddings" fund at any given time, so I always had the option to attend if I wanted and cover all those prewedding festivities. At the time, I put 25 percent of each side-hustle paycheck into the savings account. I wasn't yet self-employed and worked a full-time job in addition to freelance writing on the side. This enabled me to focus my day-job salary on other financial goals.

On a few occasions, Peach and I even leveraged a destination wedding into a longer vacation. When my best friend got married in Dallas, Peach and I rented a car and road-tripped with another friend to Austin the day after the wedding.

Unfortunately, weddings have a special ability to bring out the absolute worst in some people, which means it's even more important to prepare for straightforward conversations and to set boundaries.

Jen Glantz, founder of Bridesmaid for Hire, has worked with hundreds of brides and maids of honor, both professionally and personally, in the five-plus years she's had her business.

"I was a bridesmaid so many times for my friends in my early twenties. I was moving from Florida to New York during that time, and working an entry-level job, so I didn't have a lot of money. I made every mistake. I didn't say no, and a lot of the reasons I wasn't so financially savvy in my twenties is because I drained so much money on these weddings. The average person spends around $1,200 to $1,500 on being a bridesmaid, and I was doing that five times in a year! I was pulling into savings accounts from high school jobs to pay for this stuff. It's so unfortunate that a lot of people have to experience this, and for some people it's a huge cause of money troubles."

Glantz served as a bridesmaid for close friends, but she also noticed that people sometimes just wanted to stack their bridal party.

"I came home one night and vented to my roommate how in one

night, two distant friends asked me to be a bridesmaid. My roommate said to me, 'Oh my God, Jen. You've become a professional bridesmaid.' And that was the lightbulb moment that I could make a business out of this," says Glantz. "There is such a huge gap in the wedding industry to help a bride out with all the personal details that sometimes their friends just can't do."

Her services have ranged from being a bridesmaid to working behind the scenes to coaching and writing vows and maid-of-honor speeches.

Similar to Glantz's experience, I'd sunk around $7,000 into attending and being in other people's weddings by the time I was twenty-seven. And that's including the fact that my parents subsidized a lot of the food and accommodation costs at family weddings. Otherwise, it would've easily dipped into the $10,000 range. Seven thousand dollars might not sound like a ton, but let's say I'd invested that $7,000 at age twenty-seven and received a 7 percent return on investment. Even if I didn't put another penny toward that investment, I would have $53,285.79 in thirty years. At the time I'm typing out these words, that investment would've increased by over $2,000 just in returns. But honestly, it's not really a fair comparison, because there are plenty of weddings I'm so glad I agreed to be in and/or attend. There are some precious memories that arose out of being there on those important days. However, if we're being honest, there are also a few weddings (even ones for which I was a bridesmaid) that I wish I'd bowed out of.

If you want to say no to being in a wedding, then it's usually more palatable if you offer some sort of alternative option—just like with the aforementioned counteroffer technique.

HOW TO SAY "THANKS, BUT NO THANKS" TO A BRIDE OR GROOM

"I think what happens is people are asked to be in a wedding and then immediately respond without thinking it through, and the resentment builds up," says Glantz. "The next thing you know, the wedding is in a month and you can't back out."

Glantz suggests that if you have a gut feeling that being a bridesmaid (or groomsman) is not in your budget, the best thing you can do when someone asks you is to express your excitement for them and then set expectations on what you can offer in terms of both time and money.

> *"I am so thrilled that you two are getting married, and I would really like to be a part of your special day, but I need to be honest that I'm* [insert your reason here: "in two other weddings this year," or "paying off debt," or "saving up for something"], *and so my budget to be a bridesmaid would be approximately* [insert number here]. *I don't want you to have to plan everything around my limitations, so let me know if you think that's realistic. If it's not, I totally understand, and I'm here to support you in other ways."*

You can also fall back on the counteroffer strategy.

> *"Sorry I can't accept the offer to be in your bridal party* [not a bad idea to give a reason, if you're comfortable], *but I'd love to help you out that morning putting up decorations or whatever you'd need."*

"If a person doesn't respect that, then that person is not someone who is levelheaded enough to be a good friend to you right now," says Glantz. "You should prioritize your finances and your life over a position that could really put you into debt. And I really mean that, because being a bridesmaid has taken on a whole new meaning. Years ago, being a bridesmaid was just showing up and being there for someone. Now it's taking all these vacations and planning these Pinterest-worthy bridal showers that could really push someone into debt."

And she's right.

Unfortunately, weddings can cause friction and fallings-out. Personally, I've had a falling-out with someone with whom I was close because I set firm boundaries on how much I could spend. I had to attend seven weddings total the year I was her bridesmaid, and I was in the bridal party for two of them. Even with the explanations and expectations set early, she ultimately didn't take it well, and it caused irreparable tension in our relationship.

But saying no to attending a wedding can be awkward, and saying no to being in a bridal party is really uncomfortable, which means most people just default to yes.

HANDLING THE COST OF BEING IN A WEDDING

If you've agreed to be a bridesmaid or groomsman, here are some key tactics to get you through without feeling resentful or decimating your bank account.

Embrace the Power of No

You don't want to be the difficult bridesmaid that everyone gossips about behind the scenes or that the bride ends up wishing she'd never asked, but you do also want to advocate for yourself and your bank account!

"When you're a bridesmaid, you think you have to say yes to everything," says Glantz. "So you don't do your research, and you don't do your planning."

Obviously, that's not the way you should handle it. You can be a helpful, happy bridesmaid *and* set some boundaries about your budget. You just need to do some extra research and express your restrictions early.

Note for men: a lot of this is written from the bridesmaids' perspective, but switch "dress" to "tux" and "bridesmaid" to "groomsman" and it holds up!

Set a Budget and Express It Early

"The very first thing to do as a bridesmaid is set a budget," advises Glantz. "How much money are you willing to spend on this?"

Glantz recommends that you consider two key points when setting your budget:

- Your financial situation
- How many weddings you think you're going to be in or attend in a year

"If you're going to be a bridesmaid seven times in a year, you need to budget for that so you're not spending $1,500 per wedding," says Glantz. Being a bridesmaid seven times in a year at $1,500 means spending $10,500 in a single year on other people's weddings!

She also recommends that you don't anticipate the overall cost based on averages, but instead really set a specific budget based on what you know you'll need to buy or be a part of. The three things that are usually asked of you as a bridesmaid are:

- Some sort of outfit
- Some sort of travel
- Some sort of gift

Use this framework to determine how much you can spend total. For example:

- Dress: I can afford $100 including shoes and alterations.
- Travel: I can spend $500 total for all events.
- Gift: I can afford to spend $200 on all gifts (e.g., wedding, bridal shower, bachelorette party, engagement).

"Once you go in knowing that, if you have curveballs thrown at you, that's when you can put your foot down and say that's not in your budget and maybe you can do your own hair and makeup," says Glantz. She also points out that you should express your budget limitations early.

Keep in mind that you don't always have to go to the bride with this information. Get a sense of who is handling the planning of the bridal shower and bachelorette party and discuss your limitations with them. Be proactive about getting in touch with the maid of honor early. Start with an offer to help, and then also make your budget clear and suggest a larger conversation with the entire bridal party about budgets so it becomes easier to plan the bachelorette party/bridal shower.

"I think it's really hard, and there isn't a one-size-fits-all answer," says Lindsey Stanberry, author of Refinery 29's *Money Diaries* and deputy managing editor of CNBC's Make It. "You just have to kind of stumble through it and be prepared to have the tough conversation, or you're going to be the person bitching behind the scenes."

Cutting Costs on the Dress

"A bride usually says, 'I want this dress and I want this style,' and you'll just go to a store and buy it," says Glantz. "But you can buy used bridesmaid's dresses, or you can rent bridesmaid's dresses, or you can have a conversation with the bride: 'Rather than you picking the brand, can you pick a color and style and let us find our own dress?'"

Glantz points out that these days, the average cost of a bridesmaid's dress is over $200, but if the bride gives you flexibility to find your own dress, then you could go to a bargain store like T.J.Maxx, Marshalls, or Nordstrom Rack and find a dress for under $50. Should your bride not be amenable to that suggestion, you could go on the hunt for bridal boutiques or stores doing deals and share that discount early on with the bride and maid of honor.

I once was in a wedding where the bride picked an expensive dress, which I knew I'd need to get altered because I'm short and floor-length always means alterations for me. But this dress was also the most popular style of the season, so I ended up searching for it elsewhere and snagged a never-worn version from eBay for $75 cheaper than the retail price.

In another case, a bride went into Nordstrom Rack, saw a dress she liked, and just bought up all the sizes for us, her bridesmaids, at the astonishingly low price point of $15 a pop. I ended up selling mine for a profit after the wedding! You can also consider donating a dress that's not really your taste to charitable organizations. There are some great charities out there that provide prom dresses to young women who may otherwise not be able to afford one.

Glantz herself was asked to buy a $400 bridesmaid dress for the first wedding she was ever in, and it's still the most expensive piece of clothing she's ever owned.

Handling All the Travel Expectations

There are potentially four (and sometimes more) events to which you'll be invited as a bridesmaid or groomsman.

- Engagement party
- Bridal shower or Jack & Jill shower
- Bachelor/bachelorette party
- Wedding

And with both bachelor and bachelorette parties becoming more and more elaborate, it can cost thousands of dollars just for the travel alone.

"I don't know, straight people are different," jokes Gaby Dunn, host of the *Bad with Money* podcast, who couldn't imagine asking people to spend a bunch of money for her celebration. "My sister didn't want to tell her friend she couldn't go to her bachelorette party and I said, 'She should've checked with everyone!'"

Dunn is right. If you're a maid of honor, best man, bride, or groom, then you have to check in with people about budget expectations before deciding where the bachelorette/bachelor party is happening and the type of accommodations you're thinking of. You can't just send Venmo requests for $400 per person without checking in first!

Hacks for Handling Travel Costs

- Set travel alerts so you can get deals for flights and accommodations.
- Suggest splitting an Airbnb for the entire group instead of getting hotel rooms.
- See if you can get the bride to bundle the shower and bachelorette party into the same weekend, so you only have to travel once.

USE THE COUNTEROFFER TECHNIQUE!
"If the bride wants to have a bachelorette party in Thailand and you can't afford to go to Thailand, that's okay," says Glantz. "Offer to take her out locally instead."

Dealing with the Never-Ending Hit-Up for Gifts

First there's the engagement gift, then the bridal shower gift, and don't forget about some tacky thing for the bachelorette party before it all culminates in your needing to buy a wedding gift.

"Consolidate your gift to just one thing," recommends Glantz. "That way you don't have to spend money here and there for gifts along the way."

Hacks to Minimize the Cost of Gifts

- *Use a coupon hunter + cash-back app before you buy!* Portals like Honey or Rakuten are good examples and can be added as an extension in your browser so it's automated.
- *Buy off the registry during a holiday.* A lot of people register at stores like Macy's, Target, or Bed, Bath and Beyond, and those stores not only often have coupons (especially BB&B!) but also do big sales around holidays. As in any holiday. I swear Macy's probably has a sale for Flag Day. Buy your gift during a holiday, and then you can make your money go even further. Let's say you

planned to spend $125 on the gift. Well, you can either buy an item that retails at $125 off the registry and get it for less, or you can spend the full $125 and get, say, $160 worth of gifts. Either way, it's a win!

- *Give money at the wedding.* You can also just give the couple money at the wedding instead of buying small gifts along the way. However, if you do attend the bridal shower, it is a little awkward not to have a gift, since they're usually opened publicly. Maybe just gift something small, like a $15 item, off the registry, or make something if you're crafty!
- *Group gift.* You can either give as a group from the bridal party or buddy up with other friends invited so you collectively can get the betrothed couple a bigger item off their registry. One of my friends had a really nice Dyson vacuum on her registry, and I knew it was something she really wanted, so a few of us pooled our money together to buy it. (We thought it was very clever to write "This gift sucks" in her card.) You can also pool money to gift experiences, either for the honeymoon or just for a fun future date night.

Advice to brides: please tell your invitees no gifts for the bachelorette party or an engagement party if you have one. Plus, if you're asking the bridal party to travel a lot prior to and for the wedding, you might want to say, "Your presence at the wedding is our present. Do not feel the need to buy us something else."

Hair and Makeup

Groomsmen don't come out of the wedding process unscathed, because those rented suits/tuxes aren't cheap, and there are plenty of expectations about the bachelor party. But the one place women always get screwed over is with hair and makeup.

The final cost of being in the wedding was going to be $150 for hair and another $150 for makeup. The bride said you can just pick one, and I decided to get my hair done because I can do my own makeup, but everyone else did both. And while the bride didn't say anything to me, I felt weird and a little guilty. I just didn't want to spend $150 on it. I wanted to spend $150 the next night going out to dinner with my husband, who normally doesn't like to go out to eat.

—Lindsey Stanberry

Of all the possible negotiations and places to financially cut corners, hair and makeup tend to be among the easier ones. Unless the bride wants all the bridesmaids to have a certain hairstyle, you can usually get away with picking between hair and makeup or doing it all yourself.

Glantz agrees.

"You should never have to pay to get your hair and makeup done," she says. "That should be something that's optional."

Be Proactive with an "Other People's Weddings" Savings Fund

Setting up a savings account earmarked specifically for other people's weddings is a really effective way to handle the variable expense and ensure you aren't going to end up in debt for a wedding.

It's also a shrewd move for you to start saving up before you even begin to get hit with a lot of weddings. Depending on where you live and when people tend to get married, it never hurts to lay this groundwork in your early twenties so you're prepared. And hey, if you don't end up getting invited to a bunch of weddings, then you've got money to take a nice trip or put toward another financial goal!

Don't Be Afraid to Get Vocal

Well, don't get vocal to the point of causing a lot of tension—it's a delicate balance. But if you're willing to mention budgets, then I bet it'll alleviate a lot of stress for other members of the bridal party.

"Other people in the room are probably as stressed as you, so don't be afraid to vocalize it," says Glantz. "But try to take the emotion out of it and instead lead with facts and be assertive about what you can handle and what you can't. You are allowed to say no."

Gently Pushing Back

You know what they say about the best-laid plans . . . Even if you've had the tough conversation with a bride or groom and set the expectations, there is a good chance they could push back on your choices along the way. Then it's time to tactfully and gently reinforce your boundaries.

Again, referring back to the compliment sandwich/counteroffer technique, Glantz recommends starting off with a compliment and then providing your facts and a counteroffer, especially if you're still in the idea phase of planning. For instance, if your bride has expressed interest in an over-the-top bachelorette party in Thailand, here's a way you could respond.

> *"That's a really awesome idea, and I love that it's what you want to do, and I'm here to support you.*
>
> *"Right now, this is what my finances look like, and I want to be really transparent with you. I want to celebrate with you, but this is what I have to work with.*
>
> *"One option that may complement your idea of going to Thailand for a bachelorette party is maybe throwing a tropical-themed bachelorette party in a nearby state instead."*

A key factor in the gentle pushback is to do it early. You shouldn't agree to go to Thailand and then back out at the last minute. You need to stand your ground at the start.

ONE OF MY favorite pieces of advice on this topic is financial therapist Amanda Clayman's point that "not every friend you make is going to be a friend for life, and sometimes we need to let that go." But you need to be careful about the difference between a natural evolution and phasing someone out because maintaining the relationship would require uncomfortable conversations in order to keep your bond in your new reality.

With that in mind, here are your challenges for this section.

CHALLENGE

Challenge 1: Use the counteroffer technique for one invite. Pick one social invitation in the coming weeks upon which to use the counteroffer strategy.

Challenge 2: Say no (in a low-stakes way). Saying no is often hard to do, and it's a muscle many of us need to develop. Find an opportunity to say no to something you genuinely don't want to do, but not something that's going to cause a fight (like skipping your partner's weekly family dinner).

Challenge 3: Start your friend fund. Set up a high-yield savings account (minimum 1 percent APY) this week and nickname it "Friend Fund" (or something similar). Then commit to putting a little bit aside, even $5 each paycheck, to start building your reserves for investing in friendships.

Part 3

Talking About Money
with Family

"SHOULD SOMETHING HAPPEN to us, then you just need to call Uncle Kevin and he'll know what to do," my mom told me.

I was eleven years old.

While directly referencing your mortality to a child may sound like insane parenting to some, it was actually incredibly practical. My family is nothing if not practical.

At the time this morsel of information was shared, my parents were going on a trip out of the country. We were living in Japan and all of our extended family lived back in the United States. So, if something happened to both of our parents while they were traveling together, my younger sister and I needed to know what to do. My mom's telling me to call my uncle Kevin was basically a way to throw up an international bat signal and initiate some sort of protocol with the adult who would then be our guardian.

Now, twenty years later, I'm in my thirties with a husband of my own. This pragmatic planning has apparently been passed down. We don't have human children, but I always have a plan in place for our beloved dog in case something happens to both of us while we're traveling. (Yes, I am that intense about it and make sure my parents and at least one local friend know where our dog gets boarded and all her details, in case she needs to be picked up by someone else.)

I'm aware that 99 percent of you reading this chapter feel that story was just waaaay too morbid. And to be honest, death and money are two fairly intense topics. The combination of them evokes so many emotions, especially if you, the adult child, are initiating the conversation with your parent. It's a role reversal of the parent-child relationship in which, if it's not done tactfully, you can come off sounding concerned at best and domineering at worst.

Of course, not all the family-and-money talks are about aging and death, but let's just go ahead and start with one of the heaviest conversations you may ever have with your parents.

Chapter 7

How to Ask Your Parents If You'll Need to Take Care of Them Financially

"MY PARENTS HAD a lot of arguments about money growing up, so I feel like I had an early awareness of money and stress around money," says Judith Ohikuare, a freelance writer and development manager at NY Writers Coalition, a nonprofit organization in Brooklyn. "We came from a working-class background. Both my parents went to college and met there, but it wasn't a straight middle-class experience. My mom needed to work and my dad needed to work. The phrase 'working mom' wasn't even something I'd heard of until I was an adult, because I didn't know any moms who didn't work."

Ohikuare learned basic personal finance lessons from her parents, like the power of compound interest and the importance of saving. Her dad especially had a heavy hand in ensuring she built financial management skills.

"My dad told me a lot about the importance of putting money into a 401(k) before I even started working," says Ohikuare. "I don't think I realized it was optional, because he made it just sound like a thing you had to do, so I did it automatically when I started working."

But as Ohikuare has aged, the money conversations have started to shift to her discussing her dad's financial future.

It's a natural and important transition that should begin sooner than you think.

EVERYTHING NEEDS TO BE COMMUNICATED EARLY

"The biggest mistake people make is assuming this conversation doesn't need to happen until it has to happen," says Cameron Huddleston, a financial journalist and author of *Mom and Dad, We Need to Talk*. Huddleston's book was inspired by her own experience having to take care of her mother, who was diagnosed with Alzheimer's—a diagnosis that occurred when Cameron was just thirty-five and her mother was only sixty-five. Cameron had to step in and handle her mother's financial affairs as well as her care.

Huddleston warns that it's a mistake to wait, because you never know when a crisis may arise, leaving you in the position of having to care and make decisions for your parents with little to no direction or legal rights.

"[If you wait,] your parents might not have the legal documents to deal with an emergency that allow you to step in and help them out with their finances and make healthcare decisions for them," says Huddleston.

Those documents, which will be discussed in depth later on in this section, have to be signed when your parents are of sound mind. If you wait too long, it's possible you'd eventually have to take your parent(s) to court to get conservatorship, which involves having to prove they can no longer take care of themselves. That can be an emotionally brutal, costly, public process that no one wants to put a loved one through.

Unfortunately, many parents don't want to discuss their eventual death or think about a reality in which they don't have agency over their bodies or mental faculties. Let's be honest: it sucks to consider that potential reality. Which means it's one you need to approach gently.

"Identify the pain point and follow the distress," says financial therapist Amanda Clayman. "If this is something that you are worried about [e.g., your parents' ability to be well taken care of as they age], that's where you need to start. Think about what it is in particular that causes you worry. Are you worried about what this means for your own stability?"

Clayman recommends taking this thought process a step further to examine how you're mentally framing the situation. Are you judging your parents as financially irresponsible, which makes you angry about the financial chaos, or is this a situation in which they're blameless because they sacrificed for you, so you need to care for them?

Your anxiety over having this conversation might not even be tied to finances. The pain could simply come from thinking about a world without your loved one, which makes you completely avoid engaging the subject.

If you'd allow me to get on a soapbox for a moment, dealing with legal and financial stressors in an already chaotic or grief-stricken time just compounds the pain. Taking care of these legal and financial documents with both your parents and within your own family if you're married and/or have children is a huge act of love.

Now, how do you actually initiate this conversation with Mom and Dad (or in-laws, Grandma and Grandpa, or your siblings)?

Clayman recommends you start the dialogue with a two-pronged approach:

1. From the position of "I"
2. Using a positive

"I appreciate all that you've done for me as a [parent, grandparent, etc.]. *I know that you've sacrificed and worked hard to support us."*

Once you lay this foundation, it's time to express your concern.

"Here's what I'm concerned about. As I start to plan my own financial future, it's hard for me to think about what that future looks like if I don't also know what your future looks like, because we are connected. And I'm thinking about what that means in practical terms."

Finally, get to what you want to ask.

"I'd really love it if we could get into a concrete conversation about how you see your future and how prepared you feel and if there's anything you worry about. I just want you to know I'm open to that and I'd feel better if we could talk about it. How do you feel about it?"

Or maybe it's slightly more direct.

[Concern] *"Here's what I'm concerned about. I know we have a history of dementia in our family."*

[Ask] *"And I want to ensure we have all the legal documents in place so if that ever were to come up, we'd be prepared and could focus on your health and care right away."*

"If your parent is not experiencing distress and does not want to join you in this conversation, then there's very little you can do to force them to do so," says Clayman.

But that doesn't mean you just give up on the conversation entirely. Come back to it on occasion. Not weekly. Maybe not even monthly, but a few times a year until you see a shift. Clayman points to speaking with "I" language and using "I worry" or "I'm concerned" language as a way to motivate your parent to participate in the conversation instead of just shutting you down.

For Ohikuare, starting these conversations early means she now knows all her dad's financial details, which helps her discuss practical options for his future with him.

"I talk to my dad about when he's going to retire and about his options for where he's going to live in the country, what's affordable, and what the tax rates are," says Ohikuare. "I know how much money is in his 401(k) plan, and I know how much the house where he lives is worth."

It's also possible that you already have a gut feeling about your parents' expectations of their future and your role and responsibilities to help them. "You should know what the expectations are," says Kristin Wong, author of *Get Money*, who points out that this can be a really uncomfortable conversation for everyone involved. But it's important to know what your parents expect from you.

"Everything from your plans to have children, to where you're going to live, to your own retirement, and to your kids' college plans can be affected by the decision to take care of your parents," Wong says.

It can also be a tough sell if you're up against cultural considerations or other reasons your parents may completely shut down this conversation. Even so, you need to proceed with an open mind and not just dictate your terms.

YOU'RE TRYING TO HELP, NOT BULLDOZE

There's a common plotline in movies and television of the well-intentioned son or daughter trying to convince a parent to move into a retirement community or into the child's home because the parent recently had a health scare or is simply showing signs of aging.

This scenario typically ends with a child's exerting their will on the parent and essentially forcing them into a huge lifestyle change. Stripping your parent of their agency and autonomy is not the right way to engage in this conversation.

"It's important to show that you're trying to help and not trying to bulldoze the person," says Ohikuare. "I think that's why these conversations often get very tense with parents. They're at a stage of life where they may already know they'll no longer be able to make all their own decisions, so you want to make them feel like you're there to support them and not just trying to run the show. It should feel like a conversation."

She points out that a parent could already be worrying and thinking about retirement and their financial future, even if they haven't talked about it with you.

"Think about all the money things that stress you out now and how you'd want to be approached about that with a little bit of sensitivity, respect, consideration, and also gentleness," says Ohikuare.

TRY TO WEAVE THE CONVERSATION IN ORGANICALLY

The first time Wong broached this topic with her own parents was after they brought up a conversation about some recent financial decisions they'd made. She used it as a chance to pivot into an overall discussion about estate planning by first explaining how she was handling it herself.

"By talking about how I was doing it for myself, it didn't seem like I was planning for their death," says Wong. "Getting a will and doing some basic estate planning is just part of getting your financial life in order, so I had done it recently."

 "I just drew up my will, and here's what the process is like; it's very easy. Have you both thought about doing this too?"

(By the way, if you just read that sentence and thought, "Uhhhh, yeah, I haven't done any of that," know that this is also something you could do *with* your parents. Or you could at least be accountability buddies for each other about it.)

Personalizing it like this also makes it feel less judgmental compared to saying, "You really need to do this! It's important!"

Lindsay Bryan-Podvin, a financial therapist and founder of Mind Money Balance, suggests using someone else's recent retirement as an opportunity to ask your parents about their plans.

"Jackie's parents just retired and moved down to Florida. What do you two think you'll do when you retire?"

Ohikuare recommends asking for advice as a way to start picking up context clues and bread crumbs about what your parents may or may not have done to set themselves up financially. "Some people's parents really do feel like it's none of your business, even though they're your parent," says Ohikuare. "So this is a way to open yourself up and show it's something you're thinking about." She recommends using lines like:

"[Partner's name] and I are starting to figure out what we're going to do with our finances and what we'll do if we have kids. What did you do?"

Follow up with:

"Are you happy you did it that way or would you do it differently?"

Ohikuare points out that a gentle follow-up like this one enables you to learn what your parents did in the past as well as unearth any possible concerns about their future financial outlook.

Huddleston also likes the asking-for-advice technique. "Parents love giving advice, and their answer is going to give you a clue as to what they've done," she points out.

"I just started a new job and was debating contributing to the company retirement plan. What do you think?"

Your parent might respond with, "Well, I have a pension, so I never had to worry about setting aside money." Or they might say, "Yes, because I didn't get started when I was your age, and now I'm trying to put aside enough to retire."

This strategy can also expand beyond purely financial questions into other topics, like tying your milestones to other necessary legal documents and insurance policies such as wills and life insurance.

"Since we just [got married/had a kid], *do you think I should make a will and get life insurance?"*

"You don't just simply ask them the question and stop there," says Huddleston. "You have to act like a journalist and follow up with more questions. The key is getting a general picture initially."

An example of the difference between a general picture and a specific one is knowing where your parents bank versus knowing exactly how much is in the bank. In fact, Huddleston recommends you avoid asking directly about numbers and dollar amounts when you're first having this conversation, as it could make your parents feel uncomfortable. It's a happy surprise if your parents volunteer that information, but many won't, and it's something you can come back to as everyone gets more comfortable with this topic.

You can also turn to pop culture for an opportunity to back-door the conversation with your parents. At least once every couple of years, a famous person will die without a will or their family will duke out the details of a will and trust after the fact, which sends the financial press into a frenzy. It's a way you can broach the conversation with your parents without citing people you all actually know. But if they're gossiping about someone they know who may have been omitted from a spouse's or parent's will, then that also gives you an in.

Tying your questions to a story or pop culture reference is also highly valuable for people who may not naturally be going to parents for advice. Perhaps your parents openly say they aren't great with money and you've been a bit of a money nerd, which they know. So your coming to ask for advice about retirement plans or wills could feel inauthentic, and your parents' BS detectors would immediately start ringing.

"A friend of mine's father passed away recently and didn't have a will. He'd gotten remarried and had kids from both marriages, and it's a huge mess now. Our family situation is different, but I wanted to know if you had a will that details what you want."

You can also start the sentence with:

"[Insert celebrity name] didn't have a will and his family is already fighting each other over the estate."

Or:

"I [heard on a podcast/read in an article] about how complicated it can be to settle your parents' estate without a will . . ."

The struggle with tying it to a celebrity's death is your parents' immediate reaction of "Well, we won't have a ton of money like that." It's also really important to know that this isn't just about passing on wealth when we talk about estates. Settling an estate can also be about handling someone's debts, paying taxes, and distributing any assets that remain—no matter how modest. Huddleston recommends you point out the assets your parents do have, such as property or a car, even family heirlooms, jewelry, or paintings.

"Maybe you don't have stocks or money set aside in retirement accounts, but you have a house and a car. You don't have to be rich to have a will."

It's not uncommon for siblings to get into huge fights over items that are tied to memories but wouldn't actually sell for even a nominal sum of money.

Finally, you can also turn the conversation toward your parents' own experiences, such as the death of another family member.

When my husband's grandfather died, I was speaking to my mother-in-law about her father's estate planning situation (mostly because she was asking me questions), and I used the opportunity to say, "And do you have a will?" It clearly wasn't the time or place to ask for specifics, but it's good to start by just knowing if it exists and where it physically resides.

> IMPORTANT NOTE: Wills have been the main example in this chapter, but wills are far from the most important legal document your parents (and you!) need to have. Medical and financial powers of attorney are critical. A will is only used in death, but the medical and financial powers of attorney impact your parents while they're still alive. They give you (or the person named in each document) the ability to make decisions and actions on your loved one's behalf if they are unable to do so independently (e.g., if they're in a coma or suffering from dementia). These documents will be further discussed in chapter 8.

Can It Tie to One of Your Life Events?

Peach and I got a prenuptial agreement prior to getting married (which is detailed in chapter 11). Part of the prenup process is discussing inheritance. For example, if I were to receive an inheritance from my parents or if Peach were to receive one from his, is the other person entitled to that money if we were to divorce?

The prenup process dictates how to divide assets in the event that you split up, so it's somewhat important you have a general idea about whether or not you'd be likely to receive an inheritance (no matter the size) from parents or grandparents or other loved ones. That creates an opportunity to bring it up with your parents, which I was able to do by framing it around my life event.

"Peach and I are in the process of drafting a prenup, and part of the process is discussing the possibility of an inheritance and how we feel that money should be divided in the case of a divorce. So, I was wondering if there's any information I need from you two to put into our prenup."

This provides a way to ask about your parents' will and the status of their estate planning without the bluntness of discussing their mortality, such as "What do you want to have happen with your assets when you die?" or, more gently, "Do you have a will?"

Another thing to consider is that your own life event could result in changes to your parents' estate planning. For instance, having a child could mean that your parents would want to update their will to include a grandchild.

Can You Deploy an In-Law?

I abhor the "monster-in-law" stereotypes. Do people have awful relationships with in-laws? Of course, just like people can be enmeshed in toxic relationships with their own immediate or extended family. Your in-law situation can also be a completely healthy, happy extension of the new family you created with your spouse. If that's the case for you, a son- or daughter-in-law can be a useful tool in the "let's talk about your future" conversation.

My father-in-law often refers to me and his other daughter-in-law as his daughters. It's endearing, but ultimately, I'm not his actual child. (This has nothing to do with bloodlines and everything to do with his not being a person who raised me.) There's love and trust there, but not the same intensity of attachment as he has to the two sons and daughter he did raise. This differentiator can be really helpful when discussing a parent's mortality.

If you and your siblings have unsuccessfully tried to talk future plans (retirement, wills, estate planning) with your parents, then see if sending in an in-law will help. The in-law can use similar strategies and maybe even start the talk by saying how they recently went through this conversation with their own parents.

If the parent loves and trusts the in-law, they may find it easier to initiate this difficult conversation with a family member who isn't their child.

CONSIDER A MULTIGENERATIONAL HOUSEHOLD

Living with grandparents, parents, and children all under one roof is the norm in many cultures, but not in much of the United States. A multigenerational household certainly can provide many advantages, including socialization of children with older people, preventing grandparents from feeling isolated, financial benefits, and in some cases, additional built-in childcare.

Lisa Cini, president of Mosaic Design Studio and Best Living Tech, works with families and senior living facilities around the world to move people from fear to freedom as they're aging. Cini herself lived in a multigenerational household when her maternal grandmother, who was in her nineties and had Alzheimer's, as well as her parents moved into the home Cini already lived in with her husband and two teenage children. It was a four-generation household, and while there were trying times just like with any family, all members ultimately thrived.

"Immediately, within a couple weeks, the sparkle in their eyes and how they were able to move was so much more engaged," says Cini of her parents' and grandmother's transition into her home. "In my experience with senior living and design, you see that when you lose your purpose, you just stop engaging."

Cini's children flourished with their grandparents and great-grandmother in the home. Cini noticed they learned to slow down and be more connected and vulnerable. Plus, with two working parents, it was nice for her children to have the grandparents there when they came home from school. Cini's parents also loved the youthful energy in the house.

"My mom is seventy-nine and on Snapchat, Instagram, and Facebook," jokes Cini.

Approach the Topic from Kindness, Not Fear

Don't focus on what your parents can't do anymore or on what scares you, advises Cini, who wrote a book about her family's experience called *Hive: The Simple Guide to Multigenerational Living: How Our Family Makes It Work.*

"The first conversation that most people have is either 'You shouldn't be driving' or 'You're going to burn the house down because you left the stove on,'" says Cini, who notes that technology has really changed the game in this regard. For example, you can purchase a monitor that goes off with an alert if your parent has left the stove on. Don't just leap to chastising them and making them feel bad about themselves. Start with solutions. Now, ultimately, the best solution may be to have your parents move in, because of either finances or physical or emotional needs (or all of the above).

You should engage with your parents about how they're feeling, especially if they've already dropped a comment or two that you can use.

"You mentioned a few weeks ago that maintaining the lawn has become a lot of work for you and Dad. Would it help if we hired someone to come by and mow the lawn once a week?"

"Mom, you mentioned navigating the stairs in the house is starting to be a lot on your knees. What if we started to look for a home that better suits your needs now? Or we could even talk about the option of you living in our home."

Cini also recommends that you steer the conversation toward the benefits to not only them, but also to you if they moved in.

"My work travel has really started to pick up lately, and it'd be so much easier on me and the kids if you lived with us and could keep an eye on them while I'm gone."

"We could have regular big family dinners again and you could help me with meal planning and prep."

Not Always the Right Choice for Every Family Dynamic

Of course, the multigenerational household is not the right option for all family dynamics. It just might not be mentally healthy to cohabit with your parents, grandparents, or siblings.

Cini has seen it be healing for some families in which the child had a poor relationship with a parent in their youth. Living together helped rebuild bridges and develop a healthy, stable relationship—partly because either the parent changed or the fact that they were in need softened the dynamic.

But if you either don't want to take the risk or know it's for the best not to have your parents live with you, then you can consider providing financial assistance or help secure a home aid or find a retirement community that's a good fit for your parents' needs. Committing to a set visitation schedule can also help reduce the feeling of isolation—or even just calling on a regular basis.

BRINGING IN A THIRD PARTY

"If your parents don't want to talk to you because they're always going to see you as a kid, even if you're fifty and they're in their seventies, getting someone else involved in the conversation can help," says Huddleston.

That person could be a trusted family member, such as one of your parents' siblings, a family friend, or a religious or community leader your parents trust and from whom they seek council.

 "Hey, Aunt Sally, could you talk to Mom and Dad about how helpful it would be to share some estate planning information with me and my siblings?"

Estate Planning Lawyer

Even if you have a trusted family member to initiate the conversation, it's still really important for your parents to seek the assistance of an estate planning attorney in order to finalize their wills and execute both the power of attorney and healthcare proxy paperwork they need.

There has been a rise in online do-it-yourself wills and legal paperwork, but you really need to make sure it's legal and enforceable—especially the power of attorney. It will likely save you and your parents time, and even money, to use an actual attorney from the jump when it comes to getting all the proper paperwork done. However, if your parents are resistant to using an attorney for whatever reason, the DIY approach is better than nothing. You can turn to sites like Nolo or software like Quicken WillMaker & Trust. The instructions need to be followed exactly and it will need to be notarized properly to be legal. But again, it's certainly preferable to hire an estate planning attorney.

You and/or your parents can search for an attorney using sites like Avvo and Nolo or word-of-mouth recommendations.

Depending on your parents' financial situation, they may also need (or want) the help of a certified financial planner to ensure their plans for retirement are in order and their other financial needs are met.

> *"I'm so glad the two of you have decided to create a will. Do you want help finding an estate planning attorney? I'm happy to ask my friends who their parents used or do some research online."*

Certified Financial Planner

There are many, many types of financial planners and advisors. There's also, at the time of this writing, a terrible lack of oversight and regulations when it comes to who can call themselves a planner/advisor. One of the ways in which you can avoid scams and sales pitches, plus ensure you're getting quality advice, is to seek out a certified financial planner (CFP). CFPs are required to complete both classes and an exam in order to use the designation. They also must have a certain amount of experience, adhere to ethics standards, and be fiduciaries.

A fiduciary is someone who is required to act in your best interest.

You'd think that would be a default in financial planning, but it's not. Some people adhere to what's known as the suitability standard, meaning they have to do what's suitable—or doesn't harm you—but not necessarily what's best for you. This can be especially tricky if your financial planner gets a commission off any financial products, as they may then be incentivized to sell you an insurance policy or have you buy certain investments that aren't the best option for you.

Some resources that can help you find a CFP include: Garrett Planning Network, the CFP Board's site at LetsMakeaPlan.org, and the XY Planning Network. Notably, the latter is focused on young professionals and may not be the right fit for your parents but could be for you.

You should know who your parents use as an estate planning attorney and as their financial planner, because those are the people to whom you can reach out to try to find out more information, especially at the time of your parents' deaths. These people can also be allies while your parents are alive and you're trying to sort out their wishes and how you can best assist them. You could ask your parents' lawyer or financial planner to gently nudge your parents.

Legally, your parents' attorney and financial planner cannot just open the books to you and share all the pertinent information while your folks are alive. However, they may be able to encourage your parents to start a dialogue with you.

"I know you can't reveal this information to me, but could you please encourage my parents to have this conversation with us?"

If you're worried about your parents' financial situation, especially their ability to retire, and you want them to sit down with a professional, then you could gift them a session with a CFP.

Your Parents' Doctors

"I could see she was having memory problems, so I called her doctor, because I knew him, and said, 'Please could you encourage my mom to be tested for Alzheimer's?' and he did," says Huddleston. "And that was me just being scared. I wasn't afraid to talk to her about money, but to have to be the one to say, 'Mom, I think you're having trouble remembering things'—I didn't want to be that person. To get that third party involved made it easier."

Similar to you parents' attorney and financial planner, a doctor can't just tell you exactly what's going on. But like Huddleston did, you can ask the doctor to help you encourage your parents to get any necessary testing.

WHEN THEY FLAT-OUT REFUSE TO ENGAGE WITH YOU

There's a possibility one or both of your parents will completely and utterly shut down this conversation.

"It's not like parents are trying to set you up for failure when they're talking about money as if it's this very scarce commodity, or when they act like money is something you need to be afraid of," says Clayman. "What they're trying to do is prepare you for the reality as they see it. That's why we see certain behaviors and mentalities around money get passed through generations of a family, even though the circumstances of the individuals may change."

There are a variety of ways these mentalities about money get passed down, but certainly one of the most common manifestations is the hesitation or discomfort around talking specifics about money. Think back to your childhood and try to remember if at any point you were told it was rude or inappropriate to ask about money. If Mom and/or Dad didn't want to share their salary, how much money your family had, or how much they paid for something, maybe it's because you were a spunky kid who could've shared your family's business on the playground and to neighbors. Or maybe it's because they were deeply uncomfortable discussing money and that still holds true today.

Huddleston knows there are parents who will flat-out refuse to engage in this conversation, especially if they're feeling embarrassed or prideful. If you've made multiple efforts to bring up this topic without success, Huddleston suggests these solutions:

- *Cover the costs:* If you and your siblings (or just you) are financially stable and can afford to help, that's of course a way to solve the problem of needing to care for an aging parent.
- *Build an emergency fund:* Caring for an aging parent—or for a sibling—can be really, really expensive, so absorbing all the costs may not be an option. However, you (and/or your siblings) could start to build an emergency fund earmarked for this future reality. You could all agree to contribute to a fund that will be used to cover the shortfall between what your parents can afford and what they need. The contributions to this cash fund can be pro-rated based on incomes and life situations and doesn't have to be split evenly among the siblings.
- *Buy a long-term-care insurance policy for them:* If your parents are still healthy and under seventy (especially if they're in their fifties), you may still be able to get a reasonable long-term-care insurance policy for them. This is especially prudent for anyone who has a family history of dementia, diabetes, cancer, or other illness.
- *Create boundaries for yourself:* You need to decide the level of involvement you're willing to have, from both a financial and an emotional perspective—especially if your relationship with your parents isn't the healthiest. You can also sit with your siblings and openly discuss these boundaries both as individuals and as a group.

You should resist any urge to issue ultimatums to your parents based on their refusal to engage with you. Don't say, "Well, if you won't talk to me about this, then I won't provide any financial assistance you may need." Instead, Huddleston recommends you use a more delicate approach.

"I'm trying to have these conversations now because I'm looking out for your best interests so that we have a plan in a worst-case-scenario situation. If we don't have a plan, then I might not be able to help you." (You can also amend this to "I might not legally be able to step in" or "I might not have the financial resources to help you.")

TAKING CARE OF A PARENT OR SIBLING

Michael Lacy grew up in East Texas, where his family lived below the poverty line in what he describes as pretty dire straits. He became a first-generation college graduate when he got his diploma in marketing from the University of Houston. He then went on to work as a national sales rep for a building products manufacturer, but his mom and grandparents still live in poverty. Lacy started providing for his mom and grandparents shortly after graduating college.

"It's kind of weird to be the first one to earn a six-figure salary and then you go home and your family is asking, 'Hey, can you buy me groceries,' or 'I need new tires for my car,' or all these little day-to-day expenses that I never really think about as an adult now, but I have to provide that for family members," says Lacy.

Determining How Much You Can and Will Give

Before you offer a family member money, it's important you determine the level of help you're willing to give, because it will immediately set expectations for the future. Of course, part of the "how much" question will be answered based on your budget and how much you can afford while accommodating your own needs and goals. But your reflection on the situation should go beyond the technical and include an analysis of your comfort level with how the money will be used.

"Maybe you're comfortable giving them five hundred dollars a month, or you're comfortable picking up their grocery bill or healthcare bill, but you won't pay for anything beyond that," says Lindsay Bryan-Podvin.

The hard truth of financially supporting loved ones is that you don't get to control how they spend money.

"I once gave a little bit of support to a family member, but then the next month they called again, and it started to become a pattern," says Lacy, who hosts the podcast *Winning to Wealth*. "Then, when we hung out I noticed they had a lot of frivolous habits. I said, 'I'm not going to be stretching my budget so you can live this lifestyle that I don't even live.'"

Ultimately, for the sake of your mental health, you have to make a decision. Either you give the loved one a set amount of cash each month and don't control how they spend it—in this situation, you have to be okay with their choices and willing to set boundaries if they call asking for more money in a month—or you just pay for certain bills so you know that specific baseline needs are met and you get to control how your money is spent.

Huddleston suggests a really simple script when setting boundaries:

> *"Mom and Dad, I love you. But I am not in a position to help you out."* Or: *"I'm only in the position to pay for* [insert amount or particular bills here]."

How to Offer Help

"It goes back to seeing needs and being aware," says Lacy. "I live very differently than my parents and grandparents, so when I go visit, there are things I notice immediately going into the house. Like going to the fridge to get a drink and seeing that it's practically empty."

You can initiate the conversation by asking a simple question:

> *"Do you need anything?"*

"In the beginning there was a lot of pride and them just saying, 'We're fine, we're fine,' because I am the child and grandchild," says Lacy. "I'm sure there's pride and ego. So, it started with me just putting a twenty somewhere randomly and waiting until I got home to make a phone call and say to use that to buy that food or whatever it is that you need."

Hiding money around the house is the method Lacy figured out would work for his family when he first started supporting them, but he acknowledges that there's no one right way to offer help. Instead, he recommends you just stay persistent in offering support.

Unfortunately, not all family members are willing to accept help or have open communication like Lacy's.

"If they keep rejecting your hints and your offers to help, well, it's important to remember that they're also adults and they've figured out a way to get to where they are right now, and they'll probably be able to scrape on by, even if that means it really sucks to watch it happen," says Bryan-Podvin. She acknowledges how harsh that advice can sound, but ultimately, we can't control our loved ones and force them to accept help.

But if someone is refusing your financial assistance, that doesn't mean you have to stop providing support. Support can also come in the form of asking the important questions. Ohikuare, for instance, recently asked her dad if his doctors were helpful with estimating future costs of his necessary medication once he was retired and no longer had his employer's health insurance coverage.

"You don't necessarily have to have the answers," says Ohikuare. "But a lot of these conversations start with general questions that become more specific questions that hopefully become answers. It's important to just start asking questions, even if neither of you have the answers." She recommends that you jot down these questions and keep track of them as they either get answered or become more targeted and specific to your parents' unique situations.

Telling Your Spouse

Maybe you've already started to have these conversations with your parents. Or you may come from a background in which caring for your parents isn't even a question but rather a foregone conclusion. Perhaps you, like Lacy, have already started providing financial assistance to parents, grandparents, or siblings. Then you get married, and now your spouse is entitled to have an opinion on how the family money is getting spent. Your spouse has a right to know and discuss the specifics of providing financial assistance to family members, especially if that means that the two of you have to change your own goals and dreams.

"There are kids who feel like they have an obligation to their parents, and that's totally okay," says Ohikuare. "But your spouse or partner may not feel the same way, and if you are giving anything, or more than what your spouse is comfortable with, that can bring up so many, many issues. It can be disastrous and cause a lot of distrust and financial instability if you're not on the same page about what your priorities are."

There are many stressful money conversations you're going to have in your romantic relationship (which you'll soon read all about in part 4), but few are more dramatic than the ones where families are involved. It's incredibly important to speak to each other respectfully, calmly, and rationally and not come in verbally swinging about anyone's mother, father, sister, or brother.

"I've been sending my [mother/father/brother/sister] *money each month to help them out. It's something I'd like to keep doing after we're married, but I'd like to discuss your thoughts and feelings. We can also brainstorm other nonfinancial ways we can support them."*

You Need to Make a Plan Sooner, Not Later
"There's no getting around [this conversation with your spouse], and if you delay it, it's only going to make it more difficult. When the time comes, you will not have created your own plan to deal with it," says Huddleston. "Your spouse might be thinking, 'We're going to downsize after the kids move out, and it's going to be awesome.' And then you

might have to say, 'Sorry, we can't because we have to move my parents in.' You don't want to string your spouse along thinking that it'll be fine and then spring this on them. If you're going to have an open and honest relationship with your spouse or partner, this has to be part of the conversation."

A conversation that should happen early—even before-marriage early.

"I don't think my wife was aware I was helping my family to the extent that I was," admitted Lacy. "So, had I had that conversation while we were dating, the transition into marriage would've been a lot easier."

For Lacy, an African-American man, part of the conversation with his wife was explaining his family's history and what they had gone through as well as the societal ills that were currently affecting their situation. Lacy's wife grew up in a different socioeconomic class with grandparents who even paid for her college education, so it was harder for her to understand why Lacy would be supporting his grandparents when her experience was the reverse of his.

"[Supporting family is] something we had to talk about a lot early in our marriage," says Lacy. "It's something that my wife wasn't used to because she grew up upper-middle-class, and in her mind she wondered, 'Why can't they do it for themselves?'"

Once the two started an open dialogue about supporting his family, the key strategy was flexibility.

Lacy, who was writing large checks to his family when he and his wife first got married, had to be willing to adjust the amount of support he offered. His wife pointed out that they had goals of their own to pursue as husband and wife.

"Our solution kept that generous spirit but also took into account that my family and my household are my first priority, and if there's excess after we take care of what we need and put money toward our goals, then I can have that conversation about 'Hey, what are we able to do this month?'" says Lacy.

Here's a way to tell your spouse you want to send money to your family:

> *"It's important to me to help* [insert family member] *live a more comfortable life than they could afford on their own* [or amend with your own personal reason for why it's important to provide support]. *Part of how I've done this is by sending financial support of* [insert amount and frequency, e.g., five hundred dollars per month]. *Now that we're becoming our own family, I'd like to discuss your feelings and expectations about providing financial support to my family."*

Ohikuare points out that using your "why" in this conversation is an important strategy to get your partner to be your ally in the matter. "They may not be doing it joyfully, but at least they would understand why it's important to you," she explains.

If you'd like to open a dialogue about the amount your partner is sending to family:

> *"I understand it's important to help* [insert family member here]. *However, I'd like to have a conversation about the amount of financial support we can afford to provide while also striving to achieve our own goals as a family."*

"I knew when I married my husband that he's a foreigner and his family in another country isn't as fortunate as we are," says Huddleston. "My husband said, 'I'm going to have to help out my family sometimes.'"

In addition to opening up the conversation for the first time, Lacy suggests you both reevaluate the amount of support you send on a fairly regular basis.

"When we first got married, it was just the two of us and there was an amount we were able to give, and it was comfortable, but then we had a kid and bought a house," says Lacy. "Everything changed our financial picture." This change prompted Lacy and his wife to be more open and honest with Lacy's mom and grandparents about how the cost of being homeowners and raising a child will impact the support they can provide to family members. "Open communication and open dialogue can go a long way in these situations," says Lacy.

That open communication also needs to allow for your spouse to feel heard and even vent about a crappy situation.

Giving Your Spouse the Space to Express Their Feelings

Consider this: You find out that your parent has a terminal illness and will require hands-on care, which is going to mean you have to move back to your hometown. This move may ultimately be inevitable, but it's important to allow your spouse to share their feelings—even if those feelings border on disdain and contempt for the situation. The hard part is that you have to avoid getting defensive or angry at your spouse for feeling this way.

"It's important to let the other person know they have a say in all of it," says Wong. "Giving your spouse the space to talk about what their feelings are in all of this and coming to a compromise if you can is really important. I think a lot of times the other person just feels like, 'Okay, this is deciding my fate.' And that can be really frustrating. Even if it is true and you are going to have to move to where a family member lives or have a family member move in with you, giving your partner space to have an opinion in it is vital."

Despite the fact that pushback from a spouse is really just providing the illusion of having a say and the result isn't going to change, just give your partner a space to vent without your getting defensive or angry. "Sometimes I think all people need is an opportunity to say, 'This really sucks,'" says Wong.

You also cannot make assumptions about how your partner will ultimately handle caring for a family member, so this absolutely needs to be a conversation between the two of you, even if it's currently just hypothetical.

"Someone may not get along with their parents at all and be borderline estranged, if not completely estranged, but they may still feel obligated to support them in some way," says Ohikuare. "It's not necessarily your place to say that's wrong or doesn't make sense or is dumb or that they're taking advantage of you. Sometimes that's true and the person still wants to provide support."

In these moments, you probably just need to acknowledge how they're feeling and listen.

"I love you and I'm so sorry this situation sucks. We'll get through it together."

Your Spouse Also Needs to Know the Details for Practical Reasons

"If you're caring for a parent, it's also important that your spouse knows what you're doing, because if something were to happen to you, then your spouse might have to be the one to step in and at least stay on top of the finances," Huddleston points out. "You probably shouldn't force the caregiving entirely on the spouse. If you were to die, they might need to turn to a Medicaid-approved facility and go that route, but it has to be part of the conversation."

Changing the Amount of Support You Provide

Once you've had the hard talk with your spouse, it might mean that now you need to tell your family member that you have to scale back the amount of support you're providing. Lacy points to transparency as a key element in these conversations. He recommends saying:

"I have a family now. I have a daughter and a wife and more responsibilities than I did five years ago. I hope you can understand that I still want to help you, but that help is going to look different now."

Providing context can also make this a more palatable conversation for your family member. Lacy, for instance, would share how the cost of day care means he can't write the same size check to a family member.

> *"I have a day care bill that sits at over $1,000 a month, so I can't write you a $1,000 check anymore."*

But ultimately, he feels fairly fortunate in his situation because his family has expressed appreciation for any amount of support he's been able to provide over the years, and the fluctuations haven't led to resentment.

LOANING MONEY TO A FAMILY MEMBER

Don't expect to get it back.
—Everyone, ever

You don't have to be any sort of money expert or a psychologist to know that loaning a family member money and expecting to get paid back is setting yourself up for a falling-out. Sure, there are success stories—but there are way more examples of siblings who no longer speak to each other or adult children who resent their parents over a loan.

Personally, I'm of the belief that if you're going to loan a loved one money (family or friend), it needs to be an amount you can afford to never see again. Plus, you need to mentally earmark that money as a gift. It's a nice surprise if you get repaid—but set the mental expectation that it won't happen so you won't be disappointed and won't hang on to resentment for years to come.

Should You Draw Up Paperwork?

In some cases, especially if you're loaning large sums to your relatives, it could be prudent to draw up a contract that also has expectations of a debt repayment program. You can do this informally, use an online legal service to make a contract, or go so far as to hire a lawyer. But before you pay for a legally binding agreement, consider whether you'd actually drag your loved one to court over a loan in default. An informal agreement with a structured repayment schedule could make both of you feel better about the situation.

> *"You know that I love and trust you, but it really would be best for my peace of mind for us to have the details of this loan in writing. That way there isn't any confusion in the future about what we agreed to."*

Be Compassionate!

Going back to Paco de Leon's mantra in chapter 4: "Don't be a dick!"

No one wants to ask a family member for financial help. Whether it's your parent, sibling, grandparent, aunt, uncle, cousin—whomever—you need to come at this with a level of compassion, regardless of your answer.

Should You Charge Interest?

The answer, as with generally anything relating to personal finance, is: it depends.

"Charging them interest in some cases is also fair, depending on the size of the loan," says Wong. "That could be a lot of money you're losing that could've been invested or placed in a high-yield savings account, and they're saving money on interest because they're not taking out an expensive loan with a super-high interest rate."

Even with a repayment plan in place and a signed contract, remember that in this scenario, you should go into the loan expecting to never see that money again and only loan what you're willing to lose.

On the other hand, what you might need to offer isn't financial assistance in the form of cash in hand, but rather, a plan.

Offering Budgeting Help

I could be way off base, but if you're reading this book, then odds are pretty high that you have a general interest in personal finance and have done some of the hard work of getting your own financial house in order (if not, here's the shameless plug telling you to get my first book, *Broke*

Millennial). You could help lay the groundwork for your loved one to get their financial life together if that's part of the reason for a loan.

"As I was pumping money into one relative's household, I saw him spending frivolously on vacations and such, and I felt like I didn't understand the full financial picture," says Lacy, who points out that it's harder to go back and do this after you've already provided money a few times. "In reality, he didn't need the money assistance. He needed better financial structure."

It won't always be easy to get a family member to accept your offer to help build a budget, rehabilitate a credit score, or develop a debt repayment attack plan, especially if they just see a check that you could afford to write as an easy solution to their problems.

"I think the most important thing is consistency in the messaging you are giving family," says Bryan-Podvin. "So, if you have a sibling who is a train wreck with their money, and they're coming to you, and you've been through this cycle a few times, you have to set a firm boundary."

> *"Here are the resources I can offer you:* [e.g., a financial advisor or service, books, podcasts, etc.]. *And I'm happy to help you in a nonfinancial way. I can help you figure out how to go through your credit report and create a plan to improve your score."*

Bryan-Podvin stresses the importance of setting a boundary that feels good for you. For instance, it might be reasonable to subsidize or make a loved one's car payment or buy them a subway pass, because without transportation, they won't be able to get to their job, and that would create a worse situation.

Asking a Family Member for a Loan

On the other side, it can range from awkward to painfully embarrassing to ask a family member for money. The Bank of Mom and Dad (or a sibling) probably comes with a more favorable interest rate than an actual bank, and they won't check your credit history. So, if you're confident it won't negatively impact your relationship, it might be the easier short-term solution. That doesn't mean it's the easier emotional option.

As discussed, it's best for the lender to think of this as money they won't recoup. That will probably impact the size of the loan your loved one is willing to provide, as will the frequency with which you've come to them to ask for a loan. Whether it's your first time asking for a loan or something you've done before, it's best to come with a pitch and proposed repayment plan.

You don't have to come with a full-on slideshow presentation and formal proposal, but it doesn't hurt to behave as though you're going to the bank. Briefly overview what you need the money for and your expected repayment schedule. Be realistic. If you're between jobs and need $2,000 for rent and groceries to float you for a couple months, don't say you'll start repaying it next week. I know how strange all this sounds. It's your family after all. But treating it as a more formal transaction can also make it more comfortable for you.

You may find it helpful to provide context about why you need the money as a start, especially if your family is unaware that you're having a tough financial time.

 "I lost my job last month, and while I do have some savings, I'm finding it's taking longer than expected to get a new one." Or maybe you're self-employed: *"Unfortunately, one of my clients is taking longer than expected to pay me, and I need a short-term loan to cover expenses until that check comes in."*

Depending on your relationship with your parents or a sibling, asking for advice first before directly asking for money can make it more palatable for everyone. Once you are ready to directly make the ask, come with a plan.

 "I've outlined how I'm going to spend the money and also my expected repayment schedule."

Keep in mind that borrowing money from a loved one, just like from a friend, means they are likely to get critical about how you're spending money. If you take a vacation or make a nonessential purchase and they haven't been repaid, you might get some snide comments. Even if you don't live near your family, social media is the ultimate snitch.

ULTIMATELY, IS IT YOUR RESPONSIBILITY TO TAKE CARE OF A FAMILY MEMBER?

Let's be honest, that's the *really* loaded question behind all of this.

"You need to decide how you do or don't want to help your parents in retirement," says Bryan-Podvin. "I find so many adult children feel it's their responsibility to manage their parents financially, and I also find that a lot of people with the means to help their parents feel a little resentful and question why their parents didn't better set themselves up for a comfortable retirement."

But the question is also rooted in the idea of having a choice. Not everyone feels that's the case.

"It's so cultural," points out Kristin Wong. "It's very American culture to think, 'I didn't ask to be born, and I'm my own person,' but in other cultures it would be awful if you didn't take care of your aging parents." Wong personally doesn't believe a parent should rely on a child's taking care of them, but she does feel a responsibility to take care of her parents even so.

Cameron Huddleston agrees. Married to a non-American herself, Huddleston points out that in many communities, it's very much expected that the kids will care for the parents. However, that doesn't mean you avoid having the conversation.

"Just because you're taking care of Mom or Dad doesn't mean you're going to have access to their financial accounts," says Huddleston. "You still have to have that legal groundwork to do it." (We'll cover the specifics on how to establish that legal groundwork in the next chapter.)

How Healthy Is Your Relationship with Your Parents?

"Some people have parents who didn't take care of them, even on a basic level, and it's not that rare," says Ohikuare. "Suppose your dad neglected you. Do you have an obligation to him? Not really."

The level and type of assistance you can provide to your parents (or siblings) should be tied to how healthy (or unhealthy) the relationship is between you. Just because you love someone and are related to them doesn't mean living with them or supporting them is the mentally and emotionally correct move for you to make. While I can't assess that dynamic for you here on this page (and because I'm not a licensed professional), this is an underlying issue you will need to factor into this entire conversation about supporting and talking about money with family.

Now, that's not to say that you should cut off assistance entirely. It just may not come in the form they asked for.

You Can't Give What You Don't Have

While it's ideal to be able to support your parents, siblings, or other extended family if that's what you choose, Ohikuare points out that you can't give what you don't have. You shouldn't put your own financial security at risk in order to support a family member.

However, she acknowledges that most people are not going to let their family members flounder or drown under crushing financial obligations. It's more about setting boundaries and understanding your other obligations, such as to a spouse or child. There's also a fine line between supporting your parents and your parents' taking advantage of you and feeing entitled to your money.

"It can be a free-for-all," says Ohikuare. "So, there has to be some sort of system."

She advises that you ask yourself the following questions:

- Can you give?
- Do you want to give?

- What is reasonable? And that means what is reasonable from the standpoint of what the needs of your immediate family are (that being defined as a family unit of your spouse and/or children).
- What do your parents/siblings/extended family actually need? (E.g., do they need you to cover their medications each month or pay a percentage of the rent?)

If you can't provide financially, consider whether you can give time. As Ohikuare points out, huge problems for the aging and elderly population are isolation and lack of intellectual and emotional connection. The ability to spend time also matters if a loved one gets hurt or sick.

"Can they be secure in the knowledge that someone is aware of how they are doing on a day-to-day or weekly basis?" asks Ohikuare.

But this advice is all predicated on an important assumption: that your loved one is still fit to care for themselves.

Chapter 8

When a Loved One Requires Your Help (or Intervention)

A LOT OF this section has focused on how to navigate a conversation with your parents or siblings when they're of sound mind and able to engage with you and answer questions. But not everyone is granted that opportunity when it comes to caring for a family member. A mental health disorder or an illness could mean that you're suddenly in the position of playing defense and taking on the care of a loved one without any sort of playbook or forethought.

Oftentimes the topic of caring for a family member focuses on children and parents, this section included, but this is also applicable if you need to care for a sibling. The death of a parent could require you to assume custody of a sibling with a disability or health issue who is otherwise unable to care for themselves.

Plus, you need to have the following legal documents in place, especially if you have a spouse or dependents (and yes, I'm including pets). Before we discuss *how* you should talk about these documents with your loved ones, let's get an overview of the documents themselves.

LEGAL DOCUMENTS

- *A will:* "The will is certainly important because it spells out who gets what when you die," says Cameron Huddleston, author of *Mom and Dad, We Need to Talk.* A will is the estate planning paperwork with which most people are familiar, perhaps because it's tied to an inheritance. But a will can stipulate more than just who gets what (no matter how modest). It can also outline how someone wants to be laid to rest, which keeps family from having to guess.

  One important thing to note: Beneficiaries can override a will. A beneficiary is the person you name to receive a particular asset if you die. For example, when you set up your 401(k) or IRA, you should've named someone as your beneficiary, the person who will get the money in that account when you die. If your parent updates a will, but the beneficiary on their investment account or life insurance policy conflicts with who they named in the will, then the beneficiary could end up with the money. For example, Jane and Tom were married for twenty years and then got divorced. Tom remarried and updated his will to leave everything to his new wife, Brandi. But Tom forgot to update the beneficiary on his life insurance policy, which was still Jane. Tom died. Even though the will said Brandi got everything, the beneficiary of the life insurance policy was still Jane, so Jane got the payout. The court could also get involved to decide who gets the money based on state law.

- *Power of attorney:* A document that Huddleston deems even more important than the will. The power of attorney gives you the ability to make decisions and actions on your loved one's behalf if they are unable to do so independently. This could be because of something like a coma or dementia. Something as simple as being able to call up your mom's bank to get the mortgage paid while she is in the hospital isn't easily done without a signed power of attorney. Make sure you know where it is, because the bank will ask to see it.

- *Healthcare power of attorney/healthcare proxy:* This document lets you name a healthcare proxy/surrogate who can make healthcare decisions for you.

- *Living will:* It also enables you to detail end-of-life medical treatment you do or do not want. Do you want to be on life support or resuscitated? You can't just tell people what you want (even your family and doctor). Your doctor wants something in writing so they don't get sued by your family members.

The executor of the will doesn't have to be the same person who has power of attorney or is the healthcare proxy. A friend of mine is a nurse and her brother is a financial planner, so she's the one named on the healthcare proxy, while he's the executor of the will and would handle settling the estate. You can (and should) also have backups or name more than one person. This could be done if parents want children to work together to make decisions. It also is important because the person named as your healthcare proxy or the person who has power of attorney could predecease you.

The aforementioned legal documents are necessary in the United States. If you or your parents (or another family member for whom you care) live outside the United States, it's important to determine the appropriate and similar versions of these documents in your/their country of residence. The UK, for instance, has a lasting power of attorney (LPA), which can include personal welfare, property, and financial affairs.

If you're curious about how your state handles healthcare laws (like do-not-resuscitate orders or living wills) or estate planning (like estate taxes and probate court), you can use the site LegalConsumer.com.

What Happens If You Don't Get These Documents Handled?

"You can sort things out if there's not a will, but if a power of attorney and a living will haven't been drafted and signed by your competent parents, and something happens like a stroke or a car accident, it's too late to draft those documents," explains Huddleston. "You can't go to the bank and say, 'My mom's in the hospital because she had a stroke and I need to make sure her bills get paid.' They're going to say to you, '[Do] you [have] power of attorney?' If [you don't], and your siblings [don't], and no one [else does], no one can get access to your parents' account. Then you have to go to court to get conservatorship. In that case, you're putting your parent on trial to prove they're no longer competent to make financial decisions on their own. It's expensive. You have to hire an attorney for your parents, yourself, a doctor—sometimes two doctors—to come in and testify. And then if you get named conservator, you have to file a document with the court detailing how you spent your parents' money."

You don't have to do any of that if you have a power of attorney and living will with a named healthcare proxy.

Asking If They Have a Will

"When you're going to talk to your parents about if they have a will, you want to make it very clear that you're not having the conversation with them because you want to find out what you're getting," says Huddleston. In fact, she suggests you don't even bring up the "what am I getting" conversation.

"Mom and Dad, do you have something in writing that spells out your final wishes?"

And they'll say, "Oh no, because your mother/father is going to get everything" or "you're going to get everything." And you say:

"Well, I know that's what you might want, but unless you have an official will, the state has a will for you. And the state might divide your assets up differently than what you had planned. Unless you spell it out, your house might have to get divided between Mom/Dad and us."

Asking for a Power of Attorney

Given how much control you can assume over your parents' life with a power of attorney, some parents may balk at the idea and feel they're relinquishing too much agency over their own lives.

> *"No, Mom and Dad, it isn't giving up control, because you get to decide who has power of attorney for you. If you don't decide, a court could decide for you. Someone might step up, and it might not be the person you want to be making those decisions for you. And if you don't want to give me this control now, just simply take the document, put it someplace safe, tell me where it is, and tell me the conditions under which I'm allowed to access it."*

Asking for a Living Will/Healthcare Proxy

> *"I want to know what you want. I don't want to have to make this decision for you. It's not my decision to make. This way, you can put it in writing and spell out what you want, so we don't make the wrong choice for you, and so the family doesn't end up fighting over it."*

AARP offers free advance directive forms that are specific to each state's laws at www.aarp.org/caregiving/financial-legal/free-printable -advance-directives. That's a good starting point if your parents are feeling overwhelmed or reluctant to engage with you.

Where Are the Documents?

It's important that you not only know your parents have these documents but know where you can find them!

WHEN A MENTAL HEALTH DISORDER IS A FACTOR

Cognitive and mental changes are natural parts of the aging process, but some parents may suffer from a serious mental health disorder such as depression, bipolar disorder, or anxiety.

Whether you've grown up handling your parent's mental illness or it's a late-onset disorder, there are some practical, logistical, and legal steps you should consider.

You Need to Get the Paperwork Handled ASAP

We previously discussed the importance of power-of-attorney paperwork, which must be signed when a person is of sound mind. There is also a mental health power of attorney. It enables your parent or sibling to detail how they would want medical and treatment decisions made in a time when they may be unable to make sound decisions. It can also detail desires about things like medication, hospitalization, drug trials, interventions, and temporary custody of children. In addition, there can be times in which you need to take over control of their finances, especially if they're prone to manic episodes with a tendency to go on impulsive spending sprees.

Signing a mental health power of attorney gives your loved one the power to make those decisions preemptively without your needing to guess their desires in the future or potentially battle it out with the state about when you can legally intervene during a crisis situation. This document does have to be signed under certain conditions and standards, such as your loved one's being mentally healthy and lucid. For your family member's peace of mind, it can also carry a provision that the mental health power of attorney will only be enforceable after they have been deemed incapacitated by a licensed psychiatrist or psychologist. That will help reduce any concern that you could just come in and take over their life at any time.

In addition, it is important to have an advance healthcare directive and a medical power of attorney/healthcare proxy. One of the important reasons you should set up a medical power of attorney and an advance healthcare directive is so you can openly discuss treatment options with your family member's doctor. Otherwise, the doctor will likely be unable to openly discuss your family member's case with you due to physician-patient confidentiality laws.

You should seek legal counsel in order to ensure your mental health power of attorney and advance healthcare directive meet your state's standards. While you technically can create a power of attorney online with templates on sites like Nolo and Rocket Lawyer, it's really preferable that you meet with an experienced attorney. This isn't a situation in which you want to use an online template and hope for the best if it ever comes to a lawsuit.

Is There a System in Place for Manic Episodes?

You need to have the tough, frank conversations about the actions your loved one would want taken to protect them from themselves during any sort of manic episode. For some, these episodes can lead to drained bank accounts, large purchases, or poor investment decisions. You should discuss the point at which your family member would want you to step in and control the finances—which could include paying all bills and providing a stipend for discretionary spending.

Determine If Assisted Living Is the Right Situation

For some people, caring for a family member with a mental health disorder can become completely untenable. You may not have the expertise to handle it yourself, it may become unsafe for you and/or other members of your family, or it could be hard for you to maintain steady employment and care for your loved one, depending on their needs. While it may be painful to consider for all parties, it bears mentioning that placing your family member in an assisted living facility could be the right solution for your family.

It can take time for your loved one to adjust, especially if they suffer from paranoia or hallucinations. It's completely normal and rational for you to experience sadness, guilt, and relief after placing a loved one in an assisted living facility.

Find Support

No matter how much you love a parent or sibling, it can be really mentally and emotionally draining to be solely responsible for them. You may go through a range of emotions, from frustration to rage to sadness to resentment. It's important you take the time to care for your own mental and emotional health, such as seeking therapy or at least finding a support group with people who are going through a similar experience.

Research Other Resources

If you're struggling to handle this situation on your own either financially or emotionally, you could consider bringing in adult protective services. These services vary by city and state and are designed to help physically or mentally impaired adults live safely in their own homes. However, you need to proceed with caution if you're going to bring in a government entity, as it could result in someone else's getting guardianship over your parent(s) or sibling and making decisions on their behalf.

Be Open in Conversations with Other Family Members

Aging parents who have an adult child with a mental health disorder may experience extreme stress over what the future holds. You can't just assume your parents know that you plan to care for your sibling or financially support them. That needs to be an open conversation within the family. On the other hand, you may not plan to take full responsibility for a family member, so making plans for what will happen is also important.

CHECKLIST OF WHAT YOU NEED TO KNOW FROM A PARENT

"When my father fell ill a few years ago and I was with him at the hospital, the doctors asked me what medication he was on and I realized I didn't know the name of it," says Judith Ohikuare, a development manager at NY Writers Coalition, a nonprofit organization in Brooklyn. "I took pictures of the bottles he has, so if I didn't remember what they were called I had the picture of it with the name clearly stated."

In addition to finding out which medications your parents take, Ohikuare also recommends you sit down with your parent(s) and do an indepth dive on their monthly expenses. But don't just pick one month out of the year and be done. It's important to evaluate one month in each season since costs can and will vary.

Questions to Ask Your Parents

- What does a typical month of spending look like for them?

  - Include groceries, utilities (which can certainly vary in cost by season), transportation, housing, healthcare, medication, entertainment, supporting family members, religious and/ or charitable contributions, and travel to visit family or for pleasure.

  - You should also pull a few months of bank and credit card statements and go through them with your parents. Keep an eye out for reoccurring, automated charges and just make sure those are still services they want and use. (This is also a good practice for you to do at least once a year!)

  - While it's good to evaluate one month in each season, Ohikuare points out that not all the months look alike in a season. For instance, maybe your parent is an immigrant and likes to return to their home country each July. So, you can't just use June as your template for their financial checklist for the summer.

- Where do they bank?
- How do they pay their bills?

- Make a full list of all the bills your parents pay both monthly and annually, and include the login information for their accounts.

- Huddleston advises that you talk to your parents early about how they pay their bills and try to help them set up automatic bill pay for many, if not all. Doing so can really reduce the stress on your end if/when something happens.

❑ Where is all the login information for their accounts?

❑ Do they have wills?

❑ Do they have retirement plans?

❑ Who has power of attorney for them?

❑ Do they have a healthcare proxy?

❑ What about debt?

- What kind of debt? How much debt exists? What's the current repayment plan?

- If your parents took out student loans for you, make 100 percent certain that those debts are discharged upon their death and won't be passed on to you.

❑ Do they have long-term-care insurance?

❑ What are their Social Security numbers and how much will they receive in benefits?

- There is a lot of discussion about when to take Social Security benefits and if you should take the distribution early. There are some online calculators and resources to use. However, your parents really should have someone knowledgeable about finance (preferably a certified financial planner) give their retirement strategy a once-over before making a big decision like taking an early distribution of Social Security benefits, especially if they're higher earners.

- What's their Medicare/Medicaid number?
- What insurance policies do they have and where is all that information stored?
- What are their social media login details, so you can take control of an account after their death?
- Do they own property besides their primary residence?
- Where are the keys to any lockboxes, safes, storage units, etc.?
- Ask if they tend to hide money or other valuables—this is incredibly important for when you're cleaning out the house. You don't want to just be tossing old pieces of luggage or shoe boxes or anything that appears nondescript without checking, especially if your parents had a proclivity for hiding money.

"When they die, if you don't know what assets they have, basically you could end up losing that money," says Huddleston. "There could be a lockbox at the bank that you didn't even know about, or jewelry hidden under the bed, or accounts you don't know about."

That last one actually happened to Huddleston. Her mom lived with her for a period of time before going into assisted living, and so her mom's mail would get sent to Huddleston's house. But Huddleston and her family moved, and the new owners eventually reached out to tell her that they kept getting mail for her mom. Huddleston went to pick up the mail and discovered letters from a bank about an account she never knew existed that was about to get turned over as unclaimed property—and it had $50,000 in it. Financial institutions like banks and brokerages will report and then turn over money in dormant accounts to the state. The period of time it takes for an account to be considered dormant can vary by state, but it's often a few years with no activity at all.

"I'm sure you don't want this money that you worked hard to save to get tossed because we didn't even know it was there. Letting us know about your assets is not about counting up your

money or evaluating an inheritance. It's about having the in-
formation so that when you die, if you want to pass on a legacy,
it gets passed on."

ARE YOU ON THE HOOK FOR YOUR PARENTS' DEBT?

"Usually, no," says Huddleston. "If your name isn't on your parent's debts, then you will not inherit the parent's debt." Having power of attorney or being the healthcare proxy or beneficiary of a will also doesn't make you liable for your parents' debts, but cosigning on a loan or credit card does. Debts may need to be paid off as part of the estate settlement, but you won't be on the hook for non-cosigned debts if there isn't enough money (a.k.a. if the estate is insolvent). However, if one parent dies and the other lives, the lenders could try to get paid by the surviving spouse, especially in a community-property state. Those states are: Arizona, California, Idaho, Louisiana, Nevada, New Mexico, Texas, Washington, and Wisconsin. Alaska is an opt-in community-property state.

There is a chance you could end up liable for your parents' medical or nursing home debt if the estate is insolvent. If your state enforces a "filial responsibility" law, then it's possible you could get sued to recoup the costs. Filial responsibility typically only kicks in if your parents didn't qualify for Medicare, so it's important for you to know if that's the case. Historically, these laws have not often been enforced, but with the insane cost of healthcare, it's never safe to assume that will continue to be the case.

DISCUSSING LONG-TERM CARE

"Long-term care really isn't cheap," says Huddleston, pointing out that for most people the default long-term-care plan is family members. "There are ways to pay for long-term care, but it requires planning, and Medicare doesn't pay for long-term care. Medicaid will, but you have to have very limited assets to qualify for Medicaid."

The struggle in navigating this conversation is getting your parents to accept a reality in which they can't care for themselves. Who wants to think about needing physical assistance to do basic tasks like getting dressed or going to the bathroom if you've been able-bodied your entire life? But the reality is that it very well could be necessary. A fall, a stroke, a terminal illness, Alzheimer's—these things happen. Long-term-care insurance can help, but in order to get a policy with a reasonable rate, your parents need to still be healthy. If that's the case, it is something you should discuss with them sooner rather than later.

As much as I dislike the use of scare tactics in these conversations, it is important to come with the facts.

"Mom and Dad, did you know that two-thirds of adults aged sixty-five and older end up needing long-term care at some point in their life? Typically, they spend three years needing that care. On average it's more than $4,000 a month for assisted living or a home health aide, and a nursing home is around $8,000 a month.[1] It's not that uncommon, and Medicare doesn't pay for it. Medicaid will, but you have to have limited assets to qualify. Long-term-care insurance will cover it. There are also some life insurance policies with long-term-care benefits, or you could begin saving up for it to pay out of pocket."

Or:

"I get that you're counting on each other, and us/me, to care for you as you age. But what happens when you're eighty-five? You may not have the physical strength to help each other in and out of bed or to hold yourself up while you bathe. And I'd love to be able to help, but I have a job and kids who are counting on me to care and provide for them. I won't be able to quit my job to be a caregiver. We need to discuss how we can pay to hire someone if you'll want to stay here in your home or cover the cost of a retirement community."

"Having that conversation sooner allows you to explore the options," says Huddleston. "There aren't a ton of options, but talking earlier can give you a chance to figure out less expensive ones. You can use a network of volunteers from church, synagogue, or the community. You can even talk your parents into looking at assisted living facilities early to know preemptively what places they'd like."

TALK ABOUT SCAMS!

The National Council on Aging estimates one in ten Americans aged sixty-plus has been the victim of some kind of elder abuse.[2] Elder abuse takes many forms, but a common one is financial exploitation. This could involve someone targeting your loved ones in person, catfishing (especially on dating websites), phishing scams, or the classic Social Security or IRS scam calls.

As technology allows scammers to get more and more sophisticated, it's important we educate our parents about how easy it is to be duped. Bringing up a common scam, such as the scam in which someone calls claiming to be from the IRS and saying you owe back taxes, is a good intro to the conversation. Just be careful that you don't make it sound like you're worried your parents would fall for it just because they're older. Ageism is not a tactful basis for this discussion!

Huddleston recommends using the discussion of data breaches and scams to bring up credit history.

"If you want, I can help you check your credit report to make sure you're not already a victim of identity theft. I can show you how to do it safely online and for free.* You can see if there are any accounts you don't recognize."

---

*You're entitled to a free copy of your credit report from each reporting agency (TransUnion, Equifax, and Experian) once per year. AnnualCreditReport.com is a one-stop shop that's 100 percent free.

Another strategy is to tie it back to yourself.

> *"I got a call from someone the other day claiming to be from the IRS and saying I owed $5,000 in back taxes. But I hung up and then did some research and found out the IRS never calls you directly first and always sends a letter as the first point of contact. Have you ever gotten a call like that?"*

There are too many horror stories of elderly people being scammed out of anywhere from thousands of dollars to their entire life savings, so you want to make sure to protect your parents.

FINANCIAL ABUSE IN FAMILIES

"You're writing a book about relationships and money? Have you thought about including what to do if your parents totally fuck up your financial life?" a man asked me at a party.

"To be honest, I thought more about including financial abuse in the romance section, but you're right, it happens in families too," I responded.

"Yeah, it does," he said. "My parents annihilated my credit score by opening up credit cards in my name."

That wasn't the first time I'd heard of a situation like that. In college, I knew someone whose parents had taken out loans in his name and used the money for their own needs and desires. It's really easy for parents to commit financial abuse and fraud because they have access to all the basics: name, address, birth date, Social Security number.

It happens for a variety of reasons: family debt, addiction, or perhaps a parent wrecked their own credit and turned to the child's for a blank slate, thinking of it as a quick, one-time solution.

The problem is that rectifying the situation usually requires you to press charges against a family member, something a lot of people, no matter how toxic the relationship, aren't willing to do.

Uncovering Financial Abuse

Oftentimes adult children will find out about a parent's misdeeds when they try to apply for a loan or credit card or open a bank account and get denied. You can also be proactive by checking your own credit reports using AnnualCreditReport.com, a free website that's endorsed by the Consumer Financial Protection Bureau.[3] By federal law, you are entitled to a free copy of your credit report from each of the credit bureaus once per year.

ChexSystems is the reporting agency that banks and credit unions typically use. It's separate from your credit report, and it's what you should check if you were denied a bank account.

Your Options Once Financial Abuse Is Uncovered

Talk to Your Family Member

This is only a step you should take if you can safely confront your family member about this issue. You may want to acknowledge that you have unearthed the fraud and are taking steps to prevent it from happening again. You can also discuss what this has done to your financial life and the road to recovery for you.

Once you've either initiated this conversation and/or moved on to cleaning up the ramifications of their fraud, here are the steps you can take.

Credit Freeze

If your parents or siblings have committed identity fraud against you (or if anyone else has), you can put a credit freeze on your credit reports to mitigate further fallout. A freeze restricts access to your credit report, which means it's going to be a lot harder if someone is trying to apply for credit in your name because a potential lender won't be able to see your report unless you—the real you—grant access.

In order to put a freeze on your reports, you'll need to go to each of the three credit bureaus: Equifax, TransUnion, and Experian. You'll need your name, date of birth, Social Security number, and address, and you may be asked for other identifying information. Once the freeze has been placed, you'll receive a PIN from each bureau that can be used to either thaw the freeze or lift it entirely. Be sure to keep this PIN in a safe location where you won't lose it, or it can be a bit of a nightmare to try to thaw your report in the future.

And before you panic, a freeze won't impact your credit score. It will, however, make it slightly more challenging to apply for credit until you remove the freeze. You can "thaw" your report to give one-time access, so it's doable, but it's a more cumbersome process.

This is also a useful tool if you have a child and are worried someone may have committed child identity theft against them.

Fraud Alert

You can also place a fraud alert on your reports. It's a less extreme move than the freeze because it doesn't completely lock down your credit reports. Potential lenders or creditors can still get access to your report, but they're supposed to take extra steps to confirm your identity.

The basic fraud alert will last for a year and is useful if you think you may be at risk of identity theft. An extended fraud alert will be in place for seven years and is used by people who are confirmed victims of identity theft. Active-duty military members can also put an alert on their reports during deployment as a protective measure against fraud.

Report the Fraud to Banks and Credit Card Companies

As soon as you uncover accounts opened in your name that aren't yours, you'll need to report them to the bank, credit union, credit card company, and/or lender.

Should the issue be with a child who is a minor, it's slightly easier to solve, because you can use birth certificates and records to prove the child is underage and someone committed identity theft. If you're eighteen years of age or older, it gets a little more complicated because you'll probably need to escalate this to the police.

Change All Your Passwords and PINs

You probably won't have access to the accounts created by the identity thief, but be sure to change all your own passwords and PINs to play defense!

Report It to the Federal Trade Commission (FTC)

Go to IdentityTheft.gov to file a report and also get guidance on recovery steps. A report from the FTC will be necessary in the future when you need proof of the identity theft.

This is also a useful tool if you've been a victim of a data breach (and let's be honest, if you haven't yet, you will be).

Report It to the Police

You need to get a police report when identity theft has been committed so that you can take that report to banks or other businesses. Some banks and creditors may request a copy of a police report in order to remove the fraudulent account.

According to the FTC's guidelines, you should take a copy of the FTC identity theft report, your government-issued photo ID, proof of your address (e.g., a lease, utilities bill, or mortgage statement), and any proof of the theft you may have, such as bills or notices from the IRS, when you go to file your police report.[4]

You also should get and store a copy of the police report in a safe place, as you may need it in the future to clear the fraudulent accounts off your credit report.

Of course, this is one of the most complicated parts of the process, because you will likely get pressured by family members not to report the fraud to the proper authorities. After all, it could have legal ramifications for your family member, including potential jail time.

Dealing with Financial Abuse

Financial abuse in families goes far beyond child identity theft. Parents (and siblings) can use financial support to manipulate and control a loved one. It can feel minor at first, like a parent's dictating where you can go to college or where you can live if you're receiving financial support. But it can also extend to a parent's dictating the type of person you can have a relationship with or the type of job you can take. Those who are victims of abuse can find support and guidance from these sources:

National Domestic Violence Hotline: Financial abuse can be an extension of a physically abusive relationship. But even if physical abuse isn't part of your suffering, you can turn to the National Domestic Violence Hotline to confidentially speak to expert advocates. These advocates can help you find resources or help if you're simply questioning unhealthy aspects of your relationship dynamic with a loved one. You can visit TheHotline.org/help/ or call 1-800-799-SAFE (7233). Those who are deaf or hard of hearing can use 1-800-787-3224 or the videophone at 1-855-812-1001, or email nationaldeafhotline@adwas.org.

Therapy: Recovering from any form of abuse can be a long journey and one you shouldn't undertake alone. Finding a therapist, especially one who specializes in or has experience dealing with your particular trauma, can help you rebuild.

DO YOUR PARENTS NEED TO MOVE?

"Florida is a great place to die," a financial advisor jokingly said to me once. She and I were in a discussion about end-of-life planning and estate taxes. Florida is one of nine states that don't charge income tax (Alaska, Nevada, South Dakota, Texas, Washington, and Wyoming also don't charge personal income tax; New Hampshire and Tennessee don't tax wages). Florida also doesn't levy a "death tax" or, more formally, an estate tax—although the estate is still likely to be taxed on a federal level. The weather and the tax code are two reasons Florida is a cliché destination for retirees. Being able to stretch your money is a consideration for most retirees, and depending on the cost of living where your parents are now, it might not be tenable in retirement.

"I'm going through this situation now with my dad," says Ohikuare, who is a born-and-raised New Yorker. Her father has lived in and built his community in Brooklyn for many decades. Her siblings also live in New York, and her father doesn't have much family elsewhere in the United States.

"Telling him to move to a place that makes sense financially but where he literally has no one else is a little absurd to me," says Ohikuare. "People need people for their well-being. You need someone to check in on you."

In her situation, she's slowly started laying the groundwork of discussing which cities and states feel close enough to New York to easily either enable one sibling to move with their dad or facilitate more frequent visits if he needs to move.

"It's important to understand what you can compromise on," says Ohikuare. "It might be a hard compromise, but know what is a compromise you can make as well as what isn't possible."

For those with siblings, it's really important to start discussing your parents' futures with the entire family, especially if you don't live near each other.

TALKING TO YOUR SIBLINGS ABOUT CARING FOR PARENTS

I intensely identify with Ohikuare's situation. My sister lives in Los Angeles, I live in New York City, and our parents live in North Carolina. To further complicate things, neither of our parents are from North Carolina, and they have lived in six states and three countries—so they're no strangers to moving. However, should my parents need one of us to care for them in their later years, either my sister and I would have to uproot them from a place where they've built a life and community, or one of us would have to leave behind her life to move to North Carolina.

Because I'm married, it adds another complicated layer to this conversation. A potential move would impact Peach's life and career. Plus, we would also need to have this conversation with his siblings about their parents, since Peach and I also don't live near his family.

None of this is a simple conversation, especially when you're spread out around the country (or globe). But often, it will come down to where people are in their lives when the situation actually arises.

"If something should happen, I will handle going there and we'll figure it out," says Ohikuare, explaining that maybe she wouldn't move permanently but might possibly go for a few months at a time. In her situation, Ohikuare is the sibling with the most flexible job situation compared to her older brother, and she doesn't have a husband or children whose lives would also be impacted by this decision. Her younger sister is a decade younger than Ohikuare, who is in her early thirties, and Ohikuare doesn't feel that taking care of a parent should be part of her sister's responsibilities when she hasn't yet had the opportunity to establish herself and her career.

The other twist to consider is each sibling's dynamic with their parents.

"We can't pretend all children necessarily have equal relationships with their parents," says Ohikuare. "It's just true that some children get along better with their parents than their siblings."

And while not all siblings will have the same relationship with their parents, they also might not have healthy relationships with each other. In fact, you might be thinking right now that you'd rather be forced to sit at a never-ending dinner debating your uncle who's at the opposite end of the political spectrum than discuss your parents' care plan with your sibling(s).

However, it's important. Here are some ways to bring it up:

"Have you thought about what will happen to our parents when they get older?"

Ohikuare advises you don't immediately leap into a conversation about money or responsibilities. Just start with a foundational conversation in which you vocalize what you may not want to have to discuss: the eventuality of your parents' aging and dying. That conversation can be a natural segue into what's possible and not possible for each person to compromise on and contribute. But it doesn't have to happen all at once, and it can be an evolving conversation, especially if you start it early, before there's an immediate crisis or concern.

> *"This is just the beginning of the conversation. I haven't really talked to Mom and Dad about it before."*

You also shouldn't assume that you're the special, smart, proactive one just because you were the one to broach the subject. You have no idea how your siblings (or parents) are feeling about this, and perhaps it's been a nagging feeling in their minds that they've just been too afraid to give voice to.

Avoid language like "You need to do this" and "I'm going to handle this." Make it a true conversation with room for flexibility.

"Of course, you have to bring it back to your parents," says Ohikuare. "You can't make plans that don't involve them, since they're the ones whose lives are being impacted and discussed."

Figuring Out How Each Sibling Can Contribute

If it becomes necessary for the children to financially care for a parent, then that's a burden that's likely to be split among siblings. But it's also an uncomfortable fact that all siblings in a family don't earn the same amount of money. However, this isn't a dinner bill at the end of the night, where you can quibble over splitting it evenly, just paying for what you ate, or having one person pick up the tab. Consideration needs to be paid to a variety of factors, including:

- Will one or more siblings handle the day-to-day in-person care of a parent due to proximity?
- How much money can each sibling afford to give based on their own financial situation?
- Prorating contributions based on income and family situations is a critical part of this discussion. It's not necessarily fair to just look at the total and divide it evenly between the siblings.

- Is a sibling married to someone who is also financially taking care of a parent or family member?

Ohikuare points to the nonfinancial ways siblings can contribute to the well-being of a parent, even one you don't live near.

- Do any of the siblings call your parents and check in? That can help reduce the potential burden on siblings who are providing in-person help. And it can make the one being checked in on feel better and cared for.
- Can they help with research or finding someone who can help make this transition a little easier?

What If You're an Only Child (or Don't Have Siblings to Whom You Can Turn)?

Admittedly, a lot of this chapter has focused on how to speak to your parents and siblings and how to turn to your siblings for support. Obviously, that's not an option for everyone. You could be estranged from a sibling or have half siblings who aren't related to the parent in question, or you could be an only child.

"The conversation really becomes much more about you and your parents, or if your parent is a single person, it's just one-on-one," says Ohikuare.

Davita Scarlett, a New York–based TV writer, is an only child who was raised by a single mom. While Scarlett does have some half siblings from her father's side, she was reared mostly by her mother.

Once Scarlett's mom retired, the two started having more conversations about where she is financially and what she needs. The two have not talked specifics about her mother's nest egg, but Scarlett knows her mom is currently living off of Social Security checks.

"We grew up without a ton of money, and she made about the same amount her entire career, so I knew she wasn't sitting on a gold mine and it'd be up to me to help her," says Scarlett, who knows there aren't any big debts and her mom has enough to meet her basic needs.

The fact that you're an only child doesn't really change the information you need to get from a parent. And aside from the fact that the conversation is now between just you and your parents, the approach to the topic doesn't change all that much, either. You still need the will, the power of attorney, and the living will and healthcare proxy. You still need to discuss what your parents' financial situation is. You need to be open with each other about options for the future, especially if your support would need to be more emotional than financial.

Without siblings to bounce ideas and feelings off of, it is important for only children to have a release.

"I talk to my therapist," says Scarlett with a bit of a laugh. She also has some friends to whom she can turn who either are only children themselves or were raised by single parents.

If you have a good relationship with your extended family members, then you could also rely on cousins or aunts and uncles to assist you in the way a sibling may for others. But try to proceed with caution. Ohikuare astutely observes that sometimes adding in more people further complicates the situation because of the additional family dynamics.

The biggest way in which this conversation and relationship dynamic are different for an only child, especially the only child of a single parent, is the pressure.

"Your parent wanted so much for you and sacrificed so much, and it makes you feel like you want to give back," explains Scarlett. "It's this loop that's going back between you and your single parent. Even for an only child in a two-parent household, there's one more person to help disperse that flow. A single-parent/only-child relationship is very intense because it's so one-to-one. You can feel that they want so much for you, and you want to fulfill that and also give back to them."

TAKING ALL OF THIS SLOWLY IS A-OKAY

The hardest part of this conversation, no matter your relationship to your parents or whether or not you have siblings, is the underlying implication.

"Any conversation we have, the subtext is mortality, and I worry that I'm reminding her that she has more years behind her than ahead of her," says Scarlett. "I feel like it's something we're always dancing around."

While mortality is certainly underpinning all of these conversations, they're also some of the most critical conversations to navigate.

"We build this up in our heads to be scarier than it is," says Huddleston. "We say things to ourselves like 'We don't talk about money in our family,' or 'My parents are going to get mad at me, and it's going to ruin our relationship,' or 'This is going to be so awkward.' If you approach your parents respectfully and let them know you love them and they took good care of you and you want to return the favor, it's most likely that they aren't going to get mad and the relationship won't be ruined. They might be reluctant at first, but if you continue finding different ways to bring it up and let them know it's important, hopefully they will come around. Don't give up. It can take time with some parents—I'm talking years in some cases. But you make small inroads."

Chapter 9

Why We Normally Avoid Talking Money at the Dinner Table

MUCH OF THIS SECTION focuses on supporting or even staging a financial intervention for a family member. But sometimes we run into straight-up awkward situations that have nothing to do with needing to talk mortality with Mom and Dad. Almost all (if not all) of us will have to face awkward admissions like "Listen, we really can't afford to take that family trip" or "Your generous gift giving makes me feel uncomfortable."

WHAT HAPPENS WHEN YOU EARN MORE THAN YOUR PARENTS (OR SIBLINGS)

"Most parents say something like 'I want my child to have it better than I did,' or 'I want my child to have opportunities I didn't have,'" says Lindsay Bryan-Podvin, financial therapist and founder of Mind Money Balance. However, just because your parents may generally feel that way, that doesn't mean your reaching a different socioeconomic class is necessarily an easy or palatable situation.

Michael Lacy, host of the podcast *Winning to Wealth*, personally experienced the consequences of moving to a different socioeconomic situation when he heard an aunt had been telling family members: "Michael, he thinks he's so much better than everybody."

"That's really not my heart," says Lacy. "I'm really genuinely trying to help, and it's something I'd never considered before—how my generosity could be perceived in that negative way."

There's no quick fix to a family member's misinterpreting your different lifestyle or your offers of financial help to mean you think you're better than them now. Lacy himself admits he doesn't have an answer for the question of how to deal with that reality, but he continues to try to have the tough conversations with family members and operate from a place of pure intentions.

Jealousy Can Happen

Even if your parents, aunts and uncles, or siblings are ultimately proud of you and your accomplishments, that doesn't mean they are completely free of envy.

"You, as the adult child, have to understand that your parents might be jealous or upset or have their own feelings to process about the situation," says Bryan-Podvin.

She points out that sometimes a parent can feel embarrassed if the adult child is picking up the tab at dinner or taking them on a vacation. While you may want to do something generous, it might not be seen and accepted as the gracious gift that it is. It's natural for parents to want to spoil their children, even adult ones, and to be the givers, so reversing the natural family dynamic can cause tense feelings.

While you should give your parents or siblings room to express how it makes them feel, you can also explain why it makes you happy or why you want to use your financial resources to spoil them a little.

"You gave me so much growing up that I want to be able to spoil you too."

"I know I can't always physically be there, so it brings me a lot of joy when I can take you out to dinner or on vacation."

Always Offering to Pay Can Be Misinterpreted

Similar to the dynamic of making more than your friends, a constant compulsion to pick up the bill could easily be misinterpreted by a family member. No matter the intention behind it, it's important for you to recognize that paying every bill could lead your family member to think that you believe they can't afford to buy a cup of coffee or a lunch out.

If your sibling or parent says, "I can get it," then LET THEM GET IT!

Don't Say "I/We Can't Afford That" When You Can

It's understandable that if you're a successful person and your family knows you make a good living, a statement like "I can't afford to come visit you for Christmas" can be frustrating for your family to hear. Even if the statement is true in your reality because you're focused on other financial goals, your loved ones may not see it that way. A simple language shift can help prevent your loved one from feeling lied to.

Use different language, like:

> *"We're prioritizing* [insert goal, e.g., saving up for a down payment, saving up for a baby, or trying to pay off student loans] *right now, so we won't be coming to visit for the holidays this year."*

There will still probably be some hurt feelings, but being more direct is also a way to avoid conflict.

WHAT HAPPENS WHEN YOU DON'T EARN AS MUCH

While it can certainly feel uncomfortable to outearn your siblings and even your parents, it's equally uncomfortable to be in the opposite position, where you're not keeping up financially. Whether it's because you opted for a different career path or because success hasn't yet come your way, or perhaps circumstances in your life have been more expensive, sometimes you have to be honest with your family about your limitations.

A Family Trip

Whether it's the cost of the destination, the lack of available vacation days, or the fact that your dance card is already full this year, it's reasonable to be honest with your family about not being able to afford a family trip. What you need to decide for yourself first is whether or not you'd be willing to accept financial help from a loved one to get you there.

You also need to disclose your limitations early, as it may impact the location of the family vacation.

"I don't want to stand in the way of a family trip, but my budget for a trip would only be $X."

However, just like with talking money with your friends, you have to accept it if everyone else wants to take the originally proposed trip.

Lavish Gift Giving

Holidays and birthdays can be extremely stressful because of the potential discrepancy in gift giving.

"I understand that you really enjoy giving nice gifts, but I need to confess that it makes me feel uncomfortable because I can't afford to reciprocate. This year, could we set a maximum budget of $20 per person?"

Or you can suggest homemade gifts or experiences or challenge each other as to who can be the most creative within a certain budget.

Doing Secret Santa–style gift giving is a way to be able to spoil one person instead of trying to buy nice presents for a bunch of people. This is incredibly helpful for larger families and for expanding families (e.g., when you and your siblings start getting married).

Another idea is to do a giftless holiday or birthday. However, for some people (like myself) gift giving is a love language and something that brings a lot of joy. Asking for a giftless holiday could be upsetting for some, just like getting a lavish gift is upsetting for others. Hopefully a compromise of limiting the budget or giving experiences instead of gifts can be a helpful middle ground.

A FINAL ASIDE: LET'S BRIEFLY TALK ABOUT WEDDINGS (AGAIN)

This section has been really heavy, so let's end on a slightly lighter note: weddings. I come back to this topic because planning a wedding is generally all about having financial conversations with our parents (and future in-laws), even if you rarely directly mention money. Each requested addition to the guest list comes with a literal dollar sign—at least it did in my head.

"It comes back to money conversations we don't usually have, but they're really important to have when planning a wedding," says Jen Glantz, founder of Bridesmaid for Hire.

Weddings are also filled with potential tensions about family expectations and balancing what your parents want against what you want against what your in-laws want against what's easier for guests.

Who Is Paying?

The one who holds the purse strings gets to make the decisions.
—A totally just-made-up wedding proverb

"When you and your fiancé are the ones covering the cost, you have to be really strict with your budget and your guest list and your decisions," says Glantz. "Family members will have their own opinions, but they also don't know how expensive some of this stuff is. So I think it's very important, before you even open up your life about suggestions for your wedding, [that] you and your fiancé are clear on the budget and have clear-cut priorities as to your must-haves."

Glantz tells couples to choose the three things they must have at their wedding. Everything else becomes a nice-to-have. This is the exact same advice I've given after going through my own wedding planning, because it ties into general personal finance advice. Set your values and prioritize your spending there! For our wedding, for example, Peach and I wanted a great DJ so it'd be an epic dance party, an excellent photographer (but we passed on a videographer), and an open bar with top-shelf alcohol. Food is important, but I knew most of our guest list would care more about the quality of the beer and whiskey than the deliciousness of our dinner.

"That way, when the other small things come up, you're able to prioritize and rank them," says Glantz. "But if you're paying for the wedding yourself, family members can't really have much of a say.

"Now, if they're paying for it, that's something you have to have the conversation about ahead of time," she says. She recommends if parents are helping fund the wedding, whether partially or in full, you are all very clear about how their money is being spent.

You also have to negotiate your values and your parents' values.

Paying Is the Only Real Way to Take Back Control

Some families still operate under the traditional rule that a bride's family pays for the wedding, but for many betrothed couples today, money may be coming from both parents plus their own bank accounts. The simple truth is: the only way to take back total control is to pay for it all yourself. A parent's writing a check for the wedding does fundamentally give them some level of say. Should they be able to call all of the shots? No. It should still feel like your wedding and be an event you want to attend. But it's hard to tell your mom she can't invite her book club if she's the one paying for the entire shindig.

CHALLENGES

Challenge 1: Ask your parents if they have a will, power of attorney, and living will and healthcare proxy. Go back to the different scripts and pick which one is best for your situation. Perhaps you can personalize it by saying you just started your own estate planning (because it's important no matter your age!) and wondered if they had too. Or you can be more direct: *"Mom and Dad, do you have something in writing that spells out your final wishes?"*

Challenge 2: Be honest with a family member about one financial boundary. A few examples include: setting your boundaries about the money you can spend for a family vacation, asking to do Secret Santa or set another type of money limit on holiday gifting, or suggesting a more budget-friendly restaurant for a family dinner.

Challenge 3: Set a time with your parents to talk about their estate plan. This is particularly important if you don't live near your parents and want to do this face-to-face.

Part 4

Talking About Money with Your Romantic Partner

IN SEPTEMBER 2018, Peach and I stood on a mountaintop to declare our love and lifelong commitment to each other in front of friends and family. It was a culmination of eight years—almost to the day—together. Our wedding photos, shot during the golden hour, show a lush background of trees with the faintest hint of autumn leaves. It captures a beautiful moment in time as if we're a couple with no tension or strife, just hopelessly in love.

Of course, that's not reality.

You'd never know from the photos that a month prior we were signing our names to a document that dictated how our assets would be split up if we decided to end it all. You'd never capture even a glimmer of the fights we'd had as a couple about how to budget, spend, invest, and save our money.

But our wedding ceremony itself demonstrated how we entered our marriage: with eyes wide open. In my vows to Peach, I publicly acknowledged my shortcomings and intertwined both jokes and serious decrees about how I hoped we'd spend our lives together, like:

> *"I vow to do my best to listen, especially when we have vastly different opinions on a topic, and to compromise on what really matters."*

> *"I vow to try and be patient during football season, and do my best to avoid making plans at one p.m. on Sunday afternoons."*

We entered our union not purely from a place of romantic love, but with private and public acknowledgment that it takes more than love and attraction to make a marriage work. Of course, we didn't get here quickly and easily. It's taken years of learning how to communicate about money with each other, especially since we have vastly different emotional relationships with money. It's still an evolving journey.

While there's a whole lot more than money that can cause conflict in a romantic relationship, that's what we'll focus on in this section—starting from the beginning: when you are casually dating.

Chapter 10

From Casual to Pretty Serious

WHEN I POLLED people on Instagram and Twitter about what they'd want from a book that focused on talking about money in relationships, "Dating!" was a dominant response. The rise of social media and dating apps might make it easier than ever to initiate lots of first dates, but that also can be a financial burden. A few years ago, a friend of mine admitted he was taking time off from dating because he was sick of paying for drinks or coffees or dinners that ultimately led nowhere.

CASUAL DATING

We all know the biggest stressor in the casual dating situation . . .

Who Pays?

Oh, the ever-looming tension in casual dating. In heterosexual dating, the classic—and frankly, antiquated—advice is that the man pays. It's advice that can be problematic for both men and women. For men, the obvious issue is that it can get expensive really quickly. Even just a handful of getting-to-know-you drinks a month can eat up a sizeable amount of your monthly spending budget. For women, this dynamic can lead to a sense of expectation and obligation. (This is, of course, speaking in general terms.)

In my early twenties, I was out at a bar with a friend of mine when two men approached us and asked if they could buy us drinks. We both had boyfriends who weren't present, and my friend immediately shut down the potential drink buyers. Naturally, my response was "We could've gotten a free drink." To which she said, "I don't like it when men think I owe them so much as a dance because they bought me a drink."

On the other hand, I've been present in conversations with women who wouldn't even consider a second date with a man who didn't pick up the full tab on the first date or if they dared to suggest going Dutch.

The fact that there are no firm rules and so many expectations, judgments, and stereotypes bundled into this conversation just makes it all the more awkward. And, if you've learned nothing else at this point in the book, you know the only way through is *communicating*! (Picture me clapping my hands on every syllable.)

"It's this funny thing where I had a boyfriend who had money and he paid for stuff and it was never a big deal," says Gaby Dunn, author of *Bad with Money*. "But I've noticed when I pay for a date with a cis dude or a nonbinary person, they'll say something like 'Oh, a sugar mama.' Like it's something extraordinary for me to be paying for a 'boy.'"

That brings us to a strategy, which I personally prefer, of looking at how this situation would be handled when socialized gender norms are removed.

"It's easier to fall back on the true economics of the situation in same-sex couples because that's all there is to really look at," says Paco de Leon, founder of The Hell Yeah Group. De Leon and her wife were high school sweethearts, so she jokes that she doesn't have much experience navigating today's dating culture. However, when you have the option to view the situation based on the money alone, without the social pressures, it at least becomes a discussion as opposed to an assumption.

Of course, that's certainly easier in a longer-term dating relationship when you start to have a sense of incomes and debt burdens, but you might not know from a first date which of you is on stronger financial footing.

"If you initiate the date, you pay, and if you made the plan, then you pay," says Dunn.

But you can still check in with your potential date about their comfort level with cost. After all, not everyone wants to be wined and dined over an expensive meal on an early date, even if the other person is picking up the check. "I like to send options ahead of time and ask, 'Is this place okay? It has two dollar signs. Is that okay?' I give as much info as possible," says Dunn.

> *"I invited you on this date, so I'd like to pay. Does this* [restaurant/bar/show] *sound good to you?"*
>
> *"Here are a few of my favorite spots to* [grab a drink/get dinner] *in the neighborhood. Do you have a preference?"*

When You Should Start Talking About Money

(Because should you really be having that conversation before things are serious?)

The earlier, the better, but I'm a realist about how uncomfortable this conversation is for many people and that you might find yourself about to marry someone without ever directly discussing money. Luckily, the conversation is already happening without words.

Picking Up Context Clues

Mindy Jensen, cohost of the *BiggerPockets Money Podcast*, and her husband, Carl Jensen, founder of the site 1500 Days to Freedom, don't remember ever directly discussing money when they started dating in the early 2000s, when they were in their mid-twenties.

"We had context clues that we were on the same page," says Mindy about her relationship with Carl. "On our first date, to Carl's favorite barbecue place, he used a coupon, which I thought was awesome."

Before Carl even met Mindy, his boss told him that he needed to buy a nicer car or he'd have trouble getting married, because even though he made good money as a programmer, he needed an outward show of his financial situation to attract someone.

"I kind of wanted the opposite," says Carl. "I wanted to show myself as a solid, nice person but not with fancy possessions so people would like me for my personality."

So it was perfect that Carl's early context clue about how Mindy spent money was the fact that she drove a clunker of a car but owned her condo. Carl owned his own home, which Mindy assumed was his parents' home when she first visited, even though his parents weren't there.

"I don't think I actively sat there and thought about it, but those context clues resonated with me on a deeper level," says Carl. "I could see that her money views were probably aligned with mine, even though we didn't have to come out and say it."

ONCE YOU'RE EXCLUSIVE

Once you're in a committed, serious relationship—no longer casual but not living together—it's time to step out of the context-clues phase and start to have some preliminary money conversations.

Getting Financially Naked 101

As you get a little further along in your relationship, you'll start to go through the process of "getting financially naked."

It's a two-level process starting with the basics, which means you can still avoid a lot of the direct "how much do you make" type of questions early on but continue getting those context clues. And hey, maybe this will be a natural lead-in for a deeper financial talk.

"How much are we going to spend on presents?" (E.g., birthdays, Valentine's Day, holidays.)

"What's the budget for our vacation together?"

"How fancy are we?"

Okay, maybe that's not the exact way you'll ask, but you should start
to get a sense of each other's preferences regarding lifestyle. Some of this
will be implied by the dates you go on, where your partner lives, the
mode of transportation your partner prefers, how your partner likes to
vacation, etc.

*"Do we alternate paying for dates or just split things down the
middle, or should the person with a stronger financial footing
subsidize more expensive dates?"*

Spoiler: the last one requires that you actually start to have some open
conversations about your financial situations.

GETTING MORE SERIOUS: WE'RE MOVING IN TOGETHER

"I really believe that couples should start talking about money as soon as
they get serious about their relationship," says Aditi Shekar, founder and
CEO of Zeta, a service that helps couples manage their money together.
Shekar points out that most couples start to merge their money once they
move in together and have meaningful shared expenses. Now, this doesn't
mean joint bank accounts upon moving in, but it does mean your financial life is starting to integrate with your partner's.

What Is Your Lifestyle?

Part of integrating your financial life with your partner's is also deciding
the kind of lifestyle the two of you will live. While some people do still

function as two completely separate entities even after moving in, there are ways that your partner's lifestyle is going to impact your wallet.

"I've talked to a lot of couples who feel pressured by their partners because they were upgrading their lifestyles by moving into their partner's apartment or by living a certain way or vacationing a certain way," says Shekar. "It's easy for one person to say, 'Why don't you just join my way of doing things,' but you really have to step back and see if your way of doing things really makes sense as we become a 'we.'"

"Even though we've been in a serious relationship for a while now, we do have different lifestyle expectations. What kind of lifestyle do you envision for us after we move in together?"

You need to be ready to discuss compromises to make both of you feel comfortable with this new reality you're creating.

Stay Separate (with Possibly One Exception)

Dear Debt author Melanie Lockert and her long-term live-in boyfriend kept completely separate accounts, but they did have a shared credit card for joint expenses like groceries. It kept the need to Venmo each other back and forth to a minimum. They chose to have him become an authorized user on one of her accounts, which also helped him establish and build his credit.

Personally, I'm an advocate of keeping finances completely separate until you're married or otherwise legally committed to each other. You could open a joint account for paying bills and put in the minimum needed to cover your portion if you want some element of streamlining. Just keep in mind that your partner, even if you break up, has a right to that joint account until it's closed.

"If you get married and want to break up, you must go to court, but if you don't get married and want to break up, you might have to go to court," said Joseph Cochran, financial attorney and cofounder of One Big Happy Life, a money- and lifestyle-focused website and YouTube channel.

Technically, your partner could drain a joint bank account and you'd have little recourse except for taking them to small-claims court, which may not be worth the cost. Even then, your ex's name is on the account, so they do have the right to take money out.

Who Pays Which Bills?

"Being equal is not always being fair," says Lockert. "A few years into our relationship, it got to a point where I was making significantly more than my partner and it wasn't fair for him to be paying for half of the rent when I was making three times more than him."

"Okay, for a long time our situations were similar and it worked to split things fifty-fifty, but now that our incomes aren't balanced, this situation doesn't feel equitable. How do you feel?"

De Leon experienced this in her own relationship when her then-girlfriend, now her wife, was making more and would often pay more and provide de Leon with more support.

Should You Help Pay Off Debt?

"It's a highly personal decision," says Lockert, who notes that it can make sense to help your partner pay off their debt if you're on the same page about it and you're both excited, you're making the effort together, and you've merged your financial goals.

Once Lockert paid off her debt, she was eager to get her then-boyfriend on the same page, but she wasn't comfortable directly putting cash toward his monthly payments. Instead, she found a workaround.

"I'm comfortable paying more toward rent if you agree to pay $X more toward student loans/credit cards."

You can subsidize without directly giving your partner money toward the debt. However, you need to come to an agreement that the freed-up money will actually go toward the debt. But whatever help you decide to provide, you have to really be introspective and gut-check whether you'd be okay saying bye to that money in the case of a breakup.

"No one likes to look at worst-case scenarios, but you have to consider it briefly," says Lockert. "Just because you consider it doesn't mean it's going to happen! But if you do pay off the debt, how are you going to feel afterward?"

In retrospect, Lockert is relieved she didn't pay off his debt, because despite the many years the two were together, the relationship ended in a breakup.

Moving in Together Money Checklist

- ❏ Have utilities in both of your names
- ❏ Discuss if splitting bills evenly makes sense for your situation
- ❏ Discuss grocery budgets and what you're willing to spend
- ❏ Consider domestic labor contributions
- ❏ Talk about shared goals
- ❏ Decide on how to handle guilty-pleasure expenses

The 101 level of getting financially naked is fairly tame and doesn't require a ton of disclosure. So, when should you be getting into those really nitty-gritty, highly detailed money talks? You should have that discussion around the time you look at your partner and think, "This is someone with whom I could spend the rest of my life." Or just whenever you're both ready. But before you commit to spending your lives together, you need to achieve full-frontal financial nudity.

FULL-FRONTAL FINANCIAL NUDITY

At this point, you're already in a really serious relationship and you may even live together. You probably know—or think you know—much of your partner's financial situation. However, it's still critical to actually have "the talk."

Set the Stage

The first part of the process is to tell your partner it's coming. The fact that this conversation is happening should never blindside your partner. They may be reluctant to open this door, but you need to tell them it's going to happen.

> *"I would like for us to sit down and talk about money. It's really important we share our financial goals and situations with each other. Maybe we could even talk a bit about our financial baggage. When would be a good time for us to talk this week?"*

Once you decide the when, you should also decide the where. Personally, I think at home is best, in private, with no one else around. If you both have roommates or live together with a roommate, then try to coordinate a time when the roomies will be out. These conversations can get tense, even heated, so you don't want to worry about other people's being around. It can also lay a calm foundation if you tie it into a nice evening. Perhaps have your favorite home-cooked meal or takeout and a glass of your desired vino or beer. (Probably best not to have more than one or two though if you're going to have an important conversation.)

Determine What You're Willing to Share Right Now and What You Want to Know

Before you two actually sit down together, you both should take time to reflect on what you're willing to share at this moment. Eventually, all the information needs to be shared (hence "full-frontal financial nudity"). But since it's the first conversation, you may only be comfortable admitting to the existence of student loans or credit card debt but not sharing the number. That's okay. Just keep in mind that you eventually need to progress to sharing the details with your partner. Maybe you provide a range to contextualize it a bit. "I have more than $5,000 in credit card debt but less than $10,000." Or "I have more than $20,000 in student loans."

You also need to ruminate on what you want to know from your partner in this conversation.

Ready Your Poker Face

Can you imagine how awful it would feel to get naked in front of someone for the first time and have them laugh at you or make a face? Same goes for sharing your finances. It can feel vulnerable to get completely open about money with someone else. You *must* come into this conversation with a strong poker face. Do not have a dramatic reaction if your partner tells you about a high debt number or a credit-crushing mistake. Doing so can immediately ruin your partner's trust in you, which is essential to this conversation, and it will make it difficult to continue the talk now—or ever.

Starting the Conversation

Okay, so all that has simply been the prep work to have this conversation. The natural next question is: but how do you actually initiate the talk?!

Here are my two favorite techniques:

First, break the tension with the truth.

 "I know this is sort of an awkward conversation, but I feel it's really important as we continue to build our life together. What do you think?"

Second, and my personal favorite, is the goal-setting strategy.

 "What's a financial goal you want to achieve in the next five years?" [Partner answers.] *"And what's standing in your way?"*

The perk of the second technique is that you can hint at the debt conversation without actually saying the D-word. It also starts to give you some ideas about what your partner values and hopes to achieve in the short to medium term.

What You Need to Share

Incomes: How much do you each bring in? This is a good chance for you to pull a few recent pay stubs. You'd be surprised how many people don't know exactly how much they earn. (Or maybe you wouldn't be surprised.)

Types of debt: Credit cards, student loans, mortgage, personal loans, auto loans, etc.

How much debt you're carrying: Now that your partner knows the types of debt you have, it's time to share the actual amounts.

Credit reports and scores: You could print them out and swap if you want! Or you can show each other your credit score and your history with credit.

Savings and investments: What's your nest egg? This is also a good chance for you to check in on your retirement plan and other investments if that's not a regular practice for you.

Financial goals: You might've already mentioned one at the start of this conversation, but take the time to share what you want to financially achieve in the short (one to three years), medium (four to ten years), and long term (ten-plus years).

Your emotional relationship with money: This is one of the most important things to learn during the financially naked conversation. It's critical that you understand your partner's emotional relationship to money because it can inform so much about their decision making and reactions to financial situations.

"What's your first memory of money? And how does that make you feel?" or *"How often do you think about money? When you do think about it, how does it make you feel?"*

Other questions to ask include:

"How did you get money to spend growing up?"

"Did your parents argue a lot about money?"

"Were you told you shouldn't talk about money?"

You'll learn more about identifying your partner's relationship with money in chapter 12, "Fighting Fair About Money."

Obviously this is a book focused on how to talk about money, but there are other conversations you also need to initiate before getting married. You should discuss lifestyle choices like whether you want kids or you want to be child-free. Be open about any assistance you plan to provide to your family long term. (If you jumped around, be sure to check out the "Taking Care of a Parent or Sibling" section in chapter 7 on page 119 to learn how to navigate this conversation.)

Are You a Team or Individuals?

Is it *your* money and *my* money or *our* money?

Now, my personal bias is that you shouldn't merge finances until after you're married. It has nothing to do with the depth or seriousness of your relationship and more to do with the legal implications. Marriage brings a certain protocol for how assets are divided up in a divorce. Breakups don't. Should you have a joint bank account with your boyfriend or girlfriend, they're entitled to drain that account. Plus, if your partner creates debt that's charged to a joint account, there is a chance you could be held liable.

For married couples, the default is often joint finances—but that doesn't have to be the case. In the next chapter, we'll take a deep dive into strategies for blending money.

Handling the "Ownership Mentality"

When Peach and I were first achieving full-frontal financial nudity, before we even got engaged, he really pushed back on the idea that any of my income would go toward helping him pay off his student loans.

"They're my loans," he'd tell me. "I want to handle paying them off."

While I both understood and respected his position, I countered that if we were to get married, those loans would impact my life too. They wouldn't legally become mine—a common misconception. You don't become responsible for your spouse's student loans unless you cosign them. But the existence of the debt would still impact our life as a married couple. If we applied for a mortgage, it would matter. It stood in the way of financial goals we wanted to achieve.

Part of how we handled Peach's ownership mentality was to develop a (at the time hypothetical) strategy for handling our money as a couple that honored his feelings.

Create a Game Plan

Set your financial goals both as individuals and as a partnership, and then discuss how you can achieve them.

When we were coming up with our game plan for how we'd merge our money, one of our biggest goals was to pay off Peach's student loans ASAP. But that ownership mentality kept butting in its ugly head at first, so I suggested a hybrid strategy. After marriage, we'd focus on merging our money, but the money to pay off Peach's student loans would technically come from his paycheck, with some also going toward retirement and savings, and my income would cover our day-to-day expenses and savings/investing goals.

When you're developing your own game plan, you should discuss logistics like:

Who pays which bills? This will certainly change over time, especially if you morph from cohabitating to married and banking jointly.

Where are your salaries going? Do you comingle it all in a joint account from which every bill is paid, or are you more of a multiple-bank-accounts kind of couple? You also need to decide how much of your income is going toward bills, savings, investments, debt repayment, and spending money.

What are your financial priorities? As you discuss your financial goals, you have to decide which ones you're prioritizing and which ones get less attention—or get completely benched for a time period.

Implement Your Game Plan

People's game plans get implemented at different times. Some start to merge money upon living together, others do it after engagement, and some wait to be legally wedded. Others may stay completely separate their entire lives together—but that doesn't mean they're without a game plan and financial strategy.

By the time Peach and I actually got married, we'd really shifted our mindsets to being a team. Well, teammates who each got money for autonomous spending—but we'll get there soon. There were myriad factors as to why this happened. Going through the prenup process, becoming husband and wife, and making a serious commitment to blend our lives together just allowed the financial aspect to fall into place for us. There was less pushback about aggressively paying off Peach's student loans and less insistence on needing to use "his money," because we'd started saying our incomes were "our money." We made short-, medium-, and long-term goals together.

Another somewhat subtle way I nudged Peach toward our being a team was to change my own language after we got married. I started referring to the debt as "our student loans" instead of "your" or "his."

Set Regular Money Dates

Talking about money and being completely vulnerable with each other is critical, but so is the more tedious work of checking in on your finances and goals. One person in your relationship may run point on handling the finances—whether that means paying the bills or making investing decisions or tracking your net worth. But both of you need to be aware of your total financial picture—which requires money dates!

It should come as no surprise that I'm a fan of the monthly check-in, but for some couples a quarterly meeting (every three months) makes more sense.

Money dates also don't have to be a long, involved process. They can be as simple as a ten-or-fifteen-minute touch-base conversation with your partner to make sure you both know the progress you've made toward goals and identify any issues (like overspending the budget). But you could make a whole date out of it. I know some couples who go out to dinner and have a nice meal while discussing their finances—which I only recommend if you know there won't be any tension. Others like to open a bottle of wine and have a chat at home.

At least once a year, you should sit down together and assess if your current goals are still best serving what the two of you hope to achieve in the short (one to three years), medium (four to ten years), and long term (ten-plus years).

Should You Be Worried If Your Partner Has Made Big Money Mistakes?

Let me start by saying that the existence of debt itself shouldn't be a deal breaker. Behaviors and change (or lack thereof) should be the indicators.

There's a difference between a past financial mistake and engaging in the same pattern over and over. Let's say you've gone through the process of getting financially naked and learned that your partner has $10,000 in credit card debt and a credit score of 550. That could be a red flag and even a deal breaker for some. But it's imperative to know the context. How did your partner end up in credit card debt and what happened to cause a drop in the credit score?

Maybe your partner had a medical emergency that was financed on a credit card and missed seeing a doctor's bill that got sent to collections and demolished his credit score. Or maybe your partner wasn't earning a lot and used credit cards to make ends meet. Or maybe it was a case of overspending and living beyond his means.

The more important consideration is: What is today's behavior? Has your partner clearly taken steps to rectify past financial mistakes? If your partner continues to finance life with credit cards and amass credit card debt or misses paying bills that then get sent to collections, then it's more of a concern.

Remember: It's an Evolving Process

The foundation to the entire process of being open and transparent with each other about money and starting to merge your financial life with someone else's is to keep in mind that it's always evolving. You have to be flexible and be willing to revisit and even change your financial goals and strategies as life unfolds.

WHEN IT'S TIME TO GET HELP (OR WALK AWAY)

The way I've described this process makes it sound like magic—you will go through these steps and get totally vulnerable with each other and become this amazing financial team together. Well, reality check: sometimes that's not how it works out for people. Instead, trying to achieve full-frontal financial nudity can lead to a lot of tension and fighting. It's understandable. This situation is full of opportunities to feel judged or belittled or even betrayed. Hopefully it doesn't happen that way in your relationship, but if you are having trouble navigating this conversation with your partner without its constantly devolving into a fight, then it may be time to bring in help.

What to Do When You Don't Trust Your Partner's Money Habits

There's a classic couple cliché: "one's a spender and one's a saver." Or, more obnoxious, there's the entire "women be shopping" rhetoric, which needs to die right now. Unfortunately, your partner's money habits could leave you with a sense of foreboding. It's not always about overspending or making large-scale financial decisions without discussion—it could be that your partner makes rash decisions about how to invest money or has a tendency to loan money to friends and family members without discussing it with you.

"An important first step in handling your money differences is to acknowledge that it's rare for two people to have the same money beliefs and handle money the exact same way," explains Lindsay Bryan-Podvin, a financial therapist and the founder of Mind Money Balance.

For someone who is dealing with an overspender or someone making rash financial decisions, Bryan-Podvin's advice is to operate from a place of empathy, which probably means not immediately jumping into battle.

"Instead of starting with 'How dare you,' wait until you're both calm and ask about what's going on to cause the increase in spending and/or shopping," says Bryan-Podvin.

Beginning to unearth your partner's emotional relationship to money is also a critical part of understanding why they're engaging in behaviors that make you feel uncomfortable. There's a simple question to initiate this conversation:

"How does money make you feel?"

If that question proves too overwhelming, you can also start by asking about your partner's first memory of money and how that memory makes them feel.

It's also good for you to be honest with your partner about how their financial behaviors are impacting you.

"When you [insert behavior here], *it makes me feel* [insert feeling—e.g., betrayed, worried, uncomfortable]. *I'd like to discuss ways we can both be comfortable with how money is handled in our relationship."*

Of course, there are also more extreme steps you can take, like completely separating your money from your partner's (though if you're married, your partner's creating debt may still legally end up as your problem) or putting your partner on an allowance, but those can quickly make you seem controlling and aren't always the healthiest ways to continue a relationship.

But if you don't trust your partner's money habits, outside of ending the relationship, the next step is to bring in a neutral third party.

Who to Ask for Help
The kind of expert you turn to will depend on exactly what you need help handling. It could also be a combination of people.

> *"I love you, but we've been really struggling to communicate effectively about money. I feel like it's time to go speak to a professional. What do you think?"*

The two of you should discuss the type of person you'd want to turn to for help based on what you each feel are the issues in the relationship.

Certified Financial Planner
A certified financial planner (CFP) could be an objective third party who can help formulate a financial plan. CFPs go through a structured education and certification process, and they are required to adhere to certain standards and ethics—including being a fiduciary, which means they're required to act in your best interest. It's really the gold standard of the financial planning industry, especially given how little regulation there is for who can call themselves a financial advisor or planner.[*]

Generally, it's good to work with a CFP at some point, no matter how well you handle money as a couple. Another set of eyes on your financial plan, especially near life milestones, can be incredibly useful.

Working with a CFP could be the right fit if you're engaged or mar-

---

[*]At least little regulation at the time of writing this, in 2020. Perhaps that will change in the future!

ried and trying to figure out how to best blend your money and/or figure out how to prioritize and achieve financial goals as a couple.

You may also want to consider a money coach or counselor, but I tend to recommend CFPs because of their training and certifications. You can use the CFP Board–authorized search tool Let's Make a Plan at Lets-MakeaPlan.org or networks like the XY Planning Network or Garrett Planning Network in order to find a CFP.

Financial Therapist

If you have all the information on how to handle your finances but you keep performing a self-sabotaging action, then financial therapy might be the right fit. Keep in mind that an act of self-sabotage doesn't just have to be extreme examples like chronic overspending or gambling, but could even be extreme frugality (indicating money anxiety), financial dependence, or financial enabling with a loved one. Ultimately, financial therapy is the right fit if you have what's known as a money disorder.

Dr. Brad Klontz, a financial therapist and professor of financial psychology at Creighton University, describes money disorders as "chronic patterns of self-destructive financial behavior. We know better, but we just can't seem to stop ourselves."

Financial therapy will help you unpack your cognitive and emotional relationship to money, which may stand in the way of your having a healthy relationship to money. Should you or your partner, or both of you, struggle with a money disorder, financial therapy could be a helpful way to sort out both your emotions and your financial behaviors.

For Bryan-Podvin, having a balanced relationship with money means being able to view it as a neutral or a positive, meaning it doesn't cause angst and it isn't the foundation of your happiness either.

Financial therapy is still a fairly new field, so Klontz advises that you seek out a licensed mental health provider as your financial therapist. You can refer to the Financial Therapy Association (www.financialthera pyassociation.org/find-a-ft) in order to search for a financial therapist.

An important consideration: your financial therapist should not be the person who is managing your money, even if they are also a CFP or financial advisor of any sort.

Therapist and/or Couples' Counselor

Your fights about money could also be a symptom of a larger issue in your relationship that needs to be discussed in therapy or counseling. Couples' counseling could bring in a neutral third party to work through your disagreements.

Identifying Red Flags in Your Relationship

As mentioned earlier, previous mistakes aren't the concern here; how your partner is currently handling money should be your focus. These red flags could indicate a need to at least investigate further (if that's safe), if not disentangle yourself entirely from your partner. Some behaviors that raise red flags are:

- They always dismiss your request to talk about finances.
- They won't consider a joint bank account in marriage. (There can be good reasons people elect not to bank jointly, which will be discussed in the next chapter, but you shouldn't be completely dismissed without a discussion.)
- They refuse to share their credit score or credit reports.
- They get calls from collection agencies.
- They use payday or title loans for short-term money needs.
- They use cash advances on credit cards.
- They currently pay wage garnishment or a tax lien. (This may be a result of a prior mistake that's being rectified, but you have a right to know the details.)

Red flags could just be the result of a partner's feeling embarrassed and withholding information, which is solvable. Other times, it's an indicator of something more nefarious, like financial abuse.

Signs of Financial Abuse

Common indicators of financial abuse include:

- Using your money without permission
- Using your identity to gain access to credit and loans
- Refusing to allow you access to money without first going through them
- Hiding assets
- Not allowing you to work in order to bring in your own income
- Marginalizing your feelings or opinions because they earn more than you

You may feel comfortable confronting your partner about financial abuse (or financial infidelity), but in many cases this can be used as another means of control in a physically abusive relationship. Please prioritize your safety.

If you or someone you know is currently experiencing abuse of any kind, then here are some (United States–based) resources:

- Safe Horizon: www.safehorizon.org/get-help/contact-us/
- National Domestic Violence Hotline: www.thehotline.org/help/ or 1-800-799-SAFE (7233), which is free and available 24/7.
- Domestic Shelters: www.domesticshelters.org
- Crisis Text Line: www.crisistextline.org or text HOME to 741741

If/When a Breakup Happens

Gone are the days when couples went straight from living at Mom and Dad's to getting married. Okay, not totally gone. There are still plenty of people who don't cohabit before marriage, but the premarital shack-up is certainly prevalent in today's culture. Living together can help you decide if this is the person for you long term. You learn *a lot* about a person when you share a space! However, living together often means starting to rely on each other financially. Even if you don't merge finances, there are often shared expenses like rent, groceries, and utilities, and maybe your partner is even subsidizing some of your life if the expenses are prorated based on income. A breakup can be a huge blow financially, especially if you have to move out and get another place.

For Melanie Lockert, author of *Dear Debt*, breaking up with her long-time boyfriend was not only a heart-wrenching experience but also caused some financial headaches.

Disentangling Finances

Lockert and her partner used a joint credit card for shared finances. Because he'd become an authorized user on her credit card, Lockert had to call the credit card company after the breakup and have him removed. She also had to ask for the card back from him.

"I wasn't worried about anything shady going on, and nothing did, but whether it's hostile or amicable, you want to make sure," says Lockert.

In addition to credit cards, you also need to consider removing—and potentially buying out—your partner from:

- Insurance policies (or you may need to get your own to replace any coverage your partner provided you)
- A lease (or mortgage or deed to a house, if you purchased one together)
- Utilities
- Shared streaming services (I mean, you don't have to, but you could)

Moving Out

Lockert stayed in the apartment, so she removed her ex's name from the utilities. He also had a few of the utilities just in his name, which she cites now as a mistake, and she had to deal with transferring those over to her. While it didn't ultimately cause a problem, it was just an additional headache during an emotional and painful time.

Who Gets the Pet?

This should actually be a conversation before you get a pet together. As much as we all adore our fur babies, you do need to consider what is in the pet's best interest. If you travel all the time, then maybe your partner should have ownership.

What Resources Do You Have in Your Network?

Even before the breakup (if you know it's coming), it is important to take stock of who you can turn to at this time. It's particularly important if you and your ex share a common circle of friends. Can you crash on a friend's couch? Do you have a friend who can help you get a temp job if your partner was financially subsidizing part of your life while you pursued a creative endeavor?

Dealing with the Guilt

Lockert knew breaking up with her boyfriend would mean he'd have to move back home. This thought delayed the breakup for a while, partly because of the guilt she felt over dramatically shifting her ex-partner's lifestyle.

Despite its being one of the most painful experiences of her life, Lockert ultimately reflected on the fact that she couldn't control his situation and it wasn't her fault.

Have a Breakup Fund

"Take care of yourself financially first," says Lockert. "Just because you're being prepared about a worst-case scenario doesn't mean it's going to happen."

Lockert suggests putting two to three thousand dollars minimum in a breakup fund that should be separate from your emergency fund. This amount should cover at least one month of rent and at least another grand for any security deposits or furniture you'll have to replace.

"I can't tell you how many stories I've heard about living with an ex because neither can afford to move out," says Lockert. "Breaking up is already so hard, and to continue to share a space with someone you're no longer in a relationship with, you're delaying being able to move on and heal from it."

Not to end this chapter on a serious note, but we're moving on to something even more intense: handling money in marriage!

Chapter 11

It Just Got Really Serious: Money and Marriage

"I DON'T HAVE my debit card with me, could you take some cash out of the ATM to cover our part of the dinner bill?"

Peach looked at me with a smirk. "Normally, but you haven't sent me my allowance yet."

Peals of laughter erupted from my friends around the dinner table, most of whom were fellow personal finance writers.

The exchange immediately led to a conversation about how people handle money in their relationships, and I got a little defensive because, while funny, the way Peach worded the sentence made it sound like he was a kept man on a tight budget.

The reality was, at that point we'd recently gotten married and hadn't actually gotten around to merging all of our bank accounts. Instead, we were working with a complicated system of multiple checking and savings accounts we'd both used prior to getting married. Our monthly discretionary spending money came out of my paycheck, which meant I had to transfer his monthly spending money out of my account into our joint account. Confused yet? Yeah, it was excessive, but we'd both been dragging our feet about doing all the paperwork to officially merge our money.

As confusing as it was, it also did work for us (except for the *one time* I forgot to send Peach his allowance because I'd been on tour promoting *Broke Millennial Takes On Investing!*). Couples come up with all sorts of highly nuanced and specific systems to manage money that work for them. In this chapter, we'll break down many of those techniques.

But before Peach and I got to that dinner, before we walked down the aisle—really, before we were even engaged—we had another critical conversation for people who are on the verge of marriage (or as I like to call it, the biggest financial decision you'll make). We discussed getting a prenup.

WE'RE READY TO GET MARRIED! IS A PRENUP RIGHT FOR ME?

Prenuptial agreements, better known as prenups, desperately need to hire a top-notch brand consultant, because they have a terrible reputation. The word typically reminds people of horror stories from celebrity divorces and evokes a sense that anyone who dares get one doesn't love and trust their partner.

I get it. Prenups are inextricably tied to divorce. After all, it's an entire document outlining how you would divide up your assets in the case of a divorce from someone to whom you're not even married yet. No one wants to flip from the post-engagement love bubble to discuss the potential end of it all. Besides, isn't that bad energy? It may even be a curse just to speak of potentially ending your pending marriage one day.

Well, I don't think so. In fact, I believe we put too much emphasis on the love aspect of marriage and not enough on the financial and legal implications.

Marriage Is Ultimately a Merger of Assets

Generally, marriage today is built on the foundation of falling in love with someone and deciding to spend your lives together. Problem is, signing your name to a marriage license also means entering a legally binding agreement that you can only dissolve through the court system. This means there are implications for how your assets (and in some cases debts) would be divided up if you decided to get divorced.

"You would not enter into a new business with someone, even a really good friend, without making an operating agreement that outlines a potential dissolution plan for your partnership," says Linda Rosenthal, a matrimonial lawyer and partner at McLaughlin & Stern in New York City. "When you enter into a marriage, which is an economic contract, it's an optimal moment to make an operating agreement and a dissolution plan from a place of generosity and love."

Calling marriage a merger of assets or an economic contract sounds strong, maybe even unromantic, but whether or not you elect to combine your money after marriage, your state does have an opinion on how your property would be divided up in a divorce.

"Everyone has a prenup, it's just the default laws of your state," my attorney told me at the beginning of the prenup process.

Before we really get into the prenup talk, a topic I feel strongly about, I do want to say these conversations can be awkward at the very least and emotionally painful at worst. You will have disagreements with your future spouse and probably get into some heated discussions. However, being able to have tough talks, especially about money, and reach a compromise is a beautiful foundation for a marriage.

The Case for a Prenup

"Everyone has their own sense of fairness," says Rosenthal. "Everyone designs their own ecosystems within their marriage for how to manage their money. Without actually entering into a contract—a prenup—the law may well do an override, or at least you should understand that it presupposes what constitutes a fair ecosystem created in the marriage."

That means that what you think is fair, or even what both of you feel is fair, won't necessarily be how it all shakes out in a divorce, unless you have a prenup.

For Aditi Shekar, founder and CEO of Zeta, an online tool that helps couples manage their money, a prenup was a natural by-product of what she and her future husband felt was fair.

"We talked about the dynamics in my own parents' relationship and I said, 'Look, I'd love to start our marriage off on the right foot,'" says Shekar. "And I asked him how he wanted to handle the fact that we had different amounts of money and different salaries and different spending habits."

Her future husband turned to her and said he was fine with her keeping the assets she was bringing into the marriage, and then they would share what was earned together in the marriage. Notably neither couple brought debt into the marriage, so it was very much an asset conversation.

"So I said, 'Cool. Are you open to a prenup?' and he said, 'Whoa, I don't know. Can you find out more about that?'" explains Shekar. "I did the research and realized you needed to get your own lawyers, which was going to be shockingly expensive."

The pair went to Rocket Lawyer to download a prenup template and then went through the process, just the two of them.

"It was actually one of the best conversations we ever had, because it walked us through and at the end of it we signed it, and quite bluntly, I'm not even sure it's legally viable," admits Shekar. "But just the exercise alone was one of the best things that happened, because we knew very explicitly how each of us felt about every one of those questions."

The questionable viability aside, my favorite takeaway from this story is that the two of them walked through the process together and went into their marriage knowing all of each other's financial details and how each one responded to abstract questions like "What happens in case of a death?," "What happens to assets we gain together?," and "What happens if I start a company and you don't work for it?"

"We felt really grown-up and accomplished at the end of it," says Shekar.

For Rosenthal, part of the process that's also important to incorporate is an understanding of the rules that will govern your marriage (a.k.a. the laws of your state). She points out that a church will often require an engaged couple to have a few sessions to sit and talk through guidelines and principles. The same should hold true in the context of finances.

"You should meet with someone, even if you aren't going to get a pre-nup, so you can understand what the rules are," says Rosenthal.

One of those rules you should understand is how your state treats assets brought into the marriage, which you may think you don't have, but even something like a 401(k) is considered an asset. You should also know how debt accumulated in the marriage gets handled in a divorce per your state's laws (e.g., if your spouse creates credit card debt, even if the card is just in their name). Decide whether you both feel your state's rules handle these issues fairly. You may also want to have the alimony, a.k.a. spousal support, formula for your state explained, especially if one of you is likely to be a primary caregiver to any children.

Another important consideration for why a prenup makes sense is the way you'll treat each other today compared to future versions of your-selves.

Now Is the Time You'd Be Generous with Each Other

The engagement period is often accompanied by the cozy cocoon of a love bubble. Sure, you'll probably get in spats about the wedding itself, but this time in your relationship is such a happy one. You're about to marry the love of your life!

Now think back to Rosenthal's point about making a "dissolution plan from a place of generosity and love."

She's right. Creating a prenup means you'll be treating each other with a type of love and respect that may no longer exist at the time of a divorce. I often joked with Peach that a prenup was a way to protect him from a vindictive version of myself. Hopefully, we never need to meet our "divorce selves," but if we do, I'd rather already have the operating agree-ment in place.

A Prenup May Seem Pricey...

Prenups can be pricey. You each need your own attorney, and depending on the complexities of the prenup and cost of lawyers in your area, it's probably safe to assume a ballpark of $3,000 to $6,000. And that's for a fairly straightforward agreement. This is a price range that makes a lot of people balk. But think of it as a one-time insurance payment. Prorated out over a ten-year marriage, that'd be $50 a month for a $6,000 prenup. Not bad for an insurance policy that should help make a divorce a fairly clean and simple process. Which is good because . . .

Divorce Is Frickin' Expensive!

Divorce is expensive. To the point that it's actually a problem for lots of couples. Sometimes it's because the cost of child support, alimony, and maintaining two residences is completely untenable. Sometimes the cost of filing alone is prohibitive, especially for couples who have fallen on hard economic times. In more extreme situations, it's because there is so much animosity that the couple can't agree on anything and keep dragging out the battle—costing each other a lot of time and money. A prenup, while not a cure-all, can at least help to make the divorce process smoother, more timely, and therefore more cost-effective.

How to Ask for a Prenup

Start the Conversation Early!

I initiated the prenup conversation early—really early. So early we weren't even engaged yet!

"What do you think about prenups?"

It really was that blunt a question. At first, I just wanted to see his reaction. Would his response style be a shrug with an "I've never really thought about it" or more of an extreme "I'd never get one" situation? He fell more in the "never thought about it" camp, which enabled us to open a dialogue about why I felt it was important.

But you know your partner, and you know if they might react badly to even the whisper of the term. If that's the case, turn to Shekar's method.

"I wouldn't use the word 'prenup,'" says Shekar. "People have a lot of preconceived notions without understanding it." Shekar and her husband never actually used the term "prenup" when having the prenup conversation. Instead, they focused on what happened to their money after being legally married and how it would change their finances.

"How do you think we should handle the assets [and/or debt] we each already have after we get married?"

If you and/or your partner feel that the assets brought into the marriage should be considered separate, then it's an opportunity to explain how a prenup can help you ensure that will be the case. If your partner says, "I think we should combine everything once we're married," then you can follow up with "What if we were to split up? Would you believe the assets we'd brought into the marriage should be split evenly?"

Explain Your Why

Your why is personal to you, but here are some of the whys I used when I engaged in this conversation.

"Wanting a prenup doesn't at all mean I don't love and trust you. It's about being pragmatic. This is a big financial commitment, possibly the biggest we'll make in our lives, and to sign on the dotted line without protecting ourselves makes me feel uncomfortable. I'd never sign a business contract without knowing and agreeing to all the terms.

"Personally, I think of it as marriage insurance. Getting a prenup doesn't mean I think we'll get divorced, just like having auto insurance doesn't mean I think I'll have a car accident and renter's insurance doesn't mean I think the apartment will get robbed. I'm simply protecting myself for a possibility in life. One I hope won't happen, but realistically, it could."

Don't Blame Your Parents

Maybe you know you'll be inheriting wealth and your parents are the ones keen on your getting a prenup. Even if that's the case, you shouldn't pass off the blame to your parents. That's a really easy way to sour the relationship between your future spouse and your parents.

Return to your why and talk about what you believe is fair when receiving an inheritance or any family money. Just a warning, this particular element of the prenup conversation has a lot of potential for conflict, especially if you have vastly different relationships with money. Plus, it's not a pleasant exercise to think about a loved one's dying.

Position It as a Bonding Exercise

Shekar says she and her husband felt really grown-up and accomplished at the end of this process because it's something they did together and it wasn't forced upon them. It felt comfortable and natural because the two approached it as a conversation and not a battle.

In her own experience, Shekar has found that couples who explore the idea of a prenup together tend to find it more of a bonding experience because it's something they're figuring out as a team.

Don't Put Your Partner on the Clock

Whatever you do, never bring this up in the eleventh hour right before the wedding. This shouldn't be done under any sort of duress (plus, that would make it fairly easy to overturn), and you want time to sit with and reflect on what you each want in a prenup.

If Your Partner Keeps Resisting

If your partner just isn't getting on board, Shekar suggests you give them both the time and the space to speak to someone with experience—such as a lawyer or a friend who has been through the process—so they can ask all the awkward questions instead of allowing rumors or dramatic stories from the Internet to impact their views.

In addition, you also need to educate (and investigate for yourself) what happens if you don't have a prenup or, more dramatically, an estate plan. The bare minimum you need to understand is what the laws of your state are and how your assets are divided up. Are you comfortable with the state's default laws?

 "Based on the laws of our state, this is how our money would get split up in the case of a divorce. Are you comfortable with those terms?"

Language Not to Use

Most of this book is about the language to use when having these conversations, but here are some statements you should never make when discussing a prenup:

- "I won't marry you if you won't sign a prenup."
- "My parents said you have to sign this in order for us to get married."
- "I have more than you, so you need to sign this."
- "I don't want your debt to be my problem after we get married."

You Don't Think It'll Happen to You

One of the most common pushbacks people will give when I bring up prenups is the standard "Oh, well, I'd never leave my husband/wife."

I completely understand that a combination of true love, how you grew up, religion, personal convictions, and family and community pressure make you feel as if no matter what happens, you would never leave your partner. My response, however, is always the same: "You can't control another person."

People grow and change. Hopefully, in marriage you find ways to grow together, but sometimes, the person you fell in love with changes into someone with whom you no longer want to share your life.

"I never thought our apartment would burn down, so I never got renter's insurance, like an idiot, and then our apartment burned down," says Shekar. "We were in the apartment while it burned down and everything we owned went to shit. It was one of the most traumatizing things because I honestly never thought it would happen to us, and it made me realize anything can happen to you."

Fortunately, Shekar and her husband were safe.

While it might feel like an extreme example, it's the truth.

Is a Prenup Right for You?

There are at least three types of couples for whom Rosenthal believes a prenup is an absolute necessity:

1. Couples with children from a prior relationship who want to make sure the interests of the children are safeguarded in a trust.
2. People who come from extreme family wealth. Often it's appropriate for them to make sure they're both safeguarding family money and being generous.
3. Couples who have accumulated assets (possibly marrying in their thirties and forties) and want to make sure those separate assets are preserved.

If none of those three categories applies to you, then it's still prudent for you to have an understanding of your state's divorce laws and then decide for yourself if a prenup is the right fit.

Prenup Conversation Checklist

This is not something you should use in lieu of a lawyer, but here are questions you two should discuss before even bringing a lawyer into the mix.

- What assets are you bringing into the marriage?
- What debts are you bringing into the marriage?
- What do you feel is a fair way to split up those assets (and debts) if you were to get divorced?
- What do you feel is a fair way to split up the assets (and debts) you create in a marriage together if you were to get divorced?

- How should your assets be handled if one of you dies?
- What's a fair way to safeguard the interests of any children you're bringing into the marriage or family members for whom you're financially responsible?
- What is fair if one of you stays home to care for the kids?
- What should be done with money that one of you inherits? Is the non-inheriting spouse entitled to that money?
- Could you afford to get divorced?

Even if you're convinced you won't get a prenup, those questions are really important to discuss prior to saying "I do."

Wait, I'm Married and Didn't Get a Prenup. Is It Game Over?

Nope! You can actually get something known as a postnup. It can cover the same ground as a prenup but is created after you're married (post-nuptial). However, it's a bit harder of a sell unless you two already agreed on a prenup and ran out of time before you got married. It's difficult to say, "Honey, I want a postnup" without it sounding like you're really saying, "Honey, I'm laying the groundwork to divorce you and minimize the financial fallout."

There is one strategy to consider: a major life change.

"I'm a big proponent of postnups," says Rosenthal. "Any time someone makes a decision that impacts them financially and is somehow in reliance on the partner's earning capacity (e.g., being a stay-at-home parent to children), I think that should be an occasion for a postnup. You're changing a fundamental aspect of your economic partnership—the name of the game."

"Now that I'm staying home, for at least a few years, to focus on raising our child, I've realized that this will have financial implications for us as a couple and for me and my earning potential. What do you think about creating a postnup together in order to ease my concerns?"

You can also get a postnup even if you had a prenup. There may be a change in your lives for which you need to account—for instance, a spouse's stepping out of the workforce or wanting to start their own company.

Regardless of your initial feelings about prenups (and postnups), at least consider having the necessary conversations prior to getting married.

Or you can be like me and be so open about it that when "Gold Digger" plays at your wedding reception, all your friends and your husband will throw up their hands and scream, "We want prenup" and share in a collective giggle.

DECIDING IF MARRIAGE IS THE RIGHT (FINANCIAL) MOVE FOR YOU

Tasha and Joseph Cochran, financial attorneys and owners of One Big Happy Life, have been together for a decade and built a life together but legally aren't married. After getting engaged nine years ago, the pair sat down and examined the numbers. The math didn't work out in favor of signing a marriage license.

First, the two attorneys would be hit with, at the time, a $5,000 "marriage tax penalty" when filing taxes. Second, Tasha's student loans were paid for by her law school, and once they were married Joseph's income would start counting in the formula of how much the law school would pay on her loans, which would have resulted in tens of thousands more the couple would have to pay annually. This is similar to couples who are on an income-driven repayment plan for student loans and see a jump in monthly payments after marriage. Which also would've happened to the Cochrans, as Joseph's student loans were on an income-driven repayment plan and on track to be forgiven through Public Service Loan Forgiveness.

"On top of that, we both came into the relationship with a lot of divorce debt, and I had a ten-year-old, so we were about eight years away from having to pay for college on top of our own student loans, and we wanted to have more kids," explains Tasha. "The only way that was going to work out was for us to be as efficient as possible when it came to our money and the decisions that we were making."

By making the choice to delay a legal marriage, the pair estimate they saved themselves around $400,000.

Here are some of the topics the Cochrans advise you to consider when deciding if marriage is the best financial move:

Taxes: For high earners, getting married can actually result in a "marriage tax penalty." This means you lose some of the tax benefits you had when you were a single filer. You should also pay attention to the deductions you can take as individuals compared to filing jointly (or separately) as a married couple.

Student loans: Depending on your repayment plan, getting married could negatively impact your monthly payments. For example, getting married while on an income-driven repayment plan means your spouse's income counts into the calculation and could significantly increase how much you're paying every month.

Insurance: You could end up paying more in taxes but less in insurance by getting married, so that might offset the tax cost.

> *"I love you and want to spend my life with you, but it would cost us tens of thousands of dollars right now to be legally married—not even including a wedding. What if we combine our lives as if we're married and delay signing the papers until after [insert goal here, e.g., student loans are paid off]?"*

"You can still have a wedding ceremony and reception and everything and just not sign the marriage license," says Tasha, except she advises that you don't do that if you live in a common-law marriage state. States that may recognize a common-law marriage include: Alabama, Colorado,

Iowa, Kansas, Montana, New Hampshire, Oklahoma, Rhode Island, South Carolina, Texas, and Utah, as well as the District of Columbia.

Regardless of the reason you choose to be committed without the marriage license, there are other legal forms you should consider signing in order to bestow the proper protections and rights on each other.

Getting Legal Protections When You're Not Married

One of the frequent criticisms the Cochrans hear about their choice not to be legally wed is that they're completely unprotected legally and financially or that only married people can have certain rights. As a reminder, both Tasha and Joseph are attorneys.

"Even if we weren't in a romantic relationship and just roommates living together in a house, there are still common-law options available to anyone who entangles their lives at all," says Tasha. She cites a familiar example, one I've actually lived through, where you go in on a piece of furniture with a roommate, like a couch, and then end up going your separate ways and have to decide who gets to keep it. In my case, we came to a reasonable solution (I bought her out because she was leaving New York City and I was staying in the apartment). But such situations can also escalate to court, where a judge decides. People get petty!

"There are all sorts of common-law rights, contract rights, and property rights that exist outside of marriage," says Tasha. "The only thing about marriage is that there are presumptions made about how things should be divided up and certain automatic rights. But that doesn't mean you can't get similar protections."

Legal Protections to Consider

Cohabitation agreement: One thing that comes along with being married is property rights and a presumption about how property should be divided if you break up. A cohabitation agreement, in which you write down who owns what and who is responsible for what expenses, covers this territory as well. Getting the agreement notarized would make it harder for the validity to be disputed in the future.

Power of attorney: Basically a power of attorney allows you to make decisions for your partner if they are unable to do so. There can be limitations set.

Medical power of attorney: "Medical power of attorney is really important because [without it] if your partner is incapacitated, you [the partner] don't have the legal right to say, 'Do this procedure,' or not. The next of kin would have to do that, and if you don't agree with them, it puts you at odds with the parents," explains Joseph. When you're married, you're automatically the next of kin.

A will: A will outlines how you want your estate distributed and how any minor children should be cared for, and can also specify what should be done with your remains. A child's inheritance should also be considered in a will. Because Joseph is the stepdad to Tasha's daughter and not her biological or adoptive father, it's important he has a will that names Tasha's daughter. Otherwise she wouldn't inherit any of his estate.

Name each other as beneficiaries: "We name each other as beneficiary of different benefits like life insurance, our pensions, our 401(k)s," says Tasha. "Normally, if you're married it would default to your spouse, so without us being married it would default to our next of kin, which would be our children and then our parents."

With the exception of a cohabitation agreement, all of the documents outlined above are also legal forms married couples should have as part of a solid estate plan. However, some of these rights are automatically bestowed on married couples, like being next of kin with the power to make medical decisions, so it's extra important for unmarried but committed couples to get these legal protections.

While many of these documents are fairly straightforward, Joseph does advise you to consult an attorney to make sure your particular situation doesn't require something unusual.

Another consideration, for those who want to have a unified family name, is that you can still legally change your name without being married, which Tasha did do, so she and her daughter from a prior relationship have the same last name as Joseph and their son together.

(In case you skipped the family section, all these legal forms are discussed much more in depth on pages 136–37.)

Becoming Domestic Partners

Another option for those who are committed but elect not to proceed with a legal marriage is to be domestic partners. The legal benefits of being domestic partners vary by state—and sometimes city—but you may be able to get on your partner's health insurance policy through work, get sick or bereavement leave, have visitation rights in hospitals, get parental leave, and more. However, becoming domestic partners doesn't bestow the same level of legal protections as handling all the paperwork mentioned above.

SHOULD WE MERGE OUR MONEY? STRATEGIES FOR HANDLING MONEY IN MARRIAGE

After you've signed the marriage license, popped the bubbly, and celebrated with your loved ones, it's time to figure out exactly how the two of you want to handle your money together. Okay, really you probably should've at least discussed it before the wedding, but you had a lot going on!

There are three main camps when it comes to handling money in marriage: totally joint, totally separate, or a hybrid model.

There isn't a right or wrong answer here. It's about what works best for the two of you from an emotional perspective as well as a practical one. Let's break down how each one operates.

Totally Joint

"You have one joint account and one investment account, and you put all your money in there," explains Shekar, who notes you don't merge retirement accounts. You each have your own retirement accounts. IRA, 401(k), 403(b), pension—whatever form of retirement account you may have doesn't get consolidated with your spouse's after marriage.

This is the classic—dare I say, default—advice on how to handle money in a marriage. After all, you're a married couple now and therefore just basically one merged human being, right? Obviously not.

Now, don't take my snark for disdain of this method. It can be really, really effective for a lot of couples. It just shouldn't be assumed that married couples have to bank jointly, because this is a decision that needs to feel right for both parties.

Totally Separate

The opposite extreme is to keep your money, even in marriage, completely separate from your spouse's.

"Couples have their own personal accounts for checking, savings, and investments and typically trade off paying for expenses," says Shekar. For example, one person might pay all the childcare expenses while the other will handle housing.

This strategy certainly takes a lot more logistical legwork and communication to ensure bills are paid on time and financial goals are met.

"Some people have separate finances for twenty years and it works, some people don't," says Paco de Leon, financial advisor and founder of The Hell Yeah Group. "I've seen people hold crazy resentment toward a partner about 'I paid for this.' When you don't have oversight, you just see what's going out of your account, not what the other person is paying for."

That potential for resentment is a key reason why it's important to be transparent in this style of budgeting.

You may be wondering, "Why do people want to keep finances totally separate when it sounds like a lot of work?" Well, there are a lot of reasons. For example, there could be emotional factors, like one partner experienced financial abuse in a prior relationship and needs this level of autonomy to feel safe. It could be more on the practical side, like it's the second marriage for both parties and you have children and are blending families and for legal and logistical reasons, it's easier to not comingle assets.

The Hybrid

Both totally joint and totally separate might feel like they aren't quite right for you and your partner. But don't worry. There is of course a compromise in the hybrid model.

"You have a joint account for shared things and an individual account for individual things," says Shekar, who refers to this style as "yours, mine, and ours." Many people who operate in this hybrid model also see some of their money as truly their own, even after marriage. Often these are the assets that were brought into the marriage (and are potentially protected by a prenup). But the money earned during the marriage is considered shared.

One way to actually structure the "yours, mine, and ours" style of blending is to keep all of your money in separate accounts and just pool what is needed for shared expenses in a joint account.

However, this hybrid model can also lend itself to another spin.

Hybrid 2.0: Joint + Allowance

"I'm a big believer in the main joint account for all the joint expenses and the two allowance accounts for each person," says de Leon. "I really like it because it forces you to be on the same team."

Shekar calls this the "allowance model" and notes that it enables couples to function as a unit, more akin to the joint method, but still allows for some autonomy.

In this style, the "allowance" comes from the joint bank account and goes into separate checking accounts for each person, which gives you complete autonomy over how you can spend that amount of money.

That autonomy is something de Leon appreciates because she's still able to spend some money in ways she wants without having to run every purchasing decision by her wife.

"If I want a new guitar and I've saved up my allowance, I don't have to have a conversation with my wife about it. I just get a shiny new guitar," explains de Leon.

Setting the Allowance

I'm the one who earns a higher salary in my marriage. Truthfully, I probably also spend more than Peach. Sure, there's being a woman and the consideration of the pink tax, plus the cost of makeup, clothes for professional and media appearances, haircuts, and waxing. But really, I just tend to be the more social one who goes out to happy hours or dinners or even networking events more often. However, when we got married I felt strongly that the two of us should receive the same amount for our monthly allowances. It could be that I'm trying not to reinforce the fact that I earn more, and perhaps a small part of me worried he'd find it emasculating if I both earned more and got to put more toward my allowance.

Even though I built it up in my head, I quickly realized after marriage that Peach doesn't care. He's as proud of my accomplishments and my career as I am of his. It also helps that he, as a public school teacher, works in an environment where most of his male coworkers are married to women who outearn them.

As we started to set our allowances shortly after getting married, he even suggested I take more of the allotment. However, to this day, we still receive the same amount. It's no longer a fear of emasculating him, but simply that I don't want to set up a power dynamic in which the breadwinner gets to spend more simply due to earning more. Truthfully, I'm probably really overthinking it.

That said, the fifty-fifty split is not what works for everyone.

"This idea of fairness comes up a lot in relationships," says Shekar, noting that a lot of millennials tend to be dual-income couples compared to our parents' generation, where there were more single-income families. "But what I encourage couples to do is to not think about fairness in terms of numbers. Think of it in terms of attitude."

What she means by "attitude" is to evaluate how the two of you operate both as individuals and as a couple.

For example, she knows a couple in which the husband decided to forgo an allowance while the wife gets one because he gets no pleasure in spending money. The wife preferred to have the allowance set up so she had some autonomy to spend without having to check in with him about every little purchase.

"The important thing is creating space to ask your partner if it feels like the right amount," notes Shekar, especially as life changes and evolves.

How Do You Decide Which Style Is Right for You?

This may sound strange, but at first, it's sort of a gut thing. Fundamentally, what style of budgeting in a marriage truly sounds good to you? Maybe you want to be totally joint because that's what your parents did or because it just sounds simpler. Maybe totally separate speaks to you because you had a bad prior experience combining with a partner or because you are fiercely protective of your autonomy. Whatever it is, start to communicate that with your partner.

What Makes You Feel Comfortable?

Here are a few examples:

> *"I like banking jointly and feel it helps push us toward our goals. However, I would still like some autonomy in my spending, so what do you think about having allowances/fun money/discretionary spending?"*

> *"Being totally joint to me is symbolic of this life we're starting together and it sounds like it will just streamline our entire financial lives."*

> *"I love and trust you very much, but for my own peace of mind I do want to keep our bank accounts separate and just set up a strategy for who covers which bills and how we prioritize our savings."*

What Are Your Strengths?

"When my husband and I moved in together, I found out he was surprisingly terrible with money," says Shekar. "It was surprising because he was fantastic with managing a budget in college."

At first, her then-boyfriend, now her husband, was the one handling the at-home finances, and Shekar started to notice how high their credit card bill was each month. Her first instinct was to force him into understanding financial responsibility by making him manage the credit card bills and pay them on time. But the plan backfired. It caused the couple to fight all the time and he'd consistently pay the bills late.

"Instead of forcing him to grow his financial strengths, I actually tapped into my own," says Shekar. "I said, 'Why don't you let me take over the day-to-day financial management and have you handle the other aspects of our life?'"

Her husband enjoys thinking about food and meal prepping, so he assumed control over that area of their life instead of Shekar's trying to strong-arm him into being better with money.

"What do you see as your strengths in our relationship? Here's what I see. [List their strengths.] What do you think are my strengths in our relationship?"

Use Your Ideal Future as a Guidepost for Today

Tasha and Joseph Cochran use the hybrid model of keeping everything joint but with each of them getting a little bit of fun money. The amount of fun money each of them receives, which is the same, is decided based on the money remaining after their financial priorities are taken care of.

But the couple kicks it up another notch.

"We use a one-year spending plan, so we budget for an entire year at once," explains Tasha. Before the couple started their practice of a one-year spending plan, they had to come to an agreement on a really big issue: what type of lifestyle they wanted in retirement.

"We believe everyone should know what their minimum savings rate is, so how much money they need to save every month to retire when they want to and with the lifestyle they want," says Tasha. "Because as long as you're hitting that number every single month, then frankly, you can burn the rest of your money if you want to because your financial future is so secure."

Once the two came to a point of agreement on how much they wanted to have in retirement and therefore how much they needed to start saving now, it informed the rest of their one-year spending plan.

"What type of lifestyle do we want in retirement and when do we want to retire?"

Think about the lifestyle you want in ten years. Here are some talking points to get you started:

- Where do you live?
- Do you have kids or want more kids?
- Do you own a home?
- Have you switched jobs or careers?
- Are certain (or all) debts paid off?

Questions to Ask Each Other When Building a One-Year Spending Plan

- When do we want to go on vacation?
- What major expenses do we want to plan for? (E.g., the projected expenses of household projects, medical procedures, starting a family, or going back to school.)

Share What You Need in Order to Feel Financially Secure

We all come into relationships with different emotional attachments to money. While a lot of this may be tied to how you grew up, it also could be based on prior romantic relationships you experienced. Someone who lived through an abusive relationship may only feel secure if she's able to keep a stash of money to the side in an account her partner can't access. Or perhaps your partner grew up in a household where a parent was abused and couldn't leave because of money, which informs the way he wants to handle money now.

> *"My previous experience with an abusive relationship makes it really stressful for me to bank completely jointly without any money in my name alone. I want to talk to you about this and come to a decision on how we can ensure I feel safe but you don't feel as if I'm hiding money from you in our relationship."*

Amanda Clayman, a financial therapist, also recommends explaining if it's an inherited behavior and making sure it's not done in a secretive way or a way that suggests you have limited trust in your partner:

> *"This is advice that has been passed down in my family and I feel safer knowing I have access to this money."*

"But it doesn't need to be gendered or a statement of mistrust," says Clayman. "There is also financial advice that says you should have money that's yours, period, and your partner should also have an emergency fund that's just theirs."

Of course, all of this assumes that you are in a safe, healthy, and non-abusive relationship.

When You Want to Make a Change

An ever-present point in this book, and really in all money discussions, is the fact that life is going to evolve and change, and so too should your financial strategies. When you reach a point at which you'd like to modify how you and your partner are handling money, Shekar suggests approaching it as a question instead of just bringing a solution. Her own husband will dodge the money conversation if he can, so she will gently nudge for specifics.

"What do you think about the way that we've been managing our money?"

He'll say something like "It's going well."
She'll follow up with:

 "What do you mean by that? Can you tell me what you like about it and what you don't like about it?"

"By using this probing technique, I end up hearing a couple of things that he might not really love," says Shekar. She'll then suggest the pair sit down to have a talk about their money and she'll bring up ideas she's had to make changes and ask her husband for his ideas as well.

Don't Make a Decision Without Consulting Your Spouse or Partner

Whether you're married, engaged, or in a long-term committed relationship, it's really important you don't just assume your partner is on board with your goals and plans. You also don't get to steamroll your partner, even if you're 100 percent certain your way is the "right" way (which always reminds me of Leslie Knope in *Parks and Recreation*).

Clayman once worked with a couple who received family money from the husband's family. Due to some circumstances in the family, the husband decided against taking the money one year. He did that because of a dynamic in his relationship with his parents, but obviously his partner felt betrayed that it happened without her being an equal participant in the decision.

"But was it an option for him to make a choice that honored the primary relationship with his partner, even though he was feeling duress in the relationship with his family?" posed Clayman. "It's rarely as cut-and-dry as we want it to be."

The more relationship dynamics are present in a situation, the more complicated it tends to be. However, at least having a discussion is often a way to minimize the fallout with a partner who feels completely left out or betrayed. Now, if this man's wife had been adamant that they continue to accept the family money and he still declined, she would've also felt betrayed. But she would've at least known about the decision beforehand.

NOW THAT YOU'VE PICKED A STYLE, WHO HANDLES THE MONEY?

Honestly, I don't really know any couples who handle money in a completely fifty-fifty fashion. Usually, there is one person who is either just more interested in being the "chief financial officer" (CFO) of the relationship or more comfortable functioning in that role. It likely comes as no surprise that in my marriage, I handle much of our finances, from modeling budgets to selecting and making investments. Peach is clued in on all the details, is consulted before any big changes or decisions, and has access to both the spreadsheets with our information as well as the accounts.

Tasha and Joseph Cochran are in a different situation because they each have a high level of interest in personal finance.

Tasha takes the lead on developing the one-year projections to create the family's spending plan. Tasha actually expands on the one-year-budget idea and makes a five-year plan that includes five years of one-year budgets. "I will do the projections and the planning for the things that could happen in each year, and then we'll sit down and reevaluate together," explains Tasha.

"I tend to handle all the day-to-day stuff, from paying all the bills and handling all the investments, but of course Tasha has access to everything and knows where everything is unless I've invested in something with my fun money," says Joseph.

"If I needed to take over for Joseph tomorrow, I absolutely could," says Tasha, which is exactly where every couple should be. Brace yourself for bluntness, but life is unpredictable, and if the person who handles the day-to-day money moves in a relationship is suddenly incapacitated or dies, the last thing the grieving partner wants to do is figure out all the details of how to pay the mortgage and utilities, access investments, or do something as seemingly basic as logging into all the bank accounts.

If you're not the CFO in your relationship, here's what you need to ask:

> *"Do you have a document detailing where to track down all our financial assets, including insurance policies?"*

> *"What are the passwords for our/your financial assets?"* (Tasha and Joseph use a password manager.)

If it all feels really overwhelming—e.g., you have multiple bank accounts across various banks: *"Is there a way we could consolidate and simplify any of our financial life in case I ever need to take over?"*

SETTING GOALS TOGETHER (REGARDLESS OF HOW YOU MANAGE MONEY)

There has been ample discussion in this chapter about the importance of goal setting (and there is more to come in the next chapter, about dealing with money fights). Regardless of the budgeting style you select in your marriage—separate, joint, or hybrid—it's important to set and work toward goals together.

Shift Your Language

This might sound silly, but shifting your language can be a powerful tool for working together as a team. When Peach and I got married, I stopped referring to the student loans he brought into the marriage as "his debt" or "your debt" and started saying "our debt." The simple linguistic change kept reinforcing the fact that we were a team and working on this together. It also helped assuage any lingering guilt he felt about having debt on our marital ledger.

> *"How do you want to pay off our student loans?"*

> *"What's the current balance of our student loans?"*

> *"Why don't we put part of this tax refund toward our student loans?"*

Do You Always Have to Compromise on Financial Goals?

"I think about it more like a pendulum swinging," says Shekar. "I'm going to side with you on some decisions, and you're going to side with me on some decisions. I tell couples to not always try to meet in the middle all the time." She explains that if you want to spend $3,000 on a purchase (let's say a couch) and your partner only wants to spend $1,000, then it doesn't mean you just meet in the middle and spend $2,000. Instead, one of you takes the win in this particular situation, and the next time you let your partner's preference win out. Of course, the risk here is getting tit-for-tat in every single financial decision in your relationship. Sometimes you do need to compromise instead of just invoking the "You made the last choice, so I get to make this one" rule.

How Often Should You Check In?

"Every six months," says Shekar. "We, as a generation, go through life changes often enough that it makes sense to connect every six months and see if what we're doing is on track for our goals."

Of course, the monthly money date is ideal, admits Shekar, but it just simply might not happen. Six months also provides a window of time to really see if you're getting traction on your goals or if there's a need for some self-correction.

CHECKLIST FOR MONEY AFTER MARRIAGE

The SparkNotes version of this chapter comes down to these action items:

Before the Wedding Day

- Discuss whether a prenup is right for you and at least go through the prenup questions.
- Decide how much you can spend without checking in.
- Discuss and decide on your short-, medium-, and long-term financial goals.
- Build your budget as a couple.

After the Wedding

- Set up a joint bank account or add each other to existing ones.
- Update billing information on any bills set to autopay.
- Close accounts you don't need anymore.
- Update your beneficiaries on financial accounts and insurance policies.

Things That Are Often Put Off but Are Actually Really Important

- Wills
- Life insurance
- Powers of attorney
- Advance healthcare directives (living will and healthcare proxy)
- Creating a password document

Chapter 12

Fighting Fair About Money

PEACH HANDED ME a thick, cream-colored envelope with our names artfully written on the front.

"Oh no, not another one," I said with zero humor in my voice.

"Come on, this one is at least in New York State," he half-jokingly said, trying to get me excited about our sixth wedding invite of the year.

"I'm going to count how many weddings we've attended since I graduated college," I said in exasperation.

I wasn't kidding. At the time, Peach and I had collectively been to twenty-three weddings and had easily sunk $20,000 into attending other people's weddings. (And at the time of this writing, it's tipping toward thirty weddings.)

Whether or not to attend weddings or the pre-big-day extravaganzas (engagement party, bridal shower, stag party, bachelor party, bachelorette party, etc., etc., etc.) had become a deep-rooted money fight for us.

Peach focuses on the emotional element of attending. The celebration with loved ones. The chance to see family we don't live near. I tend to fixate on both the cost and the time. Of the twenty-three weddings, not a single one had been in our home of New York City, so every wedding and all the preliminary events required travel. Then you had the cost of gifts and outfits, if we were in the bridal parties. Plus, it took away time that would otherwise have been available for personal travel—one of my absolute highest priorities.

Ultimately, what we were actually debating wasn't so much the money but our values. Weddings aren't how I'd elect to spend time with loved ones, especially after going to so many of them in less than a decade. And feeling as if other people are spending my money, even though in actuality I have the autonomy to choose, is something that quickly gets my hackles raised. Peach does value money, but his threshold on saving and spending isn't exactly aligned with mine, and he'd prefer to use the money today, whereas I focus on saving for more flexibility in the future.

Merging your financial life with another person's is all about making compromises and figuring out how to maximize happiness for both of you while minimizing the feeling of restriction. Aligning your financial life with your partner's shouldn't be about taking anything away from them; rather, focus on playing the long game and understanding that it sometimes comes with short-term sacrifices.

"THERE PROBABLY ALWAYS will be couples' conflicts about money, because we have different beliefs around money," says Dr. Brad Klontz, a professor of financial psychology at Creighton University. "The mistake people make is they try to take that money script [how you relate to money] and beat it over the head of their partner until they yield and say, 'Okay, fine—you're right. You and your family history is right and mine is wrong.'"

The desire or belief that we are right becomes so deeply entrenched within us that it correlates to another interesting fact about conflict in relationships.

"In his work, John Gottman [a psychologist and America's foremost researcher of marriages and families] said that around seventy percent of the things couples disagree on will never get resolved," says Klontz.

While this research wasn't specifically about money conflicts, the Gottman Institute's research found that 69 percent of relationship conflict is about perpetual problems. Perpetual problems are identified as "fundamental differences in your personalities, or fundamental differences in your lifestyle needs."[1] According to the institute, all couples have perpetual problems.

"It's a fabulous number because you don't need to feel so bad about your relationship now, do you?" Klontz jokes. An example Klontz gives of a perpetual problem is when you always want to get to the airport early and your spouse doesn't, which is a problem because neither person will ever be able to convince the other their way is wrong. (Well, maybe if you miss a flight you would.)

None of this is to say that you should just give up on communicating about your problems. It's important to have a dialogue about stress points in your relationship, especially around money. You should also recognize that while you can reach a point of compromise, that doesn't mean you've fundamentally changed your partner's mind.

However, before you leap toward a resolution, Klontz encourages you to first engage in a conversation about your money scripts. Realistically, you probably won't be keen on doing this mid–money fight, so begin this discussion when you're both calm and not currently in a debate.

UNEARTH YOUR PARTNER'S MONEY SCRIPTS

When Klontz works with couples, he starts by having them engage in a listening exercise to learn more about each other's money scripts. Money scripts are unconscious beliefs that you hold about money, which are rooted in your childhood. The core money scripts Klontz has established are:

Money avoidance: a tendency to believe money is bad and the wealthy are greedy and corrupt

Money worship: a tendency to believe money is the key to happiness and the solution to your problems

Money status: a tendency to link your self-worth to your net worth

Money vigilance: a tendency to be alert and watchful over your financial health and not believe in being given financial handouts

In order to start to identify your own money scripts as well as your partner's, it's good to ask each other these questions:

- What was the money situation like for you growing up?
- What did your mother teach you about money?
- What did your father teach you about money?
- What are your financial goals?
- Did they teach you either directly or indirectly that there will never be enough money?
- Did you grow up believing there will always be enough money so you don't have to worry about it?
- What did they teach you about rich people?
- What were their opinions about poor people?
- What's your biggest fear about money?

You can also do an online assessment to find out your money script and have your partner do theirs by visiting Klontz's website: www.your mentalwealthadvisors.com/find-out-your-money-script.

"It's shocking that most couples never have that conversation and have no clue, really, what it was like for their partner growing up and the mindset they're bringing into the relationship," says Klontz. "If you understand this it does two things. One, it helps your partner get more insight into their own relationship with money. And two, you can get insight into your partner and the energy around certain purchases."

BALANCING YOUR MONEY NEUROSES

The reason it's critical to unearth your and your partner's money scripts is to figure out how to begin balancing your particular money neuroses.

"There are couples made up of spenders and savers," says Melanie Lockert, author of *Dear Debt* and host of the *Mental Health and Wealth Show* podcast. "And I'm not going to say break up and divorce. I just want to say really be honest with yourself and see if it's a reflection of different values. If so, can we make these values work together?"

"I go overboard sometimes on frugality," admits Carl Jensen, founder of 1500 Days to Freedom. "I have a hard time paying for someone else to do something because I don't value my time enough. If I can clean our gutters, I'm going to do it, even though it might not be worth my time."

The Jensens flip houses and live in a home as they're rehabilitating it to sell. There have been moments in their business when the two of them, while generally handy, struggled to complete part of a renovation project—notably, trying to size and install new gutters. After several attempts, Carl's wife, Mindy, made the call to bring in professionals, who completed the job efficiently for only $400 more than the cost of materials.

Carl errs on the side of minimalism, which sometimes puts him at odds with Mindy and their daughters. Even though the family primarily shops at thrift stores, they like to be thoughtful about how many items they're bringing into the house.

At the end of fifth grade, the Jensens' oldest daughter asked Mindy if she could buy a dress from a "real store" for her final elementary school concert.

"Instead of going to the thrift store and spending five dollars on a dress, we went to a department store and spent thirty-five dollars on a dress that she wore twice and has now outgrown," says Mindy. "But she had so much confidence in that dress that that's okay, though I remember Carl being not so excited that we spent thirty-five dollars on a dress."

"Bridesmaid's dresses are even worse!" jokes Carl. But his money script, like most of ours, links back to childhood, when he saw his parents struggle with money. He told himself he didn't want to ever be broke. So he needed to save, which resulted in a hesitancy to spend even as a kid. This tendency earned him the childhood nickname "Mr. Cheapo" from his sisters. "I'd rather be wealthy than look wealthy," says Carl.

For Lockert, money represented far more than just a difference of opinion on how to spend and save.

"In my relationship, from the surface it looked like 'This is about money,' but it was actually not," says Lockert. "What it came down to was a value system about work. A value system about what we wanted in life. Money represented power. It represented respect. It represented control and it represented our values. After a while I realized we had completely different values."

Lockert felt that she focused on wanting to travel and move toward their goals together as a couple, while her partner was more focused on his own interests, such as his passion for both music and cars.

"Whether you're in a long-term relationship or you're married, you have to think about 'us,'" says Lockert. "You can't be acting like you're financially single."

"If you're both super frugal and never want to do anything, you have to let go of some of that control and scarcity mindset with your money and enjoy it," says Lockert, pointing out that if you spend money, it doesn't have to be on yourself. It could also be charitable contributions that bring you joy. "It's tough because you want to prepare to live until you're one hundred but also prepare to die tomorrow."

When you're actually engaging in a money disagreement, it can be easy to get heated and make flippant comments about your partner's money mistakes or beliefs. It's critical to suppress that behavior and lead with another emotion.

HAVE COMPASSION AND ASK (MORE) QUESTIONS

"You should have a lot of compassion for your partner," says Farnoosh Torabi, financial expert, host of the podcast *So Money*, and bestselling author of *When She Makes More*. "Even if you think your partner is being completely irrational by doing or not doing something with their money, it's important to listen first and ask a lot of questions."

Why is this so important to you?

Why do you feel this way?

Where do you think this is coming from?

"Maybe your partner who is being stubborn or irrational from your perspective will have a lightbulb moment and realize something like 'I'm being just like my dad, and I don't like that, and I vowed never to do what he did with money,'" says Torabi. "The best is when they can call themselves out rather than you pointing fingers and saying, 'You're being this way and I don't like it.'"

You also want to be really careful not to throw around accusations like "You're cheap," or "You save too much," or "You're reckless with money," advises Torabi.

Operating from a place of compassion is also important, because admittedly, it's really easy to get your hackles up and be defensive.

"It's my belief that money conflicts are really about power, respect, control, and values," says Lockert. "Because I was making more than my ex, sometimes I was on a power trip about money," she admits. She would judge certain ways in which he would spend money—a reaction that, while natural, she finds both shameful and embarrassing today.

After the emotional foundations have been laid, it's time for the two of you to actually start working toward a solution.

KEEP YOUR GOALS FRONT AND CENTER

Goal setting is the north star of all things personal finance. Your goals— and how you prioritize your various goals—inform the financial moves you should make, both as an individual and as a team. This is true of everything from basic budgeting to paying off debt to investing.

It's also one of the best ways to resolve money conflicts in your relationship.

"You're going to fight," explains Torabi. "You're going to have differences. So it's not about me versus you. It's about what are our goals, and going back to the common ground is essential when you're at these crossroads."

 "We agreed we wanted to buy a house in the next year and we agreed we wanted to start a family in two years. At the rate we're going, those goals are going to be delayed."

"Go back to the spreadsheet," says Torabi. "Because numbers don't lie, and you want to stay as objective as possible by reminding each other what the common goals are. If those goals are no longer shared, then that's a separate conversation that you need to have."

If you don't have a spreadsheet, now is a good time to make one. It doesn't have to be tracking every penny you spend. But at least write down your goals, the timeline in which you want to complete them, and how much you'd need to save per month to get there on time. Then you can start tracking your progress.

Putting your goals front and center is one of the best ways to handle the most common of money fights: How do I get my partner on a budget?

WHAT I'M HEARING YOU SAY . . .

There's a favorite piece of advice I love to bestow when asked about techniques for handling marital disputes (and this applies to just about any fight). It's the old "What I'm hearing you say . . ." line.

We all have our moments of poor communication, especially in a heated discussion. One way to step back and make sure you're being understood and understanding your partner is to simply say, "What I'm hearing you say is [*and then complete the sentence*]."

Your partner may be completely misinterpreting the intention behind your argument and vice versa, which then spirals you into a fight that doesn't even need to happen. This technique also gives both of you a time-out and a chance to consider the other side of this discussion.

GETTING YOUR PARTNER ON A BUDGET

"People often feel like they need to spend a lot of money because there is some other part of their life that's not in alignment," says Tasha Cochran, a financial attorney and cofounder of One Big Happy Life, which she runs with her partner, Joseph. "There's something that's making them unhappy, so they turn to spending money to soothe the problem instead of actually looking at and addressing the problem."

While that process possibly requires therapy and more than just engaging your partner in some deep-thinking exercises, you can still start to lay the groundwork for getting on a budget together.

First, you should probably just ditch the B-word—especially if that's a pain point with your partner. "Spending plan" is a more palatable term.

Second, Cochran suggests you two sit down and really talk about both of your financial and life priorities.

Set your financial priorities first.

"What does a good life look like for you?"

"What things can you actually not live without?"

This can segue into a discussion with your partner about how they personally feel life is going as an individual. It's not about the state of your relationship but about whether your partner is fulfilled and satisfied.

Do a Life Satisfaction Check-In

Checking in with each other and being open to reconfiguring a household budget based on each other's wants is one of the Cochrans' strengths as a team.

The pair will sit down and ask each other:

"How is life going for you?"

"Are you happy with this right now?"

"Do you feel like you need to make a change?"

"What actually matters and is important to you?"

To use an example from the Cochrans' relationship, Joseph was training for a triathlon, which not only took time but required an extra gym membership that originally wasn't a part of the couple's budget. But it's something that was really important to Joseph and his overall life satisfaction, so they made the accommodation in their household budget.

Tasha points out that it's okay for you to want things, but you need to sit down together and determine what's a reasonable amount to spend in light of your other financial goals.

"At the end of the day, we always agree to prioritize hitting our minimum savings rate and then after that we agree to be committed to us each living our best, fullest, and happiest life," says Tasha.

Don't Forget to Reevaluate Your Budgeting Strategy

If constantly nitpicking at each other's spending habits seems to be a chronic issue in your relationship, then you may need to reevaluate how you handle your money. Going back to the strategies for budgeting in a relationship, it could be time to switch from totally joint to a "yours, mine, and ours" bank account system.

BEST PRACTICES FOR HANDLING MOST MONEY-RELATED FIGHTS IN ACTION

Tasha and Joseph Cochran walked me through one of their biggest financial "friction points," as Joseph called it, in their relationship, and how the pair implemented different strategies to reach a compromise.

It all started with deciding on how much to spend on a house—a common friction point for many couples.

Joseph preferred to focus on a house that was the best deal at the lowest price point, which had led him to purchase a foreclosure as his first home. Tasha, who'd owned multiple properties before her relationship with Joseph, jokingly described herself as "not a tiny house person."

"I always imagined myself in a house with a grand kitchen and multiple Christmas trees all over the house," says Tasha. "So we lived in his house for a year, and then we decided to start house hunting and definitely bumped heads on how much to spend."

It's a friction point in their relationship that doesn't necessarily change just because a decision got made. After all, their baseline opinions stayed the same. However, the way they deal with this, and similar money disagreements, is to "fit in everything," jokes Tasha. That means fitting everything they want into their budget. But that "fitting in everything" strategy isn't without compromise.

Start with Where You're in Agreement

It's already been well established that your first move in a money dispute should be to go back to your common ground: goals.

"Our number one priority is savings," Tasha explains. "If we're able to hit our savings goals, our financial future is secure, so everything else becomes lifestyle spending."

Debate Using Reality, Not Perception, Which Means Examining Your Numbers

"When you're sitting there and arguing over ideas and potential futures with one person looking at it optimistically and the other is being pessimistic, neither one of those are necessarily fully reflective of what's happening in reality," says Tasha. "Get your budget and actually look at it!"

When the Cochrans were disagreeing about how much to spend on a house, they looked at their numbers and asked each other about compromises each was willing to make:

"Okay, well how much will it cost for the level of house I want and what will our budget look like?"

Then they talked about it and discussed what they'd need to give up.

"Are you willing to give up international vacations for a few years until we get our income up?"

 "Are you going to give up certain beauty routines?"

"I really want to go on vacations, so I think we need to reevaluate how much we're going to spend."

You also need to make sure you both aren't fixated on the perceived positives of your version of events by challenging each other to consider the downsides.

 "Sure, that's a good possible outcome. But what would be some of the potential friction points in that plan? What do you think would be some of the friction points in my plan?"

Play the What-If Game

We've all got our particular fights in a relationship where we each get so entrenched in a viewpoint and debate back and forth, around and around, each convinced the other just isn't seeing it the "right way."

Instead of fixating on two potential results, the Cochrans encourage people to play the "what-if" game in order to brainstorm multiple solutions to a problem. For instance, let's say you're evaluating the pros and cons of a parent's staying at home with a child versus returning to work. What if you went to your employer and said, "It's important to me to be able to work from home for the first six months of my child's life, and then I'll come back full-time," or "I need to go down to a part-time schedule for the first six months. Is that something you can work with me on?"

"Maybe they'd be willing to have you move down to part-time rather than lose you entirely," says Tasha.

 "Other than these two possible outcomes, what are some of the other options we could at least try?"

Don't Rehash Your Decision

Once you've agreed on a decision, it's really easy to continue to rehash it, especially if it's something like paying more for a house than you wanted. Each month you make that payment and you're reminded that you didn't want to spend that money. It might even cause you to pick a little fight with your partner about how much you're paying and all the other things you could be doing with that money. In the now-cringy words of a kids' movie, "Let it go."

"It's really important that once you agree, you can move forward and live without resentment," says Joseph.

For Tasha, part of that process is making sure that the person who had to compromise a little more also gets something else they wanted to ensure both parties are content and can come to terms with the decision.

DEALING WITH FINANCIAL INFIDELITY

Plenty of money fights, no matter how enormous they feel in the moment, can be solved by using the techniques outlined in this chapter. But sometimes there is a breach of trust that feels irreconcilable. A breach that fractures the trust you have in your partner. A breach known as "financial infidelity."

To be completely honest, financial infidelity can be a book unto itself. In its most basic form, there is nothing insidious or spiteful about it, and it's probably more to do with your partner's feeling embarrassed about a behavior like overshopping, gambling, or making a bad investment. So they try to hide it from you while attempting to rectify the mistake.

Other times, it's a calculated move one partner is making to hide money from the other as a means of control.

Common warning signs of a partner's financial infidelity include:

- Your partner won't share household bills with you and evades the question when you ask about them.
- Your partner gets calls from banks, lenders, or debt collectors and dismisses your request to discuss it.
- Collection agencies call you for a debt you have no knowledge of.
- Your partner won't share their credit score or report with you.
- Your partner discourages you from attending meetings with a financial advisor or accountant.
- Your partner won't share financial details or bank log-ins with you.
- Bills come in the mail for financial products you didn't know your partner had or that were taken out in your name.
- Accounts show up on your credit report for which you didn't apply.

Before you start freaking out if any of these warning signs are present in your relationship, you need to reflect on one thing: "What agreements do you have around money to begin with?" asks Klontz.

Klontz has worked with very happily married couples who don't discuss how much they're making and where they're putting their money.

"But they're operating from the same assumption," says Klontz. "The infidelity means that you both had an agreement and one person violated it and held that information from the other."

Still Fighting? Bring in a Professional

Whether it's something potentially relationship ending, like financial infidelity, or more of a never-ending money fight you can't seem to resolve, you may need to bring in a professional.

"It doesn't hurt in some relationships to bring in an advisor or a money therapist or a money coach," says Torabi. "Your spouse is someone you signed up to work with for the rest of your lives. In relationships, sometimes a little bit of financial therapy can be really helpful at certain junctures."

As discussed in chapter 10, a financial therapist focuses on helping you unpack your cognitive and emotional relationship to money, which may stand in the way of your having a healthy relationship to money. Your financial therapist should not be the person who is managing your money, even if they are also a CFP or another type of financial advisor. Refer back to chapter 10 (page 189) for a refresher on financial therapy.

Chapter 13

It's All Changing: Navigating the Finances of a Major Life Change

IN MY BIASED little sampling of people I know, not a single person is still working for the same employer they started with after college graduation a decade or so ago. In 2020, I've worked four jobs, including self-employment but excluding side hustles, since leaving college in 2011. It may be a millennial cliché, but many of us, if not most of us, won't go through the rest of our lives working for the same employer. We'll also grow and change in other ways, like starting a family, starting our own business, making a move to another state or country, or retiring completely from the workforce early.

Those life changes are going to be intricately tangled with finances, which means we need to be able to discuss both the desire for change and the financial implications of those changes with our partners.

NAVIGATING A MAJOR CAREER SHIFT WITH A PARTNER

In 2019, Tasha Cochran quit her job as a financial attorney and pivoted to running One Big Happy Life, the online business she started with her partner, Joseph, full-time.

Tasha knew quitting her full-time job would be a hit on the family budget, but she also focused on making that hit a temporary situation as she committed to growing the business to the point where it could not only replace her old income but exceed it. However, in the interim and before she gave notice, the Cochrans sat down and ran the numbers in order to make an informed choice.

"We do simulated budgets for every change we're thinking about making," says Tasha, which includes everything from moving to switching jobs to expanding their family.

The pair also look at more than just the household income and also evaluate tax implications, time commitments, and the shifts in contingency plans that come with any big changes.

Then they also start to address the intangibles.

"You have to apply value to the things you can't really put a number on," says Joseph. "When it came to Tasha running the business full-time, one positive is that she'd have more free time because she wouldn't be working forty hours at a day job every week and then working almost forty hours on the business. Instead, she'd just do one. At least in the short run, that altered our budget, because we did have three full-time jobs between the two of us, but now there's more free time and there's definitely value to that."

What to ask each other about these decisions:

> *"Why do you want to make this change?"*
> *"Why is this important to you?"*
> *"What are you willing to give up, or comfortable giving up, in order to make this happen?"*

It's worth pointing out that it takes time and practice to become budgeting and planning rock stars like the Cochrans. Don't be discouraged if this feels overwhelming right now or if you miss major expenses your first few times giving simulated budgets a go.

Paco de Leon, founder of The Hell Yeah Group, helped her wife start her business. "My wife obviously knows that I handle finances, so she leans on me and trusts me and I don't have to have a battle with her," says de Leon.

That doesn't mean it was without its scary moments.

"What you have to do is realize all the risks that are involved and assess them and really think about your worst-case scenario," says de Leon. "If you can't deal with the worst-case scenario, maybe come up with some sort of runway [time before your business runs out of cash] where this has to work by a certain date."

> *"What's the worst-case scenario?"*
>
> *"That makes me really uncomfortable. Could we set a deadline so that if it's not working by then* [you'll/I'll] *pivot back to a traditional career for a while?"*

De Leon had her own experience running the numbers and evaluating whether or not a career move made sense. In 2010, she sat for the LSAT and debated going to law school. "It was one of those things where I was listening to society and wanted to be 'important,'" she said, "so I thought I wanted to go to law school to get those letters and be amazing."

After she ran the numbers on how much she'd need to borrow, her heart broke, because she realized her repayment plan would be $1,000 a month on the low end of the spectrum, which would mean she'd be stuck in that job.

"If there's any way to convince a millennial to do something or not do something, it's to make them feel trapped," joked de Leon. "Just looking at those numbers made me feel trapped, so I didn't do it."

Jokes aside, de Leon encourages you to be that black-and-white when you run the numbers and evaluate if you have the runway to make a big move. If you don't, then you need to wait a year or so to build up that runway.

"You can't just dive feet first because you could screw your relationship up," says de Leon. "I feel like finances are something you could rebuild, but the relationship is important. You can't put a price on that."

A CHANGE IN WHO EARNS MORE

"I don't want to be dethroned as the breadwinner," I admitted to my mastermind group, a part peer-mentoring and part entrepreneurial support group. It was spring of 2020 and the world was grappling with the coronavirus pandemic, social distancing, quarantine, and the subsequent financial fallout. Peach's job was stable, but my income was getting rocked as speaking engagements had to be canceled and freelance budgets at major publications were frozen while everyone waited to evaluate the longer-term financial impact. For the first time in our nearly decade-long relationship, it seemed I might close out the year earning less than my husband—a paradigm shift with which I wasn't entirely comfortable.

Here's the thing. We often talk about women outearning men and the fact that it can do a number on the relationship. While writing *When She Makes More*, Farnoosh Torabi found that the probability for divorce actually doubles when the woman earns more. This is a reality that really boils down to gender norms, what we expect from both genders and the ideals we try to uphold, says Torabi.

"We feel safer when a man is making more," says Torabi. "[When the woman earns more,] it's an unsettled feeling from both men and women in some cases because this wasn't modeled for them and they feel embarrassed or uncomfortable. Women might've been raised in a culture or family in which women weren't breadwinners, and that's what was presented to them as the ideal. Similarly, from the man's point of view, he was raised to be the breadwinner."

Veronica Dagher, host and cocreator of the *Wall Street Journal*'s *Secrets of Wealthy Women* podcast, has noticed similar trends in her interviews with successful, career-oriented women.

"Among the married heterosexual women who have been guests on my show, having a supportive partner has been key," says Dagher. "A few of the women have told me (some off the record) that they've ended a marriage or relationship because their man at the time was jealous of how much money they made or their career success. The women told me that they came to realize that if their husbands truly loved them and wanted the best for the couple, they would want them to shine at work. If he doesn't, cut your losses sooner rather than later, they say."

So, why is it that I react the way I do to the idea of my husband's out-earning me? It's not a lack of love and support for him and his career as a teacher. It's that a lot of my self-worth (to an admittedly unhealthy degree) is tied up in my identity as an earner. Peach works a job that is notoriously underpaid but comes with high career satisfaction. In my mind, I've taken a risk being self-employed and building a business, so to yield the high-earner spot to someone who works a job that's nationally noted as being underpaid makes me feel like I'm failing both myself and us. His job provides us with stability and the almighty health insurance, while mine gives us the lifestyle we both like.

All this context is to say that I often wonder if the tension in outearning a partner isn't always tied specifically to gender but also to the paradigm upon which the foundation of your relationship was built. A shift in who earns more changes that paradigm.

"What about my potentially earning more bothers you?"

For those of you experiencing a shift in who earns more, I encourage you to discuss it openly with your partner and try to identify why it's causing any animosity or tension. If you're struggling to have this be a productive, healthy conversation, then it should be one you discuss together with a couples' counselor or separately in therapy (possibly with a financial therapist, if that feels like the better fit).

"No matter who you're with, you want your partner to be your cheerleader," says Dagher. "Someone who is going to build you up and pick you up when you're down, no matter how much money either of you makes."

GOING BACK TO WORK (OR NOT) AFTER BABY

Life after a baby will be full of financial decisions, but many of those choices also manifest as values and lifestyle decisions. If one of you (or both of you) was raised in a two-parent household where one parent stayed home as the primary caregiver, then that's the model you know and might think is best. After all, it's what worked for you and your family. If you were raised with both parents working or by a single parent, it might not even be a question in your mind that you'll both continue working after having a child—especially if you have career satisfaction.

The reality could also be that even if one of you wants to stay home, it's just not financially viable. You need both incomes—even with the cost of day care—to have a comfortable lifestyle.

You get it. There are lots of choices here. But having the "life after baby" conversation, especially in reality and not the abstract, isn't always easy.

Lauren Smith Brody, the author of *The Fifth Trimester* and the founder of the Fifth Trimester consultancy, is a mother of two and studied all aspects of the return to a job for working moms.

In her research, Smith Brody found that the ideal length for maternity leave is six months. It gives the mother time to physically recover and the baby time to adjust, and research has shown this time together also helps with the health and development of the child.

You might've just literally laughed out loud reading that stat. SIX MONTHS?! Ha—six weeks is generous in many cases, and it's probably not even paid.

"The Family and Medical Leave Act (FMLA) protects twelve weeks of unpaid leave and your job will be waiting for you at the end of it. But very few Americans can afford to take a quarter of their year unpaid," says Smith Brody.

Advocating for Yourself

Part of the transition into motherhood may also require having to learn to advocate for yourself in new ways, both in your relationship and at work.

Learn to Ask for Help from Your Partner

You need to be able to rely on your partner for a lot of support, especially in the early months of raising a child. Smith Brody recommends you start practicing this by asking for really simple things, like a glass of water.

"If I'm sitting on the couch feeding our child for the twelfth time that day, I need to be able to ask for water," says Smith Brody. "Know that they can't read your mind and they need to be told as specifically as possible."

This practice should come even before the baby arrives, because after delivery there will be needs that are forced upon you as a by-product of caring for this new life and recovering yourself.

"We're so independent that we've taught ourselves to want to do everything ourselves," says Smith Brody. "As a new parent, it can bite you in the ass."

Ask Your Employer for Flexibility

Everyone's needs and opportunities will be different, but if you have the chance to advocate for yourself, then consider asking your employer for exactly what you need in your new reality. Part of this might require you to educate your employer a little bit.

"I'm so grateful for the leave that I'm able to take. I know the research points to the six-month mark as when women's bodies are more ready to be back to work and up to speed. I'd like to ask for some temporary work flexibility that will allow me to get to that point and flourish and bring in the best work for the long term."

Going back to a point Tasha made in the last chapter about playing the what-if game, you could consider using language like:

"It's important to me to be able to work from home for the first six months of my child's life. And then I'll come back full-time."

Or:

"I'd like to go down to a part-time schedule for the first six months.* Is that something you can work with me on?"

As Tasha previously pointed out, maybe they'd be willing to have you move down to part-time rather than lose you entirely.

Depending on your relationship with your employer, you could even play a light version of the what-if game.

"Other than these two possible outcomes, what are some of the other options we could at least consider?"

Feeling awkward about making the big ask? Try repositioning it to be about more than just you.

"If you're negotiating for something that will make work more sustainable, think of it beyond yourself. It's good for all people you work with and your company's business," says Smith Brody.

Communicate What You Need from Coworkers

You should also feel empowered to communicate your needs to your coworkers. For example, when you're pregnant, it should be understood you're going to need to get up and go to the bathroom more often or just leave midway through a meeting, and after the baby is born, you'll need a space to pump that's close to where you work and not floors away.

"By being a little bit more open about the things that are uncomfortable, you're helping everyone who may need support for a personal issue," says Smith Brody, "whether it's a partner at home who needs caregiving or for an aging parent. It's important for you to unbraid what's wound up

---

*Or adjust for whatever feels right for your situation.

in your own sense of self. You're asking because you want to be good and productive."

When One Person's Salary Is Eaten Up by Childcare

At this writing, I don't even have kids, and I feel like I've been privy to way too many conversations (a few in person and certainly online) that end with the conclusion "Well, your salary is pretty much eaten up by childcare, so it doesn't make sense for you to work."

The thing is, for many people, work isn't just about earning income. It can provide satisfaction in other ways and give you a sense of autonomy, success, and pride. Now, this isn't to say caring for children can't give you those feelings. But we're all wired differently.

Smith Brody points out that once your children have aged into attending school, you're essentially without a paying vocation from 8:15 a.m. to 3:15 p.m. You could always aim to get back into the workforce when your children go to school, but it is significantly harder to get back in after five years (or more) than after a maternity-leave window.

If you want to work after the baby is born and your spouse is resisting the idea, citing the financial burden of childcare or the other classic, "I don't want my kids raised by someone else," then you can consider this script from Smith Brody.

> *"Our entire job as parents is to prepare our children to be satisfied, happy, productive adults. The best way I can do that is by modeling that myself. My priority is always my children, but my work will support our children. I'll be a happier, better mom if I'm contributing to our family's income and contributing to the world and using my education. This is the right decision for me and our family."*

Smith Brody also points to a 2018 study by Harvard Business School professor Kathleen McGinn that found that adult daughters who had mothers who worked outside the home were more likely to work themselves and "hold more supervisory responsibilities, and earn higher wages than women whose mothers stayed home full time."[1] The study found that it didn't impact sons in their employment and earnings, but it did make them more egalitarian in their attitudes toward gender.

If One of You Doesn't Want to Go Back to Work

You could be on the other side of this situation. You or your spouse might not want to go back to work after the baby is born.

Reflecting on the last chapter, it's important you two think about your long-term goals (both lifestyle and financial) and then discuss if they've changed for one of you. Are you willing to give up certain lifestyle luxuries or push back a deadline on a financial goal in order to have one of you stay home with the baby? And maybe it's not your first child. Perhaps you're feeling this way with your second or third, and that's okay too.

 "Okay, if we switch to just having one salary coming in but don't have to pay for childcare, what will our finances look like?"

Run the actual numbers. Don't work in abstractions. Then begin to discuss what you might need to sacrifice, at least in the short term.

"Are you willing to give up X membership?"

"Are you willing to give up more than one vacation—or the 'just us' trip we take each year?"

"Are you willing to give up traveling during the holidays?"

"Are you willing to delay our moving into a larger home to get more space for our expanding family?"

REGARDLESS OF THE TRANSITION, THERE'S ONLY ONE WAY THROUGH . . .

I said it at the very beginning of this book, but the only way through is by setting your boundaries and communicating. Of course, part of it is also compromise, especially with your spouse or life partner.

CHALLENGES

Challenge 1: Set a time to have the first "full-frontal financial nudity" talk. If you've never fully revealed your financial life with your partner (and you're in a serious relationship), then your challenge is to start the conversation. Tell your partner you want to have this talk and set a date and time. In preparation, you should also have them read the section of this book on full-frontal financial nudity in chapter 10.

Challenge 2: Married couples: Make sure you can both function as the chief financial officer. That means you both need to know how to pay all bills, access all accounts, and know where all the legal paperwork is stored. If the primary CFO can no longer function in that role, the other one of you can seamlessly step in. Sit down together by the end of this week and make sure you both have all the necessary information.

Challenge 3: Separately write down your short-, medium-, and long-term financial goals and then compare. It's hard to pick a path if you don't know your final destination. One of the best ways for you and your partner to get on the same path and start making financial goals as a team is to determine what you want as individuals and then decide how to merge those goals.

Epilogue

You can even take it a step further and start breaking the taboo of talking about finances by having financial chats with friends or getting financially naked with your partner. Money isn't a dirty, shameful topic; in fact, our whole society would probably be a lot better off if we stopped being so afraid to discuss it. So go on and get talking.

I WROTE THOSE WORDS in the epilogue of my first book, *Broke Millennial: Stop Scraping By and Get Your Financial Life Together.* It's the book that launched this series, and it feels prophetic that I'd already shifted my focus to the importance of talking money.

You can have all the tools to handle your money yourself. You can build flawless spreadsheets, live below your means, determine what you value, and invest to build wealth. But money will still be a pain point if you can't effectively communicate about it with those around you.

Hopefully, this book has provided you with the playbook to initiate money conversations in a productive and healthy way. It's not a cure-all, and it doesn't mean you'll never have another argument about finances. (I quite literally wrote the book on this topic, and trust me, I still get into arguments with loved ones about money and sometimes struggle to set boundaries.)

Before we part ways, I encourage you to revisit the goals you set back in the introduction and write down what happened after you had these conversations. (Why yes, this is a gentle nudge for you to actually complete those goals if you haven't already!)

I want to talk to _____ about

_____ by _____.

The result was: _____

_____.

I want to ask _____ about

_____ by _____.

The result was: _____

_____.

I want to tell _____ about

_____ by _____.

The result was: _____

_____.

Speaking of gently nudging you to complete something . . .

If you've gotten to these last few pages without attempting even one of the challenges I outlined at the end of each section, then I dare you to go back and try at least one today. Whichever one feels the least daunting to you is perfectly fine, but you aren't going to progress in your ability to talk money without initiating conversations. You can flip to the appendix of this book to easily access all the scripts in case you want some extra help.

And in the last moment before you close this book, I want to thank you for taking the steps to start talking more openly about money. It's one of the ways we can all build and pass on a positive, healthy financial legacy.

Acknowledgments

To all the people in the Broke Millennial community who not only help make this book series successful but also make my job a reality, thank you.

I owe so much gratitude to Aditi Shekar, Alexandra Dickinson, Alison Green, Amanda Clayman, Brad Klontz, Caitlin Boston, Cameron Huddleston, Claire Wasserman, Davita Scarlett, Farnoosh Torabi, Gaby Dunn, Jen Glantz, Judith Ohikuare, Lauren Smith Brody, Lindsay Bryan-Podvin, Linda Rosenthal, Lindsey Stanberry, Melanie Lockert, Melody Wilding, Michael Lacy, Mindy and Carl Jensen, Paco de Leon, Tasha and Joseph Cochran, and Veronica Dagher, who volunteered their time, insights, and in many cases, deeply personal stories for this book.

To Roshe Anderson and Allyssa Fortunato, who worked so hard to make this book a hit.

Thanks to Eric Myers for taking a chance on me five years ago—here we are, three books later. All of this couldn't have happened without you.

Thank you to my editor, Lauren Appleton, for believing in the concept of this book and helping sculpt it into shape.

Many thanks to my mastermind group, who dealt with a lot of my complaining and exhaustion when the going got tough.

Thanks to my friends, for putting up with my peppering them with questions about "normal reactions" to certain money situations and for allowing me to share some of our stories in my work.

Mom and Dad—thank you for talking about money so openly with me through my entire life. It laid the foundation for everything I've built today.

Cailin—thank you for always telling me your honest critiques. You push me to be a better writer, and more important, a better person. (And thank you for being the only reason I can mount a successful book tour!)

Finally, to my husband, Peach. Thank you for your willingness to engage in every money discussion with me and for being okay with sharing many intimate details of our financial life. I love you.

Appendix:
Every Single Money Script

PART 1: TALKING ABOUT MONEY AT WORK

Chapter 1: "How Much Do You Make?"

How to Actually Ask "How Much Do You Make?"

Sentence 1: *"I'm doing research because . . .* [insert your reason].*"* For example, the reason could be that you're about to ask for a raise, trying to determine if your salary is within the standard range, or interviewing for a new position.

Sentence 2: *"And I think you have some information that could help me."*

Sentence 3: *"Would you be willing to share your ballpark salary with me?"*

Alternatively, if you're asking someone who hires for your role, is a mentor or a former boss, or is just generally in a higher position in the company, then amend the line to *"I'm thinking of asking for X. Does that sound reasonable to you?"*

•

"I am getting ready to ask for a raise. I want to make sure that my expectations aren't too high or too low. I was hoping you could help me calibrate what to expect at our company."

•

"I am getting the sense that I'm significantly underpaid compared to the men on our team and I'm hoping you can help me test that assumption."

The Power of the Cold Pitch

"Hey—I'm a UX researcher and I just found out I'm really grossly under-paid compared to some of my coworkers. As I go into the next round of job interviews, it would be helpful if you could share what you think I should be making or what salary you think I should ask for."

CHAPTER 2: Asking for More Money (a.k.a. Time to Negotiate)

"I want X for my salary. I'm not going anywhere beneath X."

"Based on [insert stats about performance], I'm at the upper end of the range here, and also X is my salary expectation. And compared to what I'm making now, I'm not prepared to move for less than X."

What to Do If You Find Out That You're Underearning

"I wanted to talk to you about my salary. I'm being paid X and I've learned that John, who does the same work that I do and manages a group of the same size [or insert your comparison here], is being paid twenty percent more than that. I'm trying to understand the reason for the difference."

Proving That You Earned That Raise

"I'm hoping we can revisit my salary; it's been [insert time here] since it was last set and I'm hoping we might be able to increase it."

Asking for Constructive Criticism

"I'd like to discuss what I can do to move up to [insert position here]. Any constructive criticism or recommendations on skills to build or improve would be really appreciated."

Common Negotiating Tactics

"How can we figure out a solution that works for everybody?" or "No doubt we can come to a compromise that everyone is happy with."

"I would like . . ."

Silence Is Powerful

"*I've done my research, and according to what I've found, the market rate for this kind of role is X, and for all the reasons that we've discussed about my performance and contributions, I'd like a raise of X percent.*"

And then just shut up!

Is It Okay to Make the First Offer?

"*In my market research I found that the top performers in this field make X amount.* [Insert context about what makes you a top performer.] *I'm looking for X amount or as close as possible to it. Is that something that's doable on your end?*"

What You Can Negotiate for Other Than Salary

"*It's really important to me to raise my salary. I think something like X dollars would be more in line with the market, but if you can't do that, it would be a great benefit to me to be able to* [insert request here, e.g., *work from home two days a week*]."

·

"*I'm covered under my spouse's healthcare plan, so I don't need healthcare coverage here. Could you increase my salary or give me a one-time bonus?*"

What If You're Turned Down?!

"*Can you give me a sense of what it would take for me to earn that raise?*"

Should You Provide a Salary Range?

Don't answer the question you were asked, answer the question you wanted to be asked!

"*Based on market rates and my skill set, my desired salary for this position is $80,000.*"

What If You Get Turned Down?

"*You know, I really appreciate your considering it, but I'm excited about the job and I'd love to accept regardless.*"

PART 2: TALKING ABOUT MONEY WITH FRIENDS

CHAPTER 3: Should You Share Your Numbers with Friends?

How to Determine Whether Sharing Your Income Is Helpful

"I'm planning to ask for a raise soon and wondered if you've had any success negotiating your salary."

•

"I'm starting to get the sense I might be underpaid in our field. This might be an awkward question, but how much do you make?"

Then, if your friend is acting awkward or uncomfortable, you pivot to the over/under strategy . . .

"It's okay if you don't want to give an exact number, but is it over or under [insert number here]?"

Another option is to ask upon hearing about a promotion or raise.

"That's so awesome you got the job offer! Are you getting a good pay bump?"

•

"To be honest, I'm not really comfortable sharing my exact numbers, but I'm happy to share the percentage of my salary I save and invest each month if you think that would be helpful."

CHAPTER 4: What Happens When You're in Significantly
Different Financial Situations?

When You Earn Less (or You're in a Lot of Debt)
DON'T LET YOUR FRIEND KEEP PICKING UP THE TAB

"I want to pay next time, but I can't afford this restaurant. Are you okay with our eating at a cheaper place?"

•

"I appreciate the kind gesture, but it doesn't feel good for me."

When You Make More

OFFER TO PAY (SOMETIMES)

"I just saw that the Backstreet Boys are doing a surprise reunion tour concert this weekend. I really want you to come with me, so I'll buy the tickets." [Friend resists.] "I hear you, but I know you were more of an NSYNC fan, so I'll get these tickets because I really want you to experience the Backstreet Boys!"

Have the Explicit Conversation

"I care about time with you and I want to ensure we don't lose our friendship with each other."

From this opening line, you can work together to brainstorm creative ways to spend time together that are enjoyable for both of you but don't hurt either person's bank account.

When Your Value Sets Just Don't Align

"Oh, we'd love to go on vacation with you, but we're trying to save up for [insert thing here]."

Creating a Plan to Work Through All This and Stay Friends

LEARN HOW TO TALK IT OUT—EVEN WHEN IT'S AWKWARD

"I love you and I want to spend time with you, and your friendship means a lot.

"I worry that as we move into this next phase of our lives when I'm a teacher and you're a banker, we are going to have different lifestyles, and it will get harder for us to just naturally hang out like we used to. I don't want that to be a factor in whether we stay friends."

CHAPTER 5: Setting Boundaries

Strategies to Set Financial Boundaries with Friends

COUNTEROFFER

"I really appreciate the invitation . . .

"But I'm focused on paying off my student loans by the end of this year," or *"It's a little out of my budget.*

"I definitely do want to spend time with you, though. Would you want to come over for game night instead?"

If your friend is inviting you to something that's already set—like a concert—then you can pick a specific night to add to your counteroffer.

"Would you want to come over next Wednesday for cocktails and game night?"

•

"I'm busy, but I can come meet you for a drink afterward."

Take Control in Order to Manage Expectations

"Could we pick a dinner spot that's no more than $20 each? I actually have a few ideas."

•

"I'd like to come out tonight, but I'm probably only going to have one drink because I'm on a budget."

Can't Afford to Split the Bill

"I'm excited to celebrate your birthday with you, but I'm really aiming to make a $500 payment toward my student loans this month, so I have to be mindful of my budget. Would it be possible for me to cover just what I order and chip in a little for your meal?"

Granted, it's not entirely fair to ask your friend to restrict options to what's in your budget, or she may already have made her selection. In either case, you can come in with a counteroffer.

"The restaurant you picked is delicious but a little out of my budget. I really do still want to celebrate with you, so I'll just come for dessert or an after-dinner drink if that's okay."

How to Decline an Invitation

"Sorry I can't come on the reunion trip, but I'd love to join digitally for a group happy hour one of the nights you're all there."

Or:

"I'd love to take you out to dinner to celebrate your new adventure."

CHAPTER 6: Let's Talk About Weddings

How to Say "Thanks, but No Thanks" to a Bride or Groom

"I am so thrilled that you two are getting married, and I would really like to be a part of your special day, but I need to be honest that I'm [insert your reason here: "in two other weddings this year," or "paying off debt," or "saving up for something"], *and so my budget to be a bridesmaid would be approximately* [insert number here]. *I don't want you to have to plan everything around my limitations, so let me know if you think that's realistic. If it's not, I totally understand, and I'm here to support you in other ways."*

You can also fall back on the counteroffer strategy.

"Sorry I can't accept the offer to be in your bridal party [not a bad idea to give a reason, if you're comfortable], *but I'd love to help you out that morning putting up decorations or whatever you'd need."*

Handling the Cost of Being in a Wedding

GENTLY PUSHING BACK

"That's a really awesome idea, and I love that it's what you want to do, and I'm here to support you.

"Right now, this is what my finances look like, and I want to be really transparent with you. I want to celebrate with you, but this is what I have to work with.

"One option that may complement your idea of going to Thailand for a bachelorette party is maybe throwing a tropical-themed bachelorette party in a nearby state instead."

PART 3: TALKING ABOUT MONEY WITH FAMILY

CHAPTER 7: How to Ask Your Parents If You'll Need to Take Care of Them Financially

Everything Needs to Be Communicated Early

"I appreciate all that you've done for me as a [parent, grandparent, etc.]. *I know that you've sacrificed and worked hard to support us."*

Once you lay this foundation, it's time to express your concern.

"Here's what I'm concerned about. As I start to plan my own financial future, it's hard for me to think about what that future looks like if I don't also know what your future looks like, because we are connected. And I'm thinking about what that means in practical terms."

Finally, get to what you want to ask.

"I'd really love it if we could get into a concrete conversation about how you see your future and how prepared you feel and if there's anything you worry about. I just want you to know I'm open to that and I'd feel better if we could talk about it. How do you feel about it?"

Or maybe it's slightly more direct.

[Concern] *"Here's what I'm concerned about. I know we have a history of dementia in our family."*

[Ask] *"And I want to ensure we have all the legal documents in place so if that ever were to come up, we'd be prepared and could focus on your health and care right away."*

Try to Weave the Conversation in Organically

"I just drew up my will, and here's what the process is like; it's very easy. Have you both thought about doing this too?"

•

"Jackie's parents just retired and moved down to Florida. What do you two think you'll do when you retire?"

•

"[Partner's name] *and I are starting to figure out what we're going to do with our finances and what we'll do if we have kids. What did you do?*"
Follow up with:
"Are you happy you did it that way or would you do it differently?"

•

"I just started a new job and was debating contributing to the company retirement plan. What do you think?"

•

"Since we just [got married/had a kid], *do you think I should make a will and get life insurance?"*

•

"A friend of mine's father passed away recently and didn't have a will. He'd gotten remarried and had kids from both marriages, and it's a huge mess now. Our family situation is different, but I wanted to know if you had a will that details what you want."
You can also start the sentence with:
"[Insert celebrity name] *didn't have a will and his family is already fighting each other over the estate."*
Or:
"I [heard on a podcast/read in an article] *about how complicated it can be to settle your parents' estate without a will . . ."*

•

"Maybe you don't have stocks or money set aside in retirement accounts, but you have a house and a car. You don't have to be rich to have a will."

Can It Tie to One of Your Life Events?
"Peach and I are in the process of drafting a prenup, and part of the process is discussing the possibility of an inheritance and how we feel that money should be divided in the case of a divorce. So, I was wondering if there's any information I need from you two to put into our prenup."

Consider a Multigenerational Household

APPROACH THE TOPIC FROM KINDNESS, NOT FEAR

> *"You mentioned a few weeks ago that maintaining the lawn has become a lot of work for you and Dad. Would it help if we hired someone to come by and mow the lawn once a week?"*

> *"Mom, you mentioned navigating the stairs in the house is starting to be a lot on your knees. What if we started to look for a home that better suits your needs now? Or we could even talk about the option of you living in our home."*

Lisa Cini, president of Mosaic Design Studio and Best Living Tech, also recommends that you steer the conversation toward the benefits to not only them, but also to you if they moved in.

> *"My work travel has really started to pick up lately, and it'd be so much easier on me and the kids if you lived with us and could keep an eye on them while I'm gone."*

> *"We could have regular big family dinners again and you could help me with meal planning and prep."*

Bringing in a Third Party

> *"Hey, Aunt Sally, could you talk to Mom and Dad about how helpful it would be to share some estate planning information with me and my siblings?"*

Estate Planning Lawyer

> *"I'm so glad the two of you have decided to create a will. Do you want help finding an estate planning attorney? I'm happy to ask my friends who their parents used or do some research online."*

Certified Financial Planner

> *"I know you can't reveal this information to me, but could you please encourage my parents to have this conversation with us?"*

When They Flat-Out Refuse to Engage with You

> *"I'm trying to have these conversations now because I'm looking out for your best interests so that we have a plan in a worst-case-scenario situa-*

tion. If we don't have a plan, then I might not be able to help you." (You can also amend this to *"I might not legally be able to step in"* or *"I might not have the financial resources to help you."*)

Taking Care of a Parent or Sibling

"Mom and Dad, I love you. But I am not in a position to help you out." Or: *"I'm only in the position to pay for* [insert amount or particular bills here]."

•

"Do you need anything?"

Telling Your Spouse

"I've been sending my [mother/father/brother/sister] *money each month to help them out. It's something I'd like to keep doing after we're married, but I'd like to discuss your thoughts and feelings. We can also brainstorm other nonfinancial ways we can support them."*

You Need to Make a Plan Sooner, Not Later

"It's important to me to help [insert family member] *live a more comfortable life than they could afford on their own* [or amend with your own personal reason for why it's important to provide support]. *Part of how I've done this is by sending financial support of* [insert amount and frequency, e.g., five hundred dollars per month]. *Now that we're becoming our own family, I'd like to discuss your feelings and expectations about providing financial support to my family."*

•

"I understand it's important to help [insert family member here]. *However, I'd like to have a conversation about the amount of financial support we can afford to provide while also striving to achieve our own goals as a family."*

Giving Your Spouse the Space to Express Their Feelings

"*I love you and I'm so sorry this situation sucks. We'll get through it together.*"

Changing the Amount of Support You Provide

"*I have a family now. I have a daughter and a wife and more responsibilities than I did five years ago. I hope you can understand that I still want to help you, but that help is going to look different now.*"

•

"*I have a day care bill that sits at over $1,000 a month, so I can't write you a $1,000 check anymore.*"

Loaning Money to a Family Member

Should You Draw Up Paperwork?

"*You know that I love and trust you, but it really would be best for my peace of mind for us to have the details of this loan in writing. That way there isn't any confusion in the future about what we agreed to.*"

Offering Budgeting Help

"*Here are the resources I can offer you:* [e.g., a financial advisor or service, books, podcasts, etc.]. *And I'm happy to help you in a nonfinancial way. I can help you figure out how to go through your credit report and create a plan to improve your score.*"

Asking a Family Member for a Loan

"*I lost my job last month, and while I do have some savings, I'm finding it's taking longer than expected to get a new one.*" Or maybe you're self-employed: "*Unfortunately, one of my clients is taking longer than expected to pay me, and I need a short-term loan to cover expenses until that check comes in.*"

•

"I've outlined how I'm going to spend the money and also my expected repayment schedule."

CHAPTER 8: When a Loved One Requires Your Help (or Intervention)

Asking If They Have a Will

"Mom and Dad, do you have something in writing that spells out your final wishes?"

And they'll say, "Oh no, because your mother/father is going to get everything" or "You're going to get everything." And you say:

"Well, I know that's what you might want, but unless you have an official will, the state has a will for you. And the state might divide your assets up differently than what you had planned. Unless you spell it out, your house might have to get divided between Mom/Dad and us."

Asking for a Power of Attorney and Living Will/
Advance Healthcare Directive

"No, Mom and Dad, it isn't giving up control, because you get to decide who has power of attorney for you. If you don't decide, a court could decide for you. Someone might step up, and it might not be the person you want to be making those decisions for you. And if you don't want to give me this control now, just simply take the document, put it someplace safe, tell me where it is, and tell me the conditions under which I'm allowed to access it."

Asking for a Living Will/Advance Healthcare Directive

"I want to know what you want. I don't want to have to make this decision for you. It's not my decision to make. This way, you can put it in writing and spell out what you want, so we don't make the wrong choice for you, and so the family doesn't end up fighting over it."

Questions to Ask Your Parents

"I'm sure you don't want this money that you worked hard to save to get tossed because we didn't even know it was there. Letting us know about

your assets is not about counting up your money or evaluating an inheritance. It's about having the information so that when you die, if you want to pass on a legacy, it gets passed on."

Discussing Long-Term Care

"Mom and Dad, did you know that two-thirds of adults aged sixty-five and older end up needing long-term care at some point in their life? Typically, they spend three years needing that care. On average it's more than $4,000 a month for assisted living or a home health aide, and a nursing home is around $8,000 a month. It's not that uncommon, and Medicare doesn't pay for it. Medicaid will, but you have to have limited assets to qualify. Long-term-care insurance will cover it. There are also some life insurance policies with long-term-care benefits, or you could begin saving up for it to pay out of pocket."

Or:

"I get that you're counting on each other, and us/me, to care for you as you age. But what happens when you're eighty-five? You may not have the physical strength to help each other in and out of bed or to hold yourself up while you bathe. And I'd love to be able to help, but I have a job and kids who are counting on me to care and provide for them. I won't be able to quit my job to be a caregiver. We need to discuss how we can pay to hire someone if you'll want to stay here in your home or cover the cost of a retirement community."

Talk About Scams!

"If you want, I can help you check your credit report to make sure you're not already a victim of identity theft. I can show you how to do it safely online and for free. You can see if there are any accounts you don't recognize."

Another strategy is to tie it back to yourself.

"I got a call from someone the other day claiming to be from the IRS and saying I owed $5,000 in back taxes. But I hung up and then did some research and found out the IRS never calls you directly first and always sends a letter as the first point of contact. Have you ever gotten a call like that?"

Talking to Your Siblings About Caring for Parents
> "Have you thought about what will happen to our parents when they get older?"

> "This is just the beginning of the conversation. I haven't really talked to Mom and Dad about it before."

CHAPTER 9: Why We Normally Avoid Talking Money at the Dinner Table

What Happens When You Earn More Than Your Parents (or Siblings)
JEALOUSY CAN HAPPEN
> "You gave me so much growing up that I want to be able to spoil you too."
> "I know I can't always physically be there, so it brings me a lot of joy when I can take you out to dinner or on vacation."

Don't Say "I/We Can't Afford That" When You Can
> "We're prioritizing [insert goal, e.g., saving up for a down payment, saving up for a baby, or trying to pay off student loans] right now, so we won't be coming to visit for the holidays this year."

There will still probably be some hurt feelings, but being more direct is also a way to avoid conflict.

What Happens When You Don't Earn as Much
A FAMILY TRIP
> "I don't want to stand in the way of a family trip, but my budget for a trip would only be $X."

LAVISH GIFT GIVING
> "I understand that you really enjoy giving nice gifts, but I need to confess that it makes me feel uncomfortable because I can't afford to reciprocate. This year, could we set a maximum budget of $20 per person?" Or you can suggest homemade gifts or experiences or challenge each other as to who can be the most creative within a certain budget.

PART 4: TALKING ABOUT MONEY WITH YOUR ROMANTIC PARTNER

CHAPTER 10: From Casual to Pretty Serious

Casual Dating
WHO PAYS?

"*I invited you on this date, so I'd like to pay. Does this* [restaurant/bar/show] *sound good to you?*"

"*Here are a few of my favorite spots to* [grab a drink/get dinner] *in the neighborhood. Do you have a preference?*"

Once You're Exclusive
GETTING FINANCIALLY NAKED 101

"*How much are we going to spend on presents?*" (E.g., birthdays, Valentine's Day, holidays.)

"*What's the budget for our vacation together?*"

"*How fancy are we?*"

·

"*Do we alternate paying for dates or just split things down the middle, or should the person with a stronger financial footing subsidize more expensive dates?*"

Getting More Serious: We're Moving in Together
WHAT IS YOUR LIFESTYLE?

"*Even though we've been in a serious relationship for a while now, we do have different lifestyle expectations. What kind of lifestyle do you envision for us after we move in together?*"

Who Pays Which Bills?

"*Okay, for a long time our situations were similar and it worked to split things fifty-fifty, but now that our incomes aren't balanced, this situation doesn't feel equitable. How do you feel?*"

Should You Help Pay Off Debt?
"I'm comfortable paying more toward rent if you agree to pay $X more toward student loans/credit cards."

Full-Frontal Financial Nudity
SET THE STAGE
"I would like for us to sit down and talk about money. It's really important we share our financial goals and situations with each other. Maybe we could even talk a bit about our financial baggage. When would be a good time for us to talk this week?"

Starting the Conversation
"I know this is sort of an awkward conversation, but I feel it's really important as we continue to build our life together. What do you think?"
Or:
"What's a financial goal you want to achieve in the next five years?" [Partner answers.] *"And what's standing in your way?"*

What You Need to Share
"What's your first memory of money? And how does that make you feel?" or *"How often do you think about money? When you do think about it, how does it make you feel?"*
Other questions to ask include:
"How did you get money to spend growing up?" "Did your parents argue a lot about money?" "Were you told you shouldn't talk about money?"

What to Do When You Don't Trust Your Partner's Money Habits
"When you [insert behavior here], *it makes me feel* [insert feeling—e.g., betrayed, worried, uncomfortable]. *I'd like to discuss ways we can both be comfortable with how money is handled in our relationship."*

Who to Ask for Help

"*I love you, but we've been really struggling to communicate effectively about money. I feel like it's time to go speak to a professional. What do you think?*"

CHAPTER 11: It Just Got Really Serious: Money and Marriage

How to Ask for a Prenup

"*What do you think about prenups?*"

Or:

"*How do you think we should handle the assets* [and/or debt] *we each already have after we get married?*"

Explain Your Why

Your why is personal to you, but here are some of the whys I used when I engaged in this conversation.

"*Wanting a prenup doesn't at all mean I don't love and trust you. It's about being pragmatic. This is a big financial commitment, possibly the biggest we'll make in our lives, and to sign on the dotted line without protecting ourselves makes me feel uncomfortable. I'd never sign a business contract without knowing and agreeing to all the terms.*

"*Personally, I think of it as marriage insurance. Getting a prenup doesn't mean I think we'll get divorced, just like having auto insurance doesn't mean I think I'll have a car accident and renter's insurance doesn't mean I think the apartment will get robbed. I'm simply protecting myself for a possibility in life. One I hope won't happen, but realistically, it could.*"

If Your Partner Keeps Resisting

"*Based on the laws of our state, this is how our money would get split up in the case of a divorce. Are you comfortable with those terms?*"

Wait, I'm Married and Didn't Get a Prenup. Is It Game Over?

"*Now that I'm staying home, for at least a few years, to focus on raising our child, I've realized that this will have financial implications for us as a couple and for me and my earning potential. What do you think about creating a postnup together in order to ease my concerns?"*

Deciding If Marriage Is the Right (Financial) Move for You

"I love you and want to spend my life with you, but it would cost us tens of thousands of dollars right now to be legally married—not even including a wedding. What if we combine our lives as if we're married and delay signing the papers until after [insert goal here, e.g., student loans are paid off]*?"*

Should We Merge Our Money? Strategies for Handling Money in Marriage
WHAT MAKES YOU FEEL COMFORTABLE?

Here are a few examples:

"I like banking jointly and feel it helps push us toward our goals. However, I would still like some autonomy in my spending, so what do you think about having allowances/fun money/discretionary spending?"

"Being totally joint to me is symbolic of this life we're starting together and it sounds like it will just streamline our entire financial lives."

"I love and trust you very much, but for my own peace of mind I do want to keep our bank accounts separate and just set up a strategy for who covers which bills and how we prioritize our savings."

What Are Your Strengths?

"What do you see as your strengths in our relationship? Here's what I see. [List their strengths.] *What do you think are my strengths in our relationship?"*

Use Your Ideal Future as a Guidepost for Today

"What type of lifestyle do we want in retirement and when do we want to retire?"

Share What You Need in Order to Feel Financially Secure

"My previous experience with an abusive relationship makes it really stressful for me to bank completely jointly without any money in my name

alone. I want to talk to you about this and come to a decision on how we can ensure I feel safe but you don't feel as if I'm hiding money from you in our relationship."

Amanda Clayman, a financial therapist, also recommends explaining if it's an inherited behavior and making sure it's not done in a secretive way or a way that suggests you have limited trust in your partner:

"This is advice that has been passed down in my family and I feel safer knowing I have access to this money."

When You Want to Make a Change

"What do you think about the way that we've been managing our money?"

He'll say something like "It's going well."

You'll follow up with:

"What do you mean by that? Can you tell me what you like about it and what you don't like about it?"

Now That You've Picked a Style, Who Handles the Money?

If you're not the CFO in your relationship, here's what you need to ask:

"Do you have a document detailing where to track down all our financial assets, including insurance policies?"

"What are the passwords for our/your financial assets?"

If it all feels really overwhelming—e.g., you have multiple bank accounts across various banks: "Is there a way we could consolidate and simplify any of our financial life in case I ever need to take over?"

Shift Your Language

"How do you want to pay off our student loans?"

"What's the current balance of our student loans?"

"Why don't we put part of this tax refund toward our student loans?"

CHAPTER 12: Fighting Fair About Money

Unearth Your Partner's Money Scripts

In order to start to identify your own money scripts as well as your partner's, it's good to ask each other these questions:

- What was the money situation like for you growing up?
- What did your mother teach you about money?
- What did your father teach you about money?
- What are your financial goals?
- Did they teach you either directly or indirectly that there will never be enough money?
- Did you grow up believing there will always be enough money so you don't have to worry about it?
- What did they teach you about rich people?
- What were their opinions about poor people?
- What's your biggest fear about money?

Have Compassion and Ask (More) Questions

- Why is this so important to you?
- Why do you feel this way?
- Where do you think this is coming from?

Keep Your Goals Front and Center

"We agreed we wanted to buy a house in the next year and we agreed we wanted to start a family in two years. At the rate we're going, those goals are going to be delayed."

What I'm Hearing You Say . . .

One way to step back and make sure you're being understood and understanding your partner is to simply say, *"What I'm hearing you say is* [and then complete the sentence]."

Getting Your Partner on a Budget

Ditch the B-word—especially if that's a pain point with your partner. "Spending plan" is a more palatable term. Then set your financial priorities.

"What does a good life look like for you?"

"What things can you actually not live without?"

Do a Life Satisfaction Check-in

The pair will sit down and ask each other:

"How is life going for you?"

"Are you happy with this right now?"

"Do you feel like you need to make a change?"

"What actually matters and is important to you?"

Debate Using Reality, Not Perception, Which Means Examining Your Numbers

"Okay, well how much will it cost for the level of house I want and what will our budget look like?"

Then talk about it and discuss what you'd need to give up.

"Are you willing to give up international vacations for a few years until we get our income up?"

"Are you going to give up certain beauty routines?"

"I really want to go on vacations, so I think we need to reevaluate how much we're going to spend."

You also need to make sure you both aren't fixated on the perceived positives of your version of events by challenging each other to consider the downsides.

"Sure, that's a good possible outcome. But what would be some of the potential friction points in that plan? What do you think would be some of the friction points in my plan?"

Play the What-If Game

"Other than these two possible outcomes, what are some of the other options we could at least try?"

CHAPTER 13: It's All Changing: Navigating the Finances of a Major Life Change

Navigating a Major Career Shift with a Partner

"Why do you want to make this change?"

"Why is this important to you?"

"What are you willing to give up, or comfortable giving up, in order to make this happen?"

•

"What's the worst-case scenario?"

"That makes me really uncomfortable. Could we set a deadline so that if it's not working by then [you'll/I'll] pivot back to a traditional career for a while?"

A Change in Who Earns More

"What about my potentially earning more bothers you?"

Going Back to Work (or Not) After Baby

ASK YOUR EMPLOYER FOR FLEXIBILITY

"I'm so grateful for the leave that I'm able to take. I know the research points to the six-month mark as when women's bodies are more ready to be back to work and up to speed. I'd like to ask for some temporary work flexibility that will allow me to get to that point and flourish and bring in the best work for the long term.

•

Going back to a point Tasha made in chapter 12 about playing the what-if game, you could consider using language like:

"It's important to me to be able to work from home for the first six months of my child's life. And then I'll come back full-time."

Or:

"I'd like to go down to a part-time schedule for the first six months. Is that something you can work with me on?"

•

"Other than these two possible outcomes, what are some of the other options we could at least consider?"

When One Person's Salary Is Eaten Up by Childcare

"Our entire job as parents is to prepare our children to be satisfied, happy, productive adults. The best way I can do that is by modeling that myself. My priority is always my children, but my work will support our children. I'll be a happier, better mom if I'm contributing to our family's income and contributing to the world and using my education. This is the right decision for me and our family."

If One of You Doesn't Want to Go Back to Work

"Okay, if we switch to just having one salary coming in but don't have to pay for childcare, what will our finances look like?"

Run the actual numbers. Don't work in abstractions. Then begin to discuss what you might need to sacrifice, at least in the short term.

"Are you willing to give up X membership?"

"Are you willing to give up more than one vacation—or the 'just us' trip we take each year?"

"Are you willing to give up traveling during the holidays?"

"Are you willing to delay our moving into a larger home to get more space for our expanding family?"

Notes

CHAPTER 1

1. National Labor Relations Board, "National Labor Relations Act," www.nlrb .gov/how-we-work/national-labor-relations-act.
2. National Labor Relations Board, "Frequently Asked Questions—NLRB," www .nlrb.gov/resources/faq/nlrb#t38n3208.
3. US Equal Employment Opportunity Commission, "The Equal Pay Act of 1963," www.eeoc.gov/laws/statutes/epa.cfm.
4. Nikki Graf, Anna Brown, and Eileen Patten, "The Narrowing, but Persistent, Gender Gap in Pay," Pew Research Center Fact Tank, March 22, 2019, www .pewresearch.org/fact-tank/2019/03/22/gender-pay-gap-facts/.
5. Eileen Patten, "Racial, Gender Wage Gaps Persist in U.S. Despite Some Progress," Pew Research Center Fact Tank, July 1, 2016, www.pewresearch.org /fact-tank/2016/07/01/racial-gender-wage-gaps-persist-in-u-s-despite-some -progress/.
6. Valentin Bolotnyy and Natalia Emanuel, "Why Do Women Earn Less Than Men? Evidence from Bus and Train Operators," Harvard Department of Economics, July 5, 2019, scholar.harvard.edu/bolotnyy/publications/why-do -women-earn-less-men-evidence-bus-and-train-operators-job-market-paper.
7. US Equal Employment Opportunity Commission, "What You Should Know: Questions and Answers About the Equal Pay Act," June 10, 2013, www.eeoc .gov/eeoc/newsroom/wysk/qanda_epa.cfm.

CHAPTER 2

1. Jaruwan Sakulku and James Alexander, "The Imposter Phenomenon," *International Journal of Behavioral Science* 6, no. 1 (2011): 75–97, www.tci -thaijo.org/index.php/IJBS/article/view/521/pdf.

CHAPTER 8

1. Genworth, "Cost of Care Survey," 2019, www.genworth.com/aging-and-you /finances/cost-of-care.html.
2. National Council on Aging, "Elder Abuse Facts," www.ncoa.org/public-policy -action/elder-justice/elder-abuse-facts/.
3. Consumer Financial Protection Bureau, "How Do I Get a Copy of My Credit Report?," ConsumerFinance.gov, March 29, 2019, www.consumerfinance.gov /ask-cfpb/how-do-i-get-a-copy-of-my-credit-reports-en-5/.
4. Federal Trade Commission, "What to Do Right Away," IdentityTheft.gov, www .identitytheft.gov/Steps.

CHAPTER 12

1. Michael Fulwiler, "Managing Conflict: Solvable vs. Perpetual Problems," Gottman Institute, July 2, 2012, www.gottman.com/blog/managing-conflict -solvable-vs-perpetual-problems/.

CHAPTER 13

1. Kathleen L. McGinn, Mayra Ruiz Castro, and Elizabeth Long Lingo, "Learning from Mum: Cross-National Evidence Linking Maternal Employment and Adult Children's Outcomes," Work, Employment and Society 33, no. 3 (April 30, 2018): journals.sagepub.com/doi/10.1177/0950017018760167.

About the Author

Erin Lowry is the author of the Broke Millennial series, which includes *Broke Millennial* and *Broke Millennial Takes On Investing*. She's appeared on the BBC, CNBC, and *CBS Sunday Morning*, and she's been quoted in the *New York Times* and the *Wall Street Journal*. She's also written for the *New York Times*, *USA Today*, *Cosmopolitan*, and CNBC. Erin lives in New York City with her husband and their rambunctious dog, Tasker. You can find her on Instagram (@BrokeMillennialBlog) and Twitter (@BrokeMillennial) and at BrokeMillennial.com.

Also by Erin Lowry